CW00408930

ALLIANCE TO CC

The First 22 Years

(1979 - 2001)

By Bob Perkins and Graham Frost

Published by:
Yore Publications
12 The Furrows, Harefield,
Middx. UB9 6AT.

© Bob Perkins and Graham Frost 2001

....

British Library Cataloguing-in-Publication Data.
A catalogue record for this book
is available from the British Library.

ISBN 1 874427 93 3

Printed and bound by
Bookcraft, Midsomer Norton, Bath.

The Authors would like to express a special
thanks to the Nationwide Conference for
their co-operation, and to Wealdstone
Football Club for permission to reproduce
the photograph shown on the back cover.
Thanks also to various Alliance/Conference
clubs (both past and present) for their help.

Occasional statistical information herein differs from that published
elsewhere. However, the Authors have checked in detail such
discrepancies in order to ensure the accuracy of information
provided.

~ Contents ~

Introduction

For many years, the ambitions of football clubs throughout the land had been stifled by their inability to gain entry to the Football League. With the introduction of Division 3 (North and South) in 1920 and 1921, the bottom two clubs in each division were compelled to seek re-election in a regionalised ballot with challengers from the non-League ranks. The two sides attaining the highest number of votes in each divisional vote would be members of the Football League the following season. When the League structure was altered to Division 3 and 4 in 1958, the re-election system was adjusted to incorporate a vote between the bottom four teams in Division 4 and those applying for membership of the League in a single nationwide vote.

The teams wishing to join the Football League were not required to meet any specified criteria and some had little or no credibility. Due to the number of teams applying, the process was lengthy and support for new clubs would tend to spread amongst the applicants meaning that few clubs were successfully voted in. The Southern League was the source of most aspiring clubs until 1968 when the Northern Premier League was formed, with the majority of its founder-members drawn from the Cheshire County League, the Lancashire Combination and the Midland League. These leagues then became feeder leagues and hence a non-League pyramid system was evolving. However, as with any pyramid, it needed an apex.

It was Football League Secretary, Alan Hardaker, who initiated talks between the Southern League and the Northern Premier League with the intention of forming an Alliance in the early 1970's. It was felt that this would further the concept of automatic promotion and relegation between the non-League clubs and the Fourth Division. Even if this did not materialise, it would help reduce the number of clubs applying for entry to the League. As late as 1975 there were 14 non-League clubs seeking election, 10 of whom received two votes or less.

A revised system was introduced in 1977, whereby a list of applicants was provided by both the Southern League and the Northern Premier League and an approved club would be chosen from each list to challenge the existing members, with any club losing Football League status gaining automatic entry to the appropriate feeder league. This was the method by which both Wimbledon and Wigan Athletic were elected to the Football League, replacing Workington and Southport respectively.

Behind the scenes, progress towards forming an Alliance was slow, until March 1978, when a Joint Steering Committee formulated a plan for amalgamating the two leagues. The plan was finally approved in April 1979 for a new league – to be known as the Alliance Premier League – consisting of twenty clubs to be formed, with the Northern Premier League, Southern League (Midland Division) and the Southern League (Southern Division) acting as feeder leagues. Of the initial twenty members, thirteen were drawn from the Southern League and seven from the Northern Premier League. The two to one southern bias was in proportion to the number of feeder leagues. Membership was based on two criteria:

1. The League position in 1977-8 and 1978-9. These were transferred into points. (Champions -1 point, runners-up – 2 points, etc) and those with the lowest combined points total were put forward for membership.
2. Suitable grading of the club in respect of ground, facilities and off the field organisation.

At the conclusion of the 1978-9 season, the tables based on the final placings over the campaigns were as follows:-

Southern League – Premier Division	Position (Points) 1977-8	Position (Points) 1978-9	Combined Total
Worcester City	4	1	5
Bath City	1	5	6
Maidstone United	3	4	7
Weymouth	2	6	8
Kettering Town	6	2	8
Telford United	9	3	12
Gravesend & Northfleet	5	12	17
Barnet	7	13	20
Yeovil Town	12	9	21
Nuneaton Borough	10	11	21
Wealdstone	8	15	23
Redditch United	17	8	25
A.P.Leamington	18	7	25

Northern Premier League	Position (Points) 1977-8	Position (Points) 1978-9	Combined Total
Southport	Div 4	5	5 *
Boston United	1	6	7
Altrincham	5	2	7
Scarborough	4	4	8
Mossley	9	1	10 *
Matlock Town	10	3	13 *
Runcorn	8	7	15 *
Stafford Rangers	7	8	15
Bangor City	3	12	15
Northwich Victoria	6	10	16
Lancaster City	11	11	22 *
Goole Town	14	9	23 *
Barrow	13	16	29

In the Southern League, the top thirteen teams were accepted for membership of the Alliance, but in the North it was not as straightforward.

* Matlock Town and Runcorn were turned down as their grounds received a 'C' grading rather than the required 'B' grade. Mossley, Lancaster City and Goole Town did not apply to join the League, while Southport were initially accepted despite only having been in the Northern Premier League for one season since their relegation from Division Four. However, Southport made a late decision to decline the offer of membership on the basis of the increased travelling costs, and Barrow replaced them in the last available spot.

Notes:

Abbreviations and other normally recognised references are generally self-explanatory. However, the following points are included to avoid confusion: For convenience, the common/original names of leagues have generally been given, i.e. Alliance/Conference has the various Sponsors' names omitted, likewise 'Southern League', 'Isthmian League' and 'N.P.L.' (which refers to the 'Northern Premier League'). Unless stated otherwise, only matches involving Alliance/ Conference clubs have been included. In the seasonal statistics sections, the 'League Cup' refers to the competition originally known as the 'Bob Lord Trophy', which subsequently incorporated various Sponsors' names. However, for the 1986/87 to 1988/89 seasons, the clubs from the top divisions of the Conference 'feeder' leagues were also included. The competition entitled 'Challenge Shield' was initially played between the winners of the League and the League Cup (up to and including 1986), and was subsequently played between the League Champions and the F.A.Trophy Winners. Under the Clubs Section, 'Career' refers to that Club's seasons in the Alliance/ Conference. Record Win/Defeat refers to Alliance/Conference league matches only; the 'record' is defined as the most clear goals for/against and the most goals scored/ conceded, i.e 8-1 overules 7-0.

1979/80

A new era in non-League football started on 18th August 1979 with the first attempt at a nationwide league competition outside of the Foot-ball League itself. The favourites for the title were Worcester City, Kettering Town and Altrincham, who had been the leading teams in their respective feeder leagues, but with each team having to face so many unknown quantities, the final outcome was uncertain.

The team with the highest profile was Altrincham due to their recent F.A.Cup exploits. They had taken both Everton and Tottenham Hotspur to third round replays in the previous five seasons and had won the F.A.Trophy in 1978. Early season form was distinctly mediocre with three defeats in their first nine games. This run was followed by eight wins on the trot, which propelled them to the top of the table by the time their annual F.A.Cup odyssey began. Crewe and Rotherham were beaten without conceding a goal before Orient won a third round replay.

Weymouth and Worcester City were flying the flag for the southern based clubs with Weymouth performing particularly well away from home. But it was Altrincham's home form that was notable. They went through the league campaign undefeated at Moss Lane and did not drop a point at home until December 29th. Towards the end of March, all three clubs were level on points, but it was the game in hand over Weymouth that proved decisive and Altrincham secured the title by two points. They were only denied a league and cup double by Northwich Victoria who won the Bob Lord Trophy after a penalty shootout.

The F.A.Trophy proved a disappointing tournament for Alliance clubs. Only Boston Utd made it through to the semi-finals, where they lost to Mossley who had already accounted for Altrincham in the third round, 5-1 away from home. No doubt Mossley felt they had a point to prove, as they had pipped Altrincham to the Northern Premier League title in 1978-9 but had decided not to apply for membership of the Alliance.

At the season's end, the first contest between the Alliance champions and the four Football League clubs seeking re-election took place and Altrincham were unlucky to lose out to Rochdale by one vote (26-25). It was discovered after the meeting that Luton Town's delegate had misunderstood the time of the voting and had arrived back from lunch after the election was over, while Grimsby Town's representative had sat in the wrong part of the room and did not vote! During their canvassing, Altrincham had been promised the support of both clubs and their failure to gain entry to the Football League was even harder to take in the circumstances, not just for the club but for the Alliance Premier League.

1979/80 Season Results Grid

	Altrincham	A.P.Leamington	Bangor City	Barnet	Barrow	Bath City	Boston United	Gravesend & Northfleet	Kettering Town	Maidstone United	Northwich Victoria	Nuneaton Borough	Redditch United	Scarborough	Stafford Rangers	Telford United	Wealdstone	Weymouth	Worcester City	Yeovil Town
Altrincham	X	3-0	5-0	1-0	3-1	4-0	3-0	4-1	0-0	1-0	0-0	3-1	2-0	2-0	3-1	2-0	2-1	3-2	3-1	1-1
A.P.Leamington	1-4	X	1-1	2-1	0-1	1-2	2-0	0-1	1-3	0-2	2-2	0-0	0-2	1-1	2-0	2-1	0-0	0-2	1-0	0-4
Bangor City	1-1	3-2	X	1-1	1-1	2-1	2-0	1-2	1-1	1-0	0-3	1-0	1-0	1-0	1-1	1-1	1-0	1-2	0-2	1-0
Barnet	2-0	1-0	1-1	X	1-1	1-0	0-0	3-0	0-2	0-1	0-2	2-1	0-0	0-0	2-1	4-1	1-3	0-2	0-0	0-3
Barrow	1-3	6-2	1-1	3-1	X	2-1	0-1	1-1	1-2	0-2	1-0	1-0	2-0	2-1	2-0	1-0	0-1	1-2		2-0
Bath City	1-1	0-0	2-1	1-2	1-0	X	0-1	2-0	3-0	1-1	0-0	1-1	1-1	1-0	2-1	1-1	4-4	4-2	0-4	1-1
Boston United	2-5	2-0	3-1	1-1	3-0	3-2	X	4-0	1-0	1-1	2-0	2-2	2-0	2-2	3-2	3-1	0-0	2-2	1-1	3-0
Gravesend & Northfleet	0-2	3-2	1-1	1-0	5-1	2-0	0-0	X	2-2	1-0	2-1	2-2	1-0	3-0	2-0	1-2	3-0	2-3	3-2	2-0
Kettering Town	1-2	1-1	0-1	1-0	0-4	1-2	3-1	0-0	X	1-1	1-0	1-1	2-1	1-1	3-6	3-2	2-0	3-1	0-0	5-3
Maidstone United	2-2	0-0	0-1	2-0	2-0	6-0	1-0	3-0	1-3	X	3-4	1-1	4-1	2-0	2-0	3-0	3-0	1-1	2-1	0-1
Northwich Victoria	1-0	2-1	4-0	2-0	6-3	6-1	0-1	0-0	2-2	0-2	X	2-1	1-0	1-1	1-0	2-1	0-0	0-0	1-0	0-1
Nuneaton Borough	2-0	1-1	2-2	2-1	3-0	1-1	2-0	3-1	2-2	4-0	2-1	X	5-1	3-1	3-1	1-1	0-1	1-2	1-0	3-0
Redditch United	0-1	3-1	1-5	1-0	1-3	1-1	0-2	0-2	0-1	0-0	0-1	1-0	X	1-2	0-2	2-2	4-1	0-2	1-1	2-2
Scarborough	1-1	5-0	0-0	0-0	2-0	6-1	2-4	1-1	2-0	1-2	2-1	2-1	3-0	X	0-0	1-2	0-0	0-0	4-1	0-0
Stafford Rangers	1-2	1-1	0-1	1-2	1-1	4-0	0-0	0-1	0-0	1-1	4-1	0-1	1-1	3-1	X	0-1	0-1	1-5	0-0	2-1
Telford United	3-2	0-1	2-0	1-2	3-2	3-1	4-1	1-2	1-0	3-1	0-0	2-1	2-1	0-1	2-2	X	1-3	3-3	0-1	0-3
Wealdstone	1-4	1-2	0-0	2-1	2-1	1-1	1-1	0-0	2-2	0-0	0-1	2-2	2-0	2-4	2-1	0-0	X	1-1	2-4	5-0
Weymouth	0-0	2-1	4-2	1-1	1-0	1-2	3-0	1-0	3-1	1-1	2-0	2-0	6-0	0-1	2-1	3-2	4-0	X	1-2	3-0
Worcester City	3-2	1-1	0-0	2-1	2-0	2-1	0-0	1-0	1-4	3-1	2-1	1-1	3-0	0-0	1-0	2-1	2-1	1-1	X	2-0
Yeovil Town	3-2	1-0	1-2	5-0	0-1	1-0	0-0	1-1	1-1	3-0	1-1	2-1	0-0	1-1	3-1	0-2	1-1	0-1	0-2	X

Final Table

	P	Home					Away					Total					
		W	D	L	F	A	W	D	L	F	A	W	D	L	F	A	Pts
Altrincham	38	16	3	0	45	9	8	5	6	34	26	24	8	6	79	35	56
Weymouth	38	13	3	3	40	14	9	7	3	33	23	22	10	6	73	37	54
Worcester City	38	12	6	1	29	15	7	5	7	24	21	19	11	8	53	36	49
Boston United	38	11	7	1	40	20	5	6	8	12	23	16	13	9	52	43	45
Gravesend & Northfleet	38	12	4	3	36	18	5	6	8	13	26	17	10	11	49	44	44
Maidstone United	38	11	4	4	38	15	5	7	7	16	22	16	11	11	54	37	43
Kettering Town	38	9	5	5	29	26	6	8	5	26	24	15	13	10	55	50	43
Northwich Victoria	38	11	5	3	31	14	5	5	9	19	24	16	10	12	50	38	42
Bangor City	38	9	6	4	21	18	5	8	6	20	28	14	14	10	41	46	42
Nuneaton Borough	38	12	5	2	41	16	1	8	10	17	28	13	13	12	58	44	39
Scarborough	38	8	8	3	32	14	4	7	8	15	24	12	15	11	47	38	39
Yeovil Town	38	8	6	5	26	17	5	4	10	20	32	13	10	15	46	49	36
Telford United	38	9	3	7	31	27	4	5	10	21	33	13	8	17	52	60	34
Barrow	38	10	3	6	27	18	4	3	12	20	37	14	6	18	47	55	34
Wealdstone	38	5	9	5	26	25	4	6	9	16	29	9	15	14	42	54	33
Bath City	38	7	9	3	26	21	3	3	13	17	48	10	12	16	43	69	32
Barnet	38	7	6	6	18	18	3	4	12	14	30	10	10	18	32	48	30
A.P.Leamington	38	5	5	9	16	27	2	6	11	16	36	7	11	20	32	63	25
Stafford Rangers	38	4	7	8	20	21	2	3	14	21	36	6	10	22	41	57	22
Redditch United	38	4	5	10	18	29	1	3	15	8	40	5	8	25	26	69	18 R

FINAL TABLE

Frickley Athletic promoted from N.P.L.

F.A.Cup

Preliminary Round		
Formby	Bangor City	2-2
Emley	Barrow	1-0
replay		
Bangor City	Formby	0-1
First Qualifying Round		
Barry Town	Bath City	2-1
Ely City	Boston Utd	1-2
East Grinstaed	Gravesend & Northfleet	1-4
Caernarfon Town	Northwich Victoria	0-0
Cinderford Town	Redditch Utd	1-2
Bilston	Telford Utd	1-2
Bridgwater Town	Yeovil Town	0-0
replay		
Northwich Victoria	Caernarfon Town	4-0
Yeovil Town	Bridgwater Town	2-0
Second Qualifying Round		
Stamford	Boston Utd	0-5
Eastbourne Town	Gravesend & Northfleet	0-2
Formby	Northwich Victoria	1-1
Bridgend Town	Redditch Utd	0-0
Coventry Sporting	Telford Utd	2-4
Liskeard Athletic	Yeovil Town	0-1
replay		
Northwich Victoria	Formby	2-0
Redditch Utd	Bridgend Town	2-3
Third Qualifying Round		
Wisbech Town	Boston Utd	1-5
Ramsgate	Gravesend & Northfleet	2-2
Oswestry Town	Northwich Victoria	1-1
Moor Green	Telford Utd	2-1
Saltash Utd	Yeovil Town	3-3
replay		
Gravesend & Northfleet	Ramsgate	2-1
Northwich Victoria	Oswestry Town	4-1
Yeovil Town	Saltash Utd	2-1
Fourth Qualifying Round		
Boston	AP Leamington	2-2
Barnet	Wycombe Wandrers	0-2
Boston Utd	Nuneaton Borough	1-1
Gravesend & Northfleet	Welling Utd	2-1
Chesham Utd	Maidstone Utd	3-1
Enderby Town	Northwich Victoria	0-1
Wealdstone	Woking	1-0
Salisbury	Worcester City	2-1
Yeovil Town	Weymouth	2-1
replay		
AP Leamington	Boston	1-0
Nuneaton Borough	Boston Utd	2-1
First Round		
Altrincham	Crewe Alexandra	3-0
Tranmere Rovers	AP Leamington	9-0
Enfield	Yeovil Town	0-1
Gravesend & Northfleet	Torquay Utd	0-1
Reading	Kettering Town	4-2
Nuneaton Borough	Northwich Victoria	3-3
Halifax Town	Scarborough	2-0
Stafford Rangers	Moor Green	3-2
Wealdstone	Southend Utd	0-1
replay		
Northwich Victoria	Nuneaton Borough	3-0

F.A.Cup

Second Round		
Rotherham Utd	Altrincham	0-2
Northwhich Victoria	Wigan Ath	0-3
(Abandoned 67 mins. - fog)		
Northwich Victoria	Wigan Ath	2-2
Blackburn Rovers	Stafford Rangers	2-0
Yeovil Town	Slough Town	1-0
replay		
Wigan Ath	Northwich Victoria	1-0
Third Round		
Altrincham	Orient	1-1
Yeovil Town	Norwich City	0-3
replay		
Orient	Altrincham	2-1

League Cup

First Round		
Scarborough	Northwich Victoria	0-0
Stafford Rangers	Nuneaton Borough	1-2
Wealdstone	Maidstone United	2-0
Worcester City	Weymouth	1-1
replay		
Northwich Victoria	Scarborough	0-0
Weymouth	Worcester City	5-1
second replay		
Northwich Victoria	Scarborough	2-0
Second Round		
Altrincham	Bangor City	1-1
AP Leamington	Kettering Town	0-4
Barnet	Bath City	2-0
Boston United	Wealdstone	1-1
Gravesend & Northfleet	Weymouth	2-2
Northwich Victoria	Redditch United	2-0
Nuneaton Borough	Yeovil Town	3-1
Telford United	Barrow	0-0
replay		
Bangor City	Altrincham	1-2
Barrow	Telford United	0-1
Wealdstone	Boston United	3-2
Weymouth	Gravesend & Northfleet	3-0
Third Round		
Altrincham	Wealdstone	2-1
Kettering Town	Weymouth	3-1
Northwich Victoria	Telford United	2-2
Nuneaton Borough	Barnet	2-2
replay		
Barnet	Nuneaton Borough	2-1
Telford United	Northwich Victoria	2-3
Semi Final (two legs)		
Barnet	Altrincham	0-1
Altrincham	Barnet	7-0
Kettering Town	Northwich Victoria	0-0
Northwich Victoria	Kettering Town	3-1
Final (two legs)		
Altrincham	Northwich Victoria	2-1
Northwich Victoria	Altrincham	1-0
(Northwich Victoria won 4-3 on pens)		

First Qualifying Round

Highgate	A.P.Leamington	1-3
Gloucester City	Redditch United	2-2
Barnet	Wealdstone	0-0
Gosport Borough	Gravesend & Northfleet	1-1

replay

Gravesend & Northfleet	Gosport Borough	2-1
Redditch United	Gloucester City	4-3
Wealdstone	Barnet	1-1

Second replay

Barnet	Wealdstone	2-0

Second Qualifying Round

Sutton Coldfield Town	Redditch United	2-3
A.P.Leamington	Boston	1-2
Leytonstone & Ilford	Barnet	1-2
Carshalton Ath	Gravesend & Northfleet	2-1

Third Qualifying Round

Barrow	Goole Town	5-2
Northwich Victoria	Lye Town	2-0
Grantham	Redditch United	3-1
Hayes	Barnet	0-1
Bath City	Trowbridge Town	2-0

First Round

Barrow	Bishop Auckland	3-2
Gainsborough Trinity	Scarborough	2-1
Oswestry Town	Northwich Victoria	2-1
Bangor City	Telford United	5-1
Runcorn	Boston United	1-1
Grantham	Altrincham	1-1
Hyde Utd	Nuneaton Borough	2-2
Stafford Rangers	Boston	1-1
Maidstone United	Yeovil Town	2-2
Tooting & Mitcham Utd	Worcester City	2-0
Dartford	Bath City	1-1
Kettering Town	Merthyr Tydfil	0-3
Hendon	Barnet	1-1
Carshalton Ath	Weymouth	0-4

replay

Boston United	Runcorn	2-1
Altrincham	Grantham	6-3
Nuneaton Borough	Hyde Utd	4-1
Boston	Stafford Rangers	1-2
Yeovil Town	Maidstone United	4-2
Bath City	Dartford	6-1
Barnet	Hendon	1-0

Second Round

Tooting & Mitcham Utd	Boston United	0-1
Leatherhead	Weymouth	0-2
Altrincham	Morecambe	2-0
Barnet	Bangor City	4-1
Nuneaton Borough	Gainsborough Trinity	2-1
Merthyr Tydfil	Bath City	0-2
Barrow	Cheltenham Town	2-0
Yeovil Town	Chorley	5-2

Third Round

Bath City	Dulwich Hamlet	1-3
Nuneaton Borough	Barnet	2-1
Altrincham	Mossley	1-5
Blyth Spartans	Yeovil Town	1-0
Boston United	Weymouth	2-2
Barrow	Hastings Utd	4-0

replay

Weymouth	Boston United	0-1

Fourth Round

Boston United	Dulwich Hamlet	0-0
Woking	Barrow	3-1
Dagenham	Nuneaton Borough	3-2

replay

Dulwich Hamlet	Boston United	0-2

Semi final

Mossley	Boston United	1-1
Boston United	Mossley	1-2

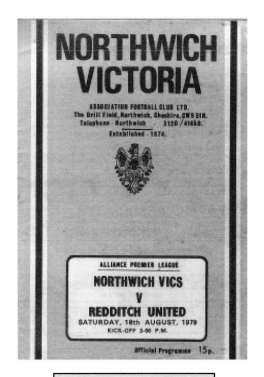

NORTHWICH VICTORIA 1
REDDITCH UNITED 0
Opening day defeat sets
trend for Redditch's season.

9

1980/81

Despite the disappointment of missing out on a place in the Football League in the cruellest fashion, Altrincham were professional enough to not only retain the Alliance Premier League title, but also secure the Bob Lord Trophy which had eluded them in 1979-80.

Alty started the campaign in unconvincing fashion. Having survived the previous season undefeated at Moss Lane, the first home fixture produced a 3-0 reverse at the hands of early pacesetters Nuneaton Borough. No single team dominated the proceedings but Altrincham, Scarborough and Kettering Town made their way to the top by the end of September and held the leading places until Christmas.

At the foot of the table, A.P.Leamington found themselves adrift with just four points from their first thirteen games. Their F.A.Cup exit at the hands of Barton Rovers signalled the end of Jimmy Knox's reign as manager; Ex-Leicester City and Cardiff City winger John Farrington took over and the form improved. A first away win was secured at Boston Utd, who were previously unbeaten at home. Six wins plus three draws in ten games took the Midlands team to seventh from bottom, but as the table at the end of January showed, all twenty teams were covered by just twelve points difference, therefore every issue was still wide open.

It was Altrincham who provided the expected F.A.Cup headlines when they reached the 3rd round yet again and this time they got drawn against the best team in the land – Liverpool. A 4-1 defeat at Anfield was no disgrace and credit must go to the Cheshire team for not letting the occasion distract them from their league endeavours. Having lost four matches in fifteen by November 8th, they only lost once more in the next five months, a run of seventeen games. Two home defeats in five days, against Telford Utd and Weymouth were a brief stumble on their march to successive championships. Kettering Town were in contention until the final run in, but defeats on each of the last two Saturdays cost them the title. It was a season of near misses as they were also runners-up in the Bob Lord Trophy. Altrincham were able to celebrate their successes at the final home game of the season against Yeovil Town in front of the season's biggest crowd, 2,864.

Sadly for Altrincham, the election for Football League status was a let-down for them after the previous years close run contest. In 1981 they amassed only fifteen votes, twenty-six less than Halifax Town. It was to prove to be the final days of one of the best non-League teams of recent years. The majority of the team were in their late twenties/early thirties, and rebuilding would clearly soon be required, and there were fresh challengers on the horizon. Each feeder league would provide a new club for the first time and to increase the number of clubs to twenty-two, two clubs were invited to join from the Isthmian League.

1980/81 Season Results Grid

	Altrincham	A.P.Leamington	Bangor City	Barnet	Barrow	Bath City	Boston United	Frickley Athletic	Gravesend & Northfleet	Kettering Town	Maidstone United	Northwich Victoria	Nuneaton Borough	Scarborough	Stafford Rangers	Telford United	Wealdstone	Weymouth	Worcester City	Yeovil Town
Altrincham	X	4-1	2-0	2-0	2-2	3-1	2-0	2-0	2-1	4-1	2-1	1-1	0-3	4-3	4-2	0-2	2-0	1-2	1-0	2-1
A.P.Leamington	2-4	X	1-0	0-1	2-2	0-4	0-0	2-2	4-1	3-3	2-3	1-1	0-1	2-0	1-1	5-0	1-1	0-1	2-1	1-0
Bangor City	4-5	1-0	X	4-2	2-6	0-1	1-1	4-3	1-1	0-1	1-1	0-0	2-5	0-3	0-0	2-0	0-2	2-0	1-1	0-2
Barnet	3-2	1-0	0-1	X	0-0	1-5	2-2	2-0	1-1	0-1	4-1	1-0	1-0	1-2	1-1	2-1	3-0	0-3	0-2	4-4
Barrow	0-4	0-2	3-0	1-1	X	0-0	0-2	0-0	3-1	2-1	4-1	2-1	1-0	0-1	5-1	0-1	1-0	0-1	1-0	2-1
Bath City	0-1	5-0	0-0	1-0	2-1	X	2-0	3-0	1-0	0-0	0-0	0-0	0-0	0-1	0-0	0-1	2-0	2-3	3-0	2-1
Boston United	1-1	2-3	1-1	3-0	0-2	4-2	X	1-2	2-1	2-1	1-2	2-3	3-1	0-3	2-2	5-3	2-1	3-1	3-1	2-0
Frickley Athletic	0-2	0-0	4-0	3-0	5-0	2-1	0-1	X	2-4	1-1	2-1	0-1	4-3	1-0	3-2	4-1	1-1	1-2	1-1	2-1
Gravesend & Northfleet	0-2	4-0	1-0	0-2	0-2	2-1	1-2	3-1	X	1-0	1-2	0-1	4-0	1-1	1-1	2-2	0-1	1-0	2-1	2-2
Kettering Town	1-1	3-0	3-1	2-1	0-1	2-2	0-0	6-1	2-0	X	3-0	3-3	3-0	1-0	2-1	0-1	1-0	1-0	4-0	1-0
Maidstone United	1-2	2-1	1-0	4-1	1-0	2-1	2-2	1-1	1-1	1-2	X	4-0	1-3	1-1	4-1	3-0	4-0	3-0	2-0	4-2
Northwich Victoria	1-0	2-0	1-0	4-1	0-0	3-1	3-1	1-3	4-0	1-1	2-1	X	0-0	2-1	1-0	0-0	0-0	3-0	1-2	3-2
Nuneaton Borough	0-0	3-0	3-2	0-1	3-1	0-0	0-2	0-1	1-2	1-5	1-1	2-0	X	0-4	2-2	3-3	2-0	1-4	2-3	3-0
Scarborough	1-0	0-0	1-1	3-0	0-0	1-0	3-2	2-1	1-0	1-2	1-2	0-0	2-1	X	0-0	1-1	4-0	2-0	0-0	2-1
Stafford Rangers	1-3	1-1	4-0	1-0	1-0	0-2	2-3	3-3	2-3	3-1	3-1	2-0	2-2	2-1	X	0-1	3-0	2-0	1-0	1-1
Telford United	3-2	2-3	1-1	0-0	5-2	2-1	2-0	1-0	0-0	0-2	1-2	1-3	2-2	0-0	1-1	X	2-1	1-0	1-2	0-1
Wealdstone	1-2	1-2	1-1	2-0	2-0	0-1	3-0	0-2	3-1	1-1	2-1	1-1	0-0	2-2	1-1	4-0	X	1-1	1-2	1-1
Weymouth	0-0	3-2	4-0	3-0	2-1	1-1	2-1	1-2	0-1	1-2	1-1	4-3	1-0	1-1	2-1	1-0	2-1	X	1-0	0-1
Worcester City	0-0	3-3	1-1	4-0	2-4	0-2	1-4	3-0	3-1	2-1	2-1	2-1	1-0	2-0	1-1	0-3	4-1	2-1	X	0-1
Yeovil Town	1-1	3-0	1-0	1-2	2-1	1-2	2-1	5-3	1-3	1-2	2-1	1-2	5-1	0-0	3-4	1-2	4-0	0-5	3-0	X

FINAL TABLE

	P	Home					Away					Total					
		W	D	L	F	A	W	D	L	F	A	W	D	L	F	A	Pts
Altrincham	38	14	2	3	40	21	9	6	4	32	20	23	8	7	72	41	54
Kettering Town	38	13	4	2	38	12	8	5	6	28	25	21	9	8	66	37	51
Scarborough	38	10	7	2	25	11	7	6	6	24	18	17	13	8	49	29	47
Northwich Victoria	38	12	4	3	32	13	5	7	7	21	27	17	11	10	53	40	45
Weymouth	38	11	4	4	30	18	8	2	9	24	22	19	6	13	54	40	44
Bath City	38	9	6	4	23	8	7	4	8	28	24	16	10	12	51	32	42
Maidstone United	38	12	4	3	42	18	4	5	10	22	35	16	9	13	64	53	41
Boston United	38	10	4	5	39	30	6	5	8	24	28	16	9	13	63	58	41
Barrow	38	10	3	6	25	18	5	5	9	25	31	15	8	15	50	49	38
Frickley Athletic	38	10	4	5	36	22	5	4	10	25	40	15	8	15	61	62	38
Stafford Rangers	38	10	4	5	34	22	1	11	7	22	34	11	15	12	56	56	37
Worcester City	38	10	4	5	33	25	4	3	12	14	29	14	7	17	47	54	35
Telford United	38	7	6	6	25	23	6	3	10	22	36	13	9	16	47	59	35
Yeovil Town	38	9	2	8	37	30	5	4	10	23	34	14	6	18	60	64	34
Gravesend & Northfleet	38	8	4	7	26	21	5	4	10	22	34	13	8	17	48	55	34
A.P.Leamington	38	6	7	6	29	26	4	4	11	18	40	10	11	17	47	66	31
Barnet	38	8	5	6	27	26	4	2	13	12	38	12	7	19	39	64	31
Nuneaton Borough	38	6	5	8	27	31	4	4	11	22	34	10	9	19	49	65	29 R
Wealdstone	38	6	8	5	27	19	3	3	13	10	37	9	11	18	37	56	29 R
Bangor City	38	5	6	8	25	34	1	6	12	10	34	6	12	20	35	68	24 R

Runcorn promoted from N.P.L., Trowbridge Town from Southern League (Midland), Dartford from Southern League (Southern)
Dagenham and Enfield joined by invitation from Isthmian League - Membership increased to 22

F.A.Cup

Preliminary Round		
Denaby Utd	Frickley Ath	1-3
Bath City	Glastonbury	7-1
First Qualifying Round		
Bangor City	Bootle	0-2
Barrow	Boldon CA	8-1
Weston-Super-Mare	Bath City	1-2
(Played at Bath City)		
Worksop Town	Frickley Ath	3-2
Boston Utd	Skegness Town	3-0
Maidstone United	Ramsgate	6-0
Northwich Victoria	New Mills	1-0
Sutton Coldfield Town	Telford United	1-0
Worcester City	Malvern Town	1-1
replay		
Malvern Town	Worcester City	0-2
Second Qualifying Round		
Barrow	Whitby Town	1-1
Barnstaple Town	Bath City	0-1
Grantham	Boston Utd	1-3
Folkestone	Maidstone United	0-2
Leek Town	Northwich Victoria	1-1
Llanelli	Worcester City	0-3
replay		
Whitby Town	Barrow	1-2
Northwich Victoria	Leek Town	1-0
Third Qualifying Round		
Horden CW	Barrow	0-0
Ton Pentre	Bath City	1-3
Boston Utd	Barton Town	2-0
Maidstone United	Bromley	2-0
Northwich Victoria	Alfreton Town	3-2
Worcester City	Barry Town	1-1
replay		
Barrow	Horden CW	2-3
Barry Town	Worcester City	2-3
Fourth Qualifying Round		
AP Leamington	Barton Rovers	0-1
Aylesbury United	Barnet	1-1
Leatherhead	Bath City	1-0
Corby Town	Boston United	0-1
Gravesend & Northfleet	Aveley	4-0
Kettering Town	Banbury United	3-0
Kidderminster Harriers	Nuneaton Borough	1-0
Kings Lynn	Stafford Rangers	1-3
Maidstone United	Barking	2-0
Northwich Victoria	Runcorn	2-1
Harlow Town	Wealdstone	1-1
Weymouth	Taunton Town	0-0
Worcester City	Wycombe Wanderers	1-1
Hayes	Yeovil Town	1-1
replay		
Barnet	Aylesbury United	0-0
Wealdstone	Harlow Town	0-1
Taunton Town	Weymouth	0-3
Wycombe Wanderers	Worcester City	1-0
Yeovil Town	Hayes	2-0
second replay		
Barnet	Aylesbury United	1-0
First Round		
Burscough	Altrincham	1-2
Barnet	Minehead	2-2
Boston United	Rotherham United	0-4
Gravesend & Northfleet	St Albans City	1-2
Kettering Town	Maidstone United	1-1
Northwich Victoria	Huddersfield Town	1-1
Burnley	Scarborough	1-0
Walsall	Stafford Rangers	3-0
Swindon Town	Weymouth	3-2
Yeovil Town	Farnborough Town	2-1
replay		
Minehead	Barnet	1-2
Maidstone United	Kettering Town	0-0
Huddersfield Town	Northwich Victoria	6-0

F.A.Cup

First Round - second replay		
Maidstone United	Kettering Town	3-1
Second Round		
Scunthorpe United	Altrincham	0-0
Barnet	Peterborough United	0-1
Gillingham	Maidstone United	0-0
Colchester United	Yeovil Town	1-1
replay		
Altrincham	Scunthorpe United	1-0
Maidstone United	Gillingham	0-0
Yeovil Town	Colchester United	0-2
second replay		
Gillingham	Maidstone United	0-2
Third Round		
Liverpool	Altrincham	4-1
Maidstone United	Exeter City	2-4

League Cup

First Round (2 legs)		
Bangor City	Worcester City	0-2
Worcester City	Bangor City	4-3
Gravesend & Northfleet	Bath City	1-3
Bath City	Gravesend & Northfleet	1-1
Maidstone United	Weymouth	1-1
Weymouth	Maidstone United	3-3
(Weymouth won 4-3 on pens)		
Telford United	Stafford Rangers	3-0
Stafford Rangers	Telford United	2-4
(Telford United disqualified, for fielding ineligible player in first leg)		
Second Round (2 legs)		
Altrincham	Boston United	4-0
Boston United	Altrincham	1-2
AP Leamington	Barnet	3-1
Barnet	AP Leamington	6-0
Bath City	Weymouth	0-0
Weymouth	Bath City	2-5
Frickley Ath	Stafford Rangers	1-1
Stafford Rangers	Frickley Ath	4-0
Nuneaton Borough	Wealdstone	0-1
Wealdstone	Nuneaton Borough	0-3
Scarborough	Barrow	0-0
Barrow	Scarborough	2-0
Worcester City	Northwich Victoria	0-0
Northwich Victoria	Worcester City	1-2
Yeovil Town	Kettering Town	0-1
Kettering Town	Yeovil Town	0-0
Third Round		
Altrincham	Nuneaton Borough	2-0
Barrow	Stafford Rangers	2-0
Bath City	Worcester City	1-1
Kettering Town	Barnet	1-1
replay		
Barnet	Kettering Town	1-4
Worcester City	Bath City	2-1
Semi Final (2 legs)		
Barrow	Kettering Town	0-2
Kettering Town	Barrow	5-1
Worcester City	Altrincham	0-1
Altrincham	Worcester City	2-1
Final (2 legs)		
Altrincham	Kettering Town	2-0
Kettering Town	Altrincham	2-1

Challenge Shield

Altrincham	Northwich Victoria	0-1

First Qualifying Round

Moor Green	A.P.Leamington	4-3
Wealdstone	Oxford City	2-4

Third Qualifying Round

Bishop Auckland	Scarborough	1-1
Morecambe	Frickley Athletic	0-0
Bedworth Utd	Telford United	1-0
Northwich Victoria	Boston	2-1
Barnet	Harlow Town	0-1
Bath City	Merthyr Tydfil	1-1
replay		
Scarborough	Bishop Auckland	4-2
Frickley Athletic	Morecambe	0-2
Merthyr Tydfil	Bath City	1-3

First Round

Runcorn	Stafford Rangers	0-1
Boston United	Gateshead	4-0
Nuneaton Borough	Ashington	1-2
Altrincham	Spennymoor United	3-2
Northwich Victoria	Barrow	3-0
Witton Albion	Bangor City	0-3
Mossley	Scarborough	2-2
Dagenham	Bath City	4-0
Hastings Utd	Maidstone United	1-1
Frome Town	Yeovil Town	1-1
Gravesend & Northfleet	Kettering Town	2-3
Minehead	Worcester City	1-3
Leatherhead	Weymouth	1-3
replay		
Scarborough	Mossley	0-1
Maidstone United	Hastings Utd	1-2
Yeovil Town	Frome Town	2-1

Second Round

Goole Town	Worcester City	1-4
Blyth Spartans	Stafford Rangers	1-0
Yeovil Town	Hastings Utd	1-1
Leytonstone & Ilford	Weymouth	1-1
Winsford Utd	Altrincham	0-2
Marine	Bangor City	0-1
Harlow Town	Northwich Victoria	0-1
Boston United	Hitchin Town	0-1
Kettering Town	Mossley	0-1
replay		
Hastings Utd	Yeovil Town	2-1
Weymouth	Leytonstone & Ilford aet	3-4

Third Round

Leytonstone & Ilford	Altrincham	0-1
Aylesbury United	Northwich Victoria	0-0
Hastings Utd	Worcester City	0-0
Bangor City	Hitchin Town	1-0
replay		
Worcester City	Hastings Utd	2-1
Northwich Victoria	Aylesbury United	1-1
second replay		
Aylesbury United	Northwich Victoria	1-0
(Played at Enderby Town)		

Fourth Round

Bishops Stortford	Worcester City	4-0
Bangor City	Mossley	5-3
Dartford	Altrincham	3-1

Semi final

Bangor City	Sutton United	2-2
Sutton United	Bangor City	4-1

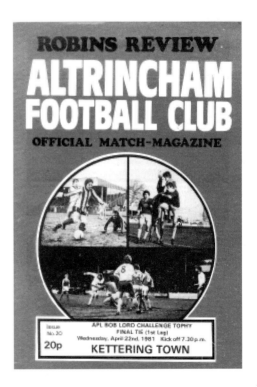

> ALTRINCHAM 2
> KETTERING TOWN 0
> *The top two sides meet
> in the League Cup Final*

1981/82

The first major injection of new faces to the Alliance provided a breath of fresh air to the league and also new champions. Dartford, champions of the Southern League Southern Division and Trowbridge Town, 3rd placed in the Southern League Midland Division were the first clubs to be promoted from their respective divisions. Runcorn were promoted as the Northern Premier League champions, while Enfield and Dagenham accepted the Alliance's invitation to move across from the Isthmian League, forming the first tangible link between the leagues and increasing the number of clubs to twenty-two. During the course of the season, agreement would be reached for the Isthmian League to gain feeder status within the Pyramid from the end of the 1982-3 campaign.

With the exception of Dartford, all the newcomers quickly adjusted to their new surroundings. Dagenham were the early leaders followed by Bath City and Runcorn, and these three were joined in late October by Enfield, who were helped by two wins over Bath City in eight days. It was Runcorn who established a lead during November that they were to maintain for the rest of the season. Having lost the third game of the season, they were not beaten in the league again until mid-February, when Enfield won 2-0 at Southbury Road. This still left the North London side seven points behind, having played one extra game.

A poor winter meant numerous postponements and all clubs faced fixture backlogs, but Runcorn's points on the board kept them in front. Enfield finished nine points adrift but were compensated by their cup heroics. In the F.A.Cup, Wimbledon were beaten 4-1, before Crystal Palace triumphed over the North London team in the 3rd round by the odd goal in five. The Bob Lord Trophy run ended in defeat to Weymouth in a two legged final, while Enfield became the first Alliance team to win the F.A.Trophy when beating Altrincham 1-0 at Wembley. Their success was well merited as they defeated five teams in the Alliance's top eleven on the way.

Teams struggled to play matches during December and January and in order to stage a game, Barnet hired Queens Park Rangers' astroturf pitch for the home fixture with A.P.Leamington. The 'visitors' would have been the happier with the point as it was only their fourth of the season. Their first victory came on 13th February, in their 27th match, away to reigning champions Altrincham. Two-nil down with 17 minutes to go, a comeback was hardly on the cards, but the winner was scored two minutes from time to at last break their duck.

Barnet, who had made the F.A.Cup headlines with their 3rd round tie against Brighton & Hove Albion, finished the season with a final day battle against relegation. Level on points with Kettering and Gravesend, a point in a goalless draw with Boston Utd preserved their status and the previous year's runners-up, Kettering, retained their status on goal difference, despite a defeat at Maidstone.

1981/82 Season Results Grid

	Altrincham	A.P.Leamington	Barnet	Barrow	Bath City	Boston United	Dagenham	Dartford	Enfield	Frickley Athletic	Gravesend & Northfleet	Kettering Town	Maidstone United	Northwich Victoria	Runcorn	Scarborough	Stafford Rangers	Telford United	Trowbridge Town	Weymouth	Worcester City	Yeovil Town
Altrincham	X	2-3	2-0	1-1	1-0	1-1	1-1	2-0	1-0	1-1	3-1	2-1	1-2	0-2	2-2	2-0	0-1	3-0	1-2	0-0	6-3	7-1
A.P.Leamington	0-1	X	0-2	1-1	0-1	2-2	0-4	0-2	2-3	1-0	3-3	3-3	1-1	0-2	1-1	1-2	1-5	0-2	0-1	2-2	0-1	2-5
Barnet	0-0	0-0	X	1-2	0-1	0-0	1-2	2-0	4-1	0-0	2-0	2-1	1-1	0-1	1-3	1-1	0-2	1-0	0-0	0-3	1-2	0-0
Barrow	1-0	4-2	2-1	X	0-1	1-0	2-2	2-0	0-2	2-0	3-1	7-2	2-0	6-1	1-1	3-2	1-1	2-0	1-0	2-0	0-0	3-1
Bath City	1-1	7-0	2-1	0-0	X	1-2	0-3	1-1	0-1	1-3	1-0	3-2	1-1	1-1	0-2	2-0	1-1	1-2	1-1	2-1	2-3	2-0
Boston United	1-1	2-0	1-1	2-1	4-0	X	3-4	3-2	1-0	3-1	2-2	4-2	6-0	2-0	0-1	2-1	2-1	4-2	1-0	1-2	3-2	0-0
Dagenham	2-0	0-0	1-1	1-0	0-1	2-0	X	2-1	2-4	2-0	1-1	2-1	1-1	2-1	0-0	2-2	2-2	3-2	1-2	1-1	1-2	3-0
Dartford	0-1	2-2	2-1	0-2	1-1	2-1	0-3	X	0-2	1-0	0-1	2-2	2-1	0-1	1-2	0-1	2-2	2-0	1-0	0-0	0-2	5-0
Enfield	1-1	6-1	0-0	7-2	5-1	4-0	3-2	1-1	X	3-0	4-0	1-1	3-2	1-0	2-0	1-4	2-0	3-4	2-1	3-0	1-2	2-0
Frickley Athletic	1-1	4-1	0-0	2-1	1-3	4-1	3-1	3-0	1-1	X	1-1	3-2	0-3	1-0	2-0	2-3	0-0	2-0	0-1	1-2	2-1	1-1
Gravesend & Northfleet	1-1	4-1	2-3	3-1	0-2	3-1	1-2	1-0	1-2	4-1	X	1-3	2-2	0-1	2-4	3-0	1-1	0-2	1-1	2-1	1-1	1-1
Kettering Town	5-4	1-2	5-2	0-2	1-3	1-1	3-1	4-4	0-1	0-0	2-1	X	2-2	0-0	0-1	1-2	3-0	1-3	4-0	1-2	0-1	1-1
Maidstone United	0-0	4-0	0-0	1-0	1-0	0-2	2-2	5-1	1-4	0-0	0-1	2-0	X	6-1	1-2	0-2	3-1	2-2	3-0	0-1	2-2	0-1
Northwich Victoria	2-0	3-0	1-1	2-0	2-1	1-0	3-0	3-4	2-1	0-0	1-0	2-0	3-1	X	1-1	2-1	1-2	2-2	0-0	0-2	3-0	1-1
Runcorn	5-4	3-0	1-0	0-0	5-1	4-0	1-0	4-2	2-0	1-1	1-0	3-2	1-1	0-1	X	2-0	1-0	2-3	3-1	5-2	5-1	3-0
Scarborough	1-3	6-1	1-0	2-0	1-1	1-1	1-1	2-0	1-4	0-1	5-0	1-0	0-0	0-4	3-0	X	1-0	0-0	3-1	1-0	1-0	2-2
Stafford Rangers	2-0	3-1	1-0	1-1	2-0	0-0	0-0	0-3	0-1	0-0	1-0	1-1	1-1	2-2	0-1	1-1	X	1-2	0-2	3-0	0-2	3-1
Telford United	4-3	2-0	3-0	0-0	0-2	4-1	0-2	2-0	0-0	7-1	1-0	1-0	1-2	2-1	1-1	1-1	0-3	X	2-0	2-0	3-2	2-1
Trowbridge Town	0-2	2-1	1-1	1-1	1-1	1-0	0-1	2-1	2-2	2-0	2-1	0-1	1-0	3-0	0-0	1-3	1-1	1-2	X	1-1	1-1	2-4
Weymouth	1-0	1-2	0-2	3-0	2-1	1-1	2-1	2-2	5-0	1-2	2-3	1-0	0-0	3-1	1-1	0-1	1-0	1-0	1-0	X	3-2	1-1
Worcester City	4-3	2-1	3-1	4-0	2-0	0-0	2-1	2-0	1-2	3-2	2-1	1-1	4-1	0-1	0-0	2-4	1-1	2-1	3-1	0-0	X	0-1
Yeovil Town	2-1	3-2	4-1	0-0	2-0	0-1	1-4	1-1	1-2	1-2	2-1	1-1	1-0	4-1	1-3	0-0	2-1	1-2	2-0	1-4	3-0	X

Final Table

	Home					Away					Total					
	P	W	D	L	F	A	W	D	L	F	A	W	D	L	F	A	Pts
Runcorn	42	17	2	2	48	18	11	7	3	27	19	28	9	5	75	37	93
Enfield	42	14	4	3	55	22	12	4	5	35	24	26	8	8	90	46	86
Telford United	42	13	4	4	38	20	10	4	7	32	31	23	8	11	70	51	77
Worcester City	42	12	4	5	38	23	9	4	8	32	37	21	8	13	70	60	71
Dagenham	42	10	6	5	32	23	9	6	6	37	28	19	12	11	69	51	69
Northwich Victoria	42	12	6	3	35	17	8	3	10	21	29	20	9	13	56	46	69
Scarborough	42	11	6	4	34	20	8	5	8	31	32	19	11	12	65	52	68
Barrow	42	15	4	2	45	17	3	7	11	14	33	18	11	13	59	50	65
Weymouth	42	11	4	6	33	21	7	5	9	23	26	18	9	15	56	47	63
Boston United	42	14	4	3	46	23	3	7	11	15	34	17	11	14	61	57	62
Altrincham	42	10	6	5	39	22	4	7	10	27	34	14	13	15	66	56	55
Bath City	42	7	7	7	30	26	8	3	10	20	31	15	10	17	50	57	55
Yeovil Town	42	10	4	7	33	27	4	7	10	23	41	14	11	17	56	68	53
Stafford Rangers	42	7	8	6	22	19	5	8	8	26	28	12	16	14	48	47	52
Frickley Athletic	42	11	4	6	35	23	3	6	12	12	37	14	10	18	47	60	52
Maidstone United	42	8	6	7	33	22	3	9	9	22	37	11	15	16	55	59	48
Trowbridge Town	42	8	7	6	26	23	4	4	13	12	31	12	11	19	38	54	47
Barnet	42	5	8	8	17	20	4	6	11	19	32	9	14	19	36	52	41
Kettering Town	42	6	7	8	35	32	3	6	12	29	44	9	13	20	64	76	40
Gravesend & Northfleet	42	7	6	8	34	31	3	4	14	17	38	10	10	22	51	69	40 R
Dartford	42	7	5	9	23	25	3	4	14	24	44	10	9	23	47	69	39 R
APLeamington	42	1	7	13	20	44	3	3	15	20	61	4	10	28	40	105	22 R

FINAL TABLE

CUP COMPETITIONS

F.A.Cup

Preliminary Round		
Dartford	Redhill	2-2
Telford United	Oswestry Town	4-0
replay		
Redhill	Dartford	1-0
First Qualifying Round		
South Bank	Barrow	3-2
Boston United	Sutton Town	2-1
Frickley Ath	Whitby Town	2-0
Runcorn	Leek Town	3-0
Belper Town	Telford United	0-6
Frome Town	Trowbridge Town	2-1
Worcester City	Moreton Town	5-2
Bath City	Mangotsfield Utd	3-0
Second Qualifying Round		
Alfreton Town	Boston Utd	0-2
(Played at Boston Utd)		
Goole Town	Frickley Ath	2-3
Shifnal Town	Runcorn	0-3
Telford United	Burcough	3-0
Bridgend Town	Worcester City	1-3
Cheltenham Town	Bath City	2-2
replay		
Bath City	Cheltenham Town	1-2
Third Qualifying Round		
Boston United	North Ferriby United	4-0
Bishop Auckland	Frickley Ath	3-0
Runcorn	Prescot Cables	4-1
Telford United	Caernarfon Town	1-2
Worcester City	Devizes Town	4-1
Fourth Qualifying Round		
Barnet	Corinthian Casuals	2-0
Boston United	Dunstable	3-1
Gravesend & Northfleet	Dagenham	0-0
Kettering Town	Kings Lynn	2-1
Maidstone United	Barking	0-1
Penrith	Northwich Victoria	1-0
Spennymoor United	Runcorn	0-1
Scarborough	Blyth Spartans	2-3
Stafford Rangers	AP Leamington	3-0
Weymouth	Farnborough Town	3-0
Minehead	Worcester City	1-0
Yeovil Town	Merthy Tydfil	3-0
replay		
Dagenham	Gravesend & Northfleet	6-3
First Round		
Sheffield United	Altrincham	2-2
Harlow Town	Barnet	0-0
Boston United	Kettering Town	0-1
Dagenham	Yeovil Town	2-2
Enfield	Hastings United	2-0
Burnley	Runcorn	0-0
Stafford Rangers	York City	1-2
Weymouth	Northampton Town	0-0
replay		
Altrincham	Sheffield United	3-0
Barnet	Harlow Town	1-0
Runcorn	Burnley	1-2
Northampton Town	Weymouth	6-2
Yeovil Town	Dagenham	0-1
Second Round		
York City	Altrincham	0-0
Barnet	Wycombe Wanderers	2-0
Dagenham	Millwall	1-2
Enfield	Wimbledon	4-1
Kettering Town	Blackpool	0-3

F.A.Cup

Second Round - replay		
Altrincham	York City	4-3
Third Round		
Burnley	Altrincham	6-1
Barnet	Brighton & Hove Albion	0-0
Enfield	Crystal Palace	2-3
replay		
Brighton & Hove Albion	Barnet	3-1

League Cup (All Rounds two legs)

First Round		
AP Leamington	Enfield	1-4
Enfield	AP Leamington	4-0
Dagenham	Barnet	1-0
Barnet	Dagenham	2-1
(Dagenham won on away goals)		
Dartford	Trowbridge Town	0-1
Trowbridge Town	Dartford	1-3
Stafford Rangers	Runcorn	2-2
Runcorn	Stafford Rangers	2-0
Worcester City	Telford United	2-4
Telford United	Worcester City	2-1
Yeovil Town	Gravesend & Northfleet	0-2
Gravesend & Northfleet	Yeovil Town	0-0
Second Round		
Barrow	Altrincham	2-1
Altrincham	Barrow	4-2
Boston United	Frickley Ath	0-0
Frickley Ath	Boston United	1-3
Dagenham	Bath City	5-0
Bath City	Dagenham	2-2
Dartford	Weymouth	2-3
Weymouth	Dartford	2-1
Gravesend & Northfleet	Maidstone United	1-1
Maidstone United	Gravesend & Northfleet	2-2
(Gravesend & Northfleet won on away goals)		
Northwich Victoria	Kettering Town	3-3
Kettering Town	Northwich Victoria	0-2
Runcorn	Scarborough	2-1
Scarborough	Runcorn	2-2
Telford United	Enfield	1-1
Enfield	Telford United	2-1
Third Round		
Altrincham	Northwich Victoria	1-0
Northwich Victoria	Altrincham	1-3
Boston United	Runcorn	2-1
Runcorn	Boston United	1-0
(Runcorn won on away goals)		
Dagenham	Enfield	1-2
Enfield	Dagenham	2-1
Gravesend & Northfleet	Weymouth	0-1
Weymouth	Gravesend & Northfleet	2-0
Semi Final		
Runcorn	Enfield	1-1
Enfield	Runcorn	2-0
Weymouth	Altrincham	1-0
Altrincham	Weymouth	2-4
Final		
Enfield	Weymouth	1-2
Weymouth	Enfield	4-3

Challenge Shield

Altrincham	Kettering Town	4-2

16

First Qualifying Round		
Enderby Town	A.P.Leamington	3-1
Telford United	Moor Green	1-1
Trowbridge Town	Shepton Mallet Town	2-1
Second Qualifying Round		
Bilston	Telford United	1-2
Trowbridge Town	Barnstaple Town	4-0
replay		
Moor Green	Telford United	0-2
Third Qualifying Round		
Telford United	Nantwich Town	5-0
Hendon	Barnet	2-1
Workington	Frickley Athletic	0-1
Epsom & Ewell	Gravesend & Northfleet	1-1
Maidstone United	Bognor Regis Town	2-1
Minehead	Trowbridge Town	3-1
Bath City	Bridgwater Town	3-0
replay		
Gravesend & Northfleet	Epsom & Ewell	3-3
second replay		
Gravesend & Northfleet	Epsom & Ewell	0-1
First Round		
Boston United	Hyde Utd	0-1
Telford United	Burton Albion	1-0
Marine	Scarborough	0-1
Frickley Athletic	Bishop Auckland	0-1
Runcorn	Stafford Rangers	2-0
Kidderminster Harriers	Barrow	0-0
Northwich Victoria	Bangor City	3-2
Kettering Town	Mossley	0-1
Altrincham	Nuneaton Borough	1-0
Slough Town	Bath City	4-2
Minehead	Worcester City	1-1
Weymouth	Enfield	0-1
Dartford	Leatherhead	2-1
Yeovil Town	Bishops Stortford	2-3
Maidstone United	Hastings Utd	1-1
Dagenham	Hitchin Town	1-0
replay		
Barrow	Kidderminster Harriers	2-2
Worcester City	Minehead	5-2
Hastings Utd	Maidstone United	0-2
second replay		
Kidderminster Harriers	Barrow	2-1
Second Round		
Wealdstone	Dagenham	1-2
St Albans City	Scarborough	0-1
Epsom & Ewell	Altrincham	0-1
Bishops Stortford	Maidstone United	3-0
Telford United	Bedford Town	0-0
Runcorn	Lancaster City	4-0
Merthyr Tydfil	Enfield	1-6
Worcester City	Croydon	4-1
Dartford	Northwich Victoria	0-2

Second Round - replay		
Bedford Town	Telford United	0-3
Third Round		
Altrincham	Mossley	2-0
Kidderminster Harriers	Dagenham	4-3
Telford United	Enfield	0-1
Scarborough	Slough Town	1-1
Northwich Victoria	Runcorn	3-0
Sutton United	Worcester City	1-1
replay		
Slough Town	Scarborough	1-2
Worcester City	Sutton United	5-2
Fourth Round		
Altrincham	Bishops Stortford	2-2
Northwich Victoria	Worcester City	2-1
Enfield	Scarborough	4-2
replay		
Bishops Stortford	Altrincham	1-3
Semi Final		
Altrincham	Wycombe Wanderers	1-1
Wycombe Wanderers	Altrincham	0-3
Northwich Victoria	Enfield	0-0
Enfield	Northwich Victoria	1-0
Final (@ Wembley)		
Altrincham	Enfield	0-1

BARNET 0
BRIGHTON & H.A. 0
Barnet's F.A. Cup highlight in an
otherwise disappointing season.

1982/83

Despite the regional bias in favour of clubs from the Midlands and the South. The Championship Trophy had so far been the exclusive property of clubs from Cheshire. Enfield's title success in 1982-3 heralded a four year period of South-east superiority. This was particularly emphasised by their main challengers, Maidstone Utd and Wealdstone, who each won the title in the following two years.

From the start, Enfield set a pace that the others found difficult to match. The Southbury Road side lost only one of their first nineteen games, at home to basement club Stafford Rangers - who gained their only away win of the season. Maidstone Utd lost their first two matches, then won ten and drew one of the next eleven. Wealdstone remained unbeaten for the longest period, but due to their early start in the F.A.Cup, their were behind on games played. It was unlucky 13 for the Stones as they lost their thirteenth league game of the season on November 13th at home to Weymouth, and this reverse heralded a run of three defeats in four matches. Enfield's form dipped around the Christmas/New Year period with four defeats in five games, yet they were still able to hold onto the top spot, although all the chasing clubs had games in hand.

The 'E's and Maidstone United fought nip and tuck for the leadership, but in mid-March it appeared that the Kent side had the overall supremacy. Enfield lost 5-1 at Harrow Borough in the F.A.Trophy and followed this with a 5-2 midweek reversal at Frickley Athletic. This situation prompted some personnel changes which proved successful, as Enfield collected 24 points from their final eleven games, compared to Maidstone United's 18, and Wealdstone's 17, in the same number of matches. The pendulum had swung back in Enfield's favour and on the final day of the season Maidstone had to hope that their rivals lost at Runcorn while Scarborough had to be beaten, and a five goal deficit in goal difference had to be overhauled. This was achieved as Scarborough were thrashed 6-0, but Enfield twice fought back from a goal down to secure the necessary point to take the title.

Conference sides suffered in the F.A.Trophy at the hands of Northern Counties (East) side Ilkeston Town. Stafford Rangers were accounted for in a first round replay, while Barnet were defeated at Underhill in the second. However, the latter match was marred by crowd troubles, with pitch invasions and a supporter falling through the roof behind one goal. Barnet appealed to the F.A., claiming players and officials had been intimidated, but this was rejected. But in round three, at home to Enfield, the Cup match was interrupted on several occasions, before finally being abandoned with 15 minutes left, and the visitors leading 5-1. The tie was awarded to Enfield, Ilkeston Town's big day having been ruined by a large number of trouble-makers, who - typically - were not to be found at Ilkeston's Manor Ground on any ordinary matchday.

1982/83 Season Results Grid

	Altrincham	Bangor City	Barnet	Barrow	Bath City	Boston United	Dagenham	Enfield	Frickley Athletic	Kettering Town	Maidstone United	Northwich Victoria	Nuneaton Borough	Runcorn	Scarborough	Stafford Rangers	Telford United	Trowbridge Town	Wealdstone	Weymouth	Worcester City	Yeovil Town
Altrincham	X	2-0	3-0	2-2	0-0	2-2	2-0	2-2	2-2	3-1	0-2	3-0	1-2	2-1	2-1	4-0	1-0	2-0	0-1	1-0	2-0	4-1
Bangor City	1-0	X	1-0	2-2	0-0	0-1	1-1	0-0	1-0	4-2	2-2	1-1	5-2	1-2	0-3	1-0	1-1	4-3	2-2	4-3	0-2	2-2
Barnet	2-1	1-3	X	2-1	2-1	1-4	2-2	1-3	4-1	2-3	1-3	4-2	1-0	2-0	2-3	1-0	0-2	1-3	0-0	1-2	3-1	4-4
Barrow	2-2	1-5	0-1	X	0-1	1-1	1-2	0-3	2-0	2-0	0-3	0-0	2-2	1-2	1-2	2-1	0-5	3-2	0-2	3-0	1-0	3-1
Bath City	0-2	1-2	0-2	4-1	X	3-2	3-1	2-2	4-3	2-1	0-1	3-0	3-0	2-1	2-3	5-1	0-0	2-0	3-2	0-1	0-0	2-0
Boston United	3-0	4-3	1-0	2-1	2-2	X	3-3	0-2	2-1	2-1	1-0	1-0	1-1	2-4	1-0	1-1	4-0	3-0	0-0	3-2	4-1	6-3
Dagenham	1-1	1-1	1-2	0-0	0-1	1-1	X	1-0	4-1	2-3	0-1	3-1	0-0	3-1	1-1	3-3	1-1	0-1	1-2	1-2	3-3	3-0
Enfield	2-1	6-2	5-0	2-0	3-0	4-2	2-1	X	2-2	5-2	1-0	2-1	1-1	0-0	5-3	0-1	6-2	2-0	0-1	2-1	4-0	3-1
Frickley Athletic	3-0	3-3	0-1	1-1	2-1	2-0	1-2	5-2	X	3-2	2-1	0-0	2-1	0-2	2-1	3-0	2-2	2-2	2-2	1-2	1-2	3-0
Kettering Town	3-2	3-4	3-1	3-1	4-2	2-0	1-2	0-2	4-1	X	1-3	1-4	0-0	3-1	2-2	2-1	1-2	1-1	1-3	1-1	1-1	5-2
Maidstone United	3-2	6-1	2-0	2-0	0-1	2-0	1-3	1-1	4-0	5-1	X	1-0	2-0	2-0	6-0	1-0	1-0	6-0	0-3	3-0	5-0	2-1
Northwich Victoria	2-1	1-4	1-0	1-0	3-0	1-1	3-0	3-1	2-1	2-1	2-1	X	2-2	2-0	1-1	2-1	2-1	6-3	3-3	1-1	3-0	5-0
Nuneaton Borough	3-1	2-1	1-0	1-1	5-0	1-2	1-1	0-2	5-1	0-0	2-2	2-1	X	0-2	0-2	1-1	2-1	2-0	1-1	2-0	2-0	3-1
Runcorn	1-0	1-2	2-0	2-1	1-0	3-2	5-1	2-2	3-3	6-0	1-1	1-1	3-1	X	2-1	4-1	0-0	3-2	2-1	1-0	3-1	4-1
Scarborough	1-1	2-0	0-2	1-1	0-1	0-0	1-1	0-2	1-2	3-0	2-1	5-1	3-0	3-2	X	2-1	1-1	5-2	1-2	2-0	4-1	2-2
Stafford Rangers	2-3	1-1	1-0	2-0	1-1	0-2	1-2	0-3	1-1	1-1	2-3	1-1	1-2	0-1	0-0	X	1-1	3-2	2-1	1-2	0-0	1-3
Telford United	1-1	2-0	3-0	1-3	2-0	3-2	3-0	4-3	1-1	2-1	3-1	3-0	2-0	4-0	0-2	2-0	X	3-1	0-0	2-0	2-0	3-2
Trowbridge Town	3-2	3-2	0-2	2-1	1-1	1-2	2-2	2-1	2-0	2-1	0-2	0-2	0-2	1-2	1-1	5-3	2-0	X	0-0	0-0	2-3	2-1
Wealdstone	1-1	2-0	6-0	4-0	1-1	0-0	3-1	1-3	2-0	4-0	0-0	2-1	1-2	2-2	3-2	2-0	4-0	2-0	X	2-4	2-0	2-0
Weymouth	2-0	2-1	1-3	1-1	1-0	4-2	0-1	1-0	0-0	4-1	0-0	3-0	3-0	1-1	2-0	0-0	0-0	2-1	4-1	X	4-2	2-0
Worcester City	1-0	1-1	4-2	2-1	1-4	1-1	1-4	1-1	4-4	6-2	1-1	3-0	1-1	1-3	3-0	1-0	4-1	1-3	3-3	X	2-1	
Yeovil Town	2-1	3-2	4-2	2-2	1-0	0-4	2-0	1-3	2-1	2-1	0-0	2-4	6-2	1-1	2-1	0-0	3-4	0-1	1-5	0-2	3-0	X

		Home					Away					Total					
	P	W	D	L	F	A	W	D	L	F	A	W	D	L	F	A	Pts
Enfield	42	16	3	2	57	21	9	6	6	38	27	25	9	8	95	48	84
Maidstone United	42	17	1	3	55	13	8	7	6	28	21	25	8	9	83	34	83
Wealdstone	42	13	5	3	45	17	9	8	4	35	24	22	13	7	80	41	79
Runcorn	42	15	5	1	50	21	7	3	11	23	32	22	8	12	73	53	74
Boston United	42	14	5	2	46	25	6	7	8	31	32	20	12	10	77	57	72
Telford United	42	16	3	2	46	17	4	8	9	23	31	20	11	11	69	48	71
Weymouth	42	13	6	2	37	14	7	4	10	26	34	20	10	12	63	48	70
Northwich Victoria	42	15	5	1	48	22	3	5	13	20	41	18	10	14	68	63	64
Scarborough	42	10	6	5	39	23	7	6	8	32	35	17	12	13	71	58	63
Bath City	42	12	3	6	41	25	5	6	10	17	30	17	9	16	58	55	60
Nuneaton Borough	42	11	6	4	36	20	4	7	10	21	40	15	13	14	57	60	58
Altrincham	42	13	5	3	40	17	2	5	14	22	39	15	10	17	62	56	55
Bangor City	42	8	9	4	33	29	6	4	11	38	48	14	13	15	71	77	55
Dagenham	42	5	9	7	30	26	7	6	8	30	39	12	15	15	60	65	51
Barnet	42	9	3	9	37	39	7	0	14	18	39	16	3	23	55	78	51
Frickley Athletic	42	11	6	4	41	25	1	7	13	25	52	12	13	17	66	77	49
Worcester City	42	10	7	4	43	33	2	3	16	15	54	12	10	20	58	87	46
Trowbridge Town	42	9	5	7	31	30	3	2	16	25	58	12	7	23	56	88	43
Kettering Town	42	9	5	7	45	37	2	2	17	24	62	11	7	24	69	99	40
Yeovil Town	42	10	4	7	37	36	1	3	17	26	63	11	7	24	63	99	40
Barrow	42	7	4	10	26	35	1	8	12	20	39	8	12	22	46	74	36 R
Stafford Rangers	42	4	8	9	22	30	1	6	14	18	45	5	14	23	40	75	29 R

FINAL TABLE

Gateshead promoted from N.P.L., Kidderminster Harriers from Southern League.

F.A. Cup

Preliminary Round		
Barrow	Crook Town	2-0
Frickley Ath	Shildon	5-3
First Qualifying Round		
Ferryhill Ath	Barrow	0-1
Netherfield	Frickley Ath	0-2
Macclesfield Town	Bangor City	3-1
Thackley	Runcorn	0-0
Telford United	Buxton	3-0
Stamford	Nuneaton Borough	1-1
Alvechurch	Worcester City	2-4
Wealdstone	Hertford Town	5-0
Trowbridge Town	Ton Pentre	2-0
Bath City	Taunton Town	2-2
replay		
Runcorn	Thackley	2-1
Taunton Town	Bath City	2-4
Nuneaton Borough	Stamford	5-0
Second Qualifying Round		
Lancaster City	Barrow	0-0
Frickley Ath	Harrogate Town	3-1
Runcorn	Curzon Ashton	3-0
Telford United	Congleton Town	3-2
Nuneaton Borough	Gainsborough Trinity	3-3
Worcester City	Rothwell Town	3-1
Hendon	Wealdstone	1-1
Trowbridge Town	Bristol Manor Farm	3-0
Bath City	Barnstaple Town	4-2
replay		
Barrow	Lancaster City	1-0
Gainsborough Trinity	Nuneaton Borough	2-0
Wealdstone	Hendon	3-2
Third Qualifying Round		
Barrow	Annfield Plain	8-0
Frickley Ath	Spennymoor Utd	1-1
Chorley	Runcorn	2-2
Eastwood Town	Telford United	2-2
Sutton Coldfield Town	Worcester City	2-4
Dulwich Hamlet	Wealdstone	0-0
Trowbridge Town	Cheltenham Town	1-1
Wimborne Town	Bath City	1-0
replay		
Spennymoor Utd	Frickley Ath	1-1
Runcorn	Chorley	4-0
Telford United	Eastwood Town	4-0
Wealdstone	Dulwich Hamlet	2-1
Cheltenham Town	Trowbridge Town	1-0
second replay		
Frickley Ath	Spennymoor Utd	2-3
Fourth Qualifying Round		
Boston United	Shifnal Town	4-1
Cheltenham Town	Weymouth	0-0
Dagenham	Tooting & Mitcham Utd	2-0
Gravesend & Northfleet	Maidstone United	1-2
Horwich RMI	Runcorn	2-2
Kettering Town	AP Leamington	3-1
Macclesfield Town	Stafford Rangers	3-1
North Shields	Barrow	2-1
Northwich Victoria	Blyth Spartans	3-0
Scarborough	Spennymoor Utd	4-2
Telford United	Grantham	3-0
Wealdstone	Sutton United	3-1
Worcester City	Wellingborough Town	2-1
Yeovil Town	Bognor Regis Town	4-2
replay		
Runcorn	Horwich RMI	0-1
Weymouth	Cheltenham Town	4-0
First Round		
Altrincham	Rochdale	2-1
Boston United	Crewe Alexandra	3-1
Carshalton Ath	Barnet	4-0
Chesham Utd	Yeovil Town	0-1
Chester	Northwich Victoria	1-1
Enfield	Newport County	0-0
Gillingham	Dagenham	1-0
Macclesfield Town	Worcester City	1-5
Swindon Town	Wealdstone	2-0
Tranmere Rovers	Scarborough	4-2
Walsall	Kettering Town	3-0
Weymouth	Maidstone United	4-3
Wigan Ath	Telford United	0-0

F.A. Cup

First Round - replay		
Newport County	Enfield	4-2
Northwich Victoria	Chester	3-1
Telford United	Wigan Ath	2-1
Second Round		
Altrincham	Huddersfield Town	0-1
Boston United	Sheffield United	1-1
Cardiff City	Weymouth	2-3
Scunthorpe Utd	Northwich Victoria	2-1
Southend Utd	Yeovil Town	3-0
Telford United	Tranmere Rovers	1-1
Worcester City	Wrexham	2-1
replay		
Sheffield United	Boston United	5-1
Tranmere Rovers	Telford United	2-1
Third Round		
Cambridge Utd	Weymouth	1-0
Coventry City	Worcester City	3-1

League Cup (All Rounds two legs)

First Round		
Frickley Ath	Altrincham	2-0
Altrincham	Frickley Ath	5-0
Bangor City	Kettering Town	6-1
Kettering Town	Bangor City	1-1
Barnet	Trowbridge Town	3-0
Trowbridge Town	Barnet	0-2
Bath City	Wealdstone	0-1
Wealdstone	Bath City	0-2
Maidstone United	Yeovil Town	4-1
Yeovil Town	Maidstone United	1-3
Stafford Rangers	Nuneaton Borough	0-1
Nuneaton Borough	Stafford Rangers	0-2
Second Round		
Barnet	Weymouth	2-0
Weymouth	Barnet	0-1
Barrow	Bangor City	2-0
Bangor City	Barrow	3-1
(Barrow won on away goals)		
Scarborough	Boston United	5-0
Boston United	Scarborough	3-1
Dagenham	Enfield	3-2
Enfield	Dagenham	4-2
Bath City	Maidstone United	0-2
Maidstone United	Bath City	7-1
Northwich Victoria	Altrincham	2-2
Altrincham	Northwich Victoria	1-2
Runcorn	Stafford Rangers	3-0
Stafford Rangers	Runcorn	1-1
Worcester City	Telford United	1-0
Telford United	Worcester City	0-2
Third Round		
Maidstone United	Enfield	1-3
Enfield	Maidstone United	2-1
Scarborough	Northwich Victoria	2-1
Northwich Victoria	Scarborough	1-1
Barrow	Runcorn	2-1
Runcorn	Barrow	2-0
Barnet	Worcester City	0-2
Worcester City	Barnet	3-3
Semi final		
Enfield	Runcorn	3-2
Runcorn	Enfield	3-1
Worcester City	Scarborough	1-3
Scarborough	Worcester City	2-2
Final		
Runcorn	Scarborough	1-1
Scarborough	Runcorn	2-2
(Runcorn won on away goals)		

Challenge Shield

Runcorn	Weymouth	4-0

Third Qualifying Round		
Frickley Athletic	Colwyn Bay	1-1
Barnet	Metropolitan Police	2-1
Kettering Town	Barking	2-2
Bromley	Trowbridge Town	4-0
Gravesend & Northfleet	Maidstone United	1-1
replay		
Colwyn Bay	Frickley Athletic	2-0
(Played at Rhyl)		
Barking	Kettering Town	0-0
Maidstone United	Gravesend & Northfleet	3-0
second replay		
Barking	Kettering Town	0-2
First Round		
Bishop Auckland	Nuneaton Borough	1-3
Bangor City	Kings Lynn	1-1
Barrow	Rhyl	2-1
Corby Town	Altrincham	1-1
Boston United	Marine	3-0
Kidderminster Harriers	Northwich Victoria	0-3
Burton Albion	Telford United	0-1
Runcorn	Scarborough	0-1
Stafford Rangers	Ilkeston Town	2-2
Yeovil Town	Sutton United	2-4
Wycombe Wanderers	Wealdstone	2-1
Maidstone United	Aylesbury United	1-0
Slough Town	Dagenham	0-1
Weston Super Mare	Weymouth	0-0
Woking	Barnet	0-2
Enfield	Bishops Stortford	2-1
Bath City	Worcester City	1-2
Dulwich Hamlet	Kettering Town	4-2
replay		
Kings Lynn	Bangor City	0-2
Altrincham	Corby Town	6-0
Ilkeston Town	Stafford Rangers	3-2
(Played at Eastwood Town)		
Weymouth	Weston Super Mare	1-0
Second Round		
Stalybridge Celtic	Scarborough	1-3
Dorchester Town	Enfield	2-3
Wycombe Wanderers	Boston United	0-0
Tow Law Town	Altrincham	2-2
Barnet	Ilkeston Town	1-2
Weymouth	Leytonstone & Ilford	1-0
Worcester City	Dagenham	0-3
Spennymoor Utd	Telford United	0-0
Maidstone United	Dulwich Hamlet	2-2
Ashington	Barrow	1-1
Blyth Spartans	Nuneaton Borough	3-2
Northwich Victoria	Croydon	1-0
Bangor City	Mossley	1-0
replay		
Boston United	Wycombe Wanderers aet	1-1
Altrincham	Tow Law Town	3-0
Telford United	Spennymoor Utd	2-1
Dulwich Hamlet	Maidstone United	0-3
Barrow	Ashington	1-0
second replay		
Wycombe Wanderers	Boston United	0-2
(Played at Kettering Town)		

Third Round			
Barrow	Harrow Borough		1-1
Blyth Spartans	Altrincham		2-0
Boston United	Maidstone United		2-1
Dagenham	Weymouth		3-0
Ilkeston Town	Enfield		1-5
(abandoned 76 mins. Crowd disturbance, result stands)			
Northwich Victoria	Bangor City		1-1
Telford United	Scarborough		3-0
replay			
Harrow Borough	Barrow	aet	1-1
Bangor City	Northwich Victoria	aet	2-2
second replay			
Barrow	Harrow Borough		0-2
(Played at Stafford Rangers)			
Bangor City	Northwich Victoria		0-1
(Played at Wrexham)			
Fourth Round			
Blyth Spartans	Northwich Victoria		1-1
Dagenham	Boston United		2-1
Harrow Borough	Enfield		5-1
Telford United	Dartford		4-1
replay			
Northwich Victoria	Blyth Spartans		3-2
Semi final			
Telford United	Harrow Borough		0-2
Harrow Borough	Telford United		1-5
Northwich Victoria	Dagenham		3-2
Dagenham	Northwich Victoria		0-1
Final (@ Wembley)			
Northwich Victoria	Telford United		1-2

BOSTON UNITED 3
CREWE ALEXANDRA 1
As an A.P.L. member, Boston claim their only League scalp.

1983/84

It was a case of second Utd, as they went one season, to capture their first occasion a final day 6-0 home victory was over long time challengers Nuneaton Borough. time lucky for Maidstone better than the previous Alliance championship. On this sufficient to give them a one point margin

Runcorn had started the season with five straight wins, but by late September, Nuneaton were topping the table from The Cheshire trio of Altrincham, Northwich Victoria and Runcorn. Wealdstone were also mounting a challenge, as they went until mid November undefeated and had games in hand. After losing their lead with a mid-season lapse, Nuneaton surged back to the top, but were vulnerable to Maidstone and Wealdstone, who had games in hand. The Kent side in particular kept up their relentless progress, and lost only two games after October 1st. They topped the table on 11th April, and held a one point lead over Nuneaton when they had to travel to Manor Park for the penultimate fixture. They managed a 2-2 draw, and despite Nuneaton's final day win at Runcorn the title went to Kent.

This was an era of outstanding goalscorers. Paul Culpin (Nuneaton Borough) scored 41 league goals, thereby averaging more than a goal a game. He missed the opening two games when returning from playing in Finland, but still scored nearly 60% of his side's goals. His total broke the Alliance record set twelve months earlier, when John Bartley netted 36 for Maidstone. By his own high standards, Bartley's return of 27 goals was disappointing, but during the season he clocked up his 500th career goal, to go with his 100th hat-trick that he achieved the previous season. He had started playing for Welling Utd, at 15, where he scored over 430 goals. Fifteen months at Millwall produced 8 goals, before joining the Stones in the summer of 1982 - and he was still only 25 years old.

A.P.Leamington had won the Southern League in 1982-3, but were denied the opportunity to renew their Alliance status as revised grading meant that the Windmill Ground was no longer acceptable. Kidderminster, who were runners-up, took the place of the Midland's team. The Harriers also took Leamington's manager Graham Allner and several players duly followed. From this point, the fortunes of the two clubs went in opposite directions - Allner had fifteen years in charge at Aggborough, leading the club to their most successful period, whereas A.P.Leamington were relegated, lost their financial backing, and were eventually disbanded in 1988.

Barnet striker, Steve Ragan, had mixed fortunes in the early season games. When Barnet beat Trowbridge 10-0 in the Bob Lord Trophy, he scored four goals, the first Barnet player to achieve this feat for thirteen years. Eighteen days later, with Barnet leading 1-0 at Yeovil, Ragan collided with the goalpost, causing sufficient damage to the woodwork for the referee to abandon the match!

1983/84 Season Results Grid

	Altrincham	Bangor City	Barnet	Bath City	Boston United	Dagenham	Enfield	Frickley Athletic	Gateshead	Kettering Town	Kidderminster Harriers	Maidstone United	Northwich Victoria	Nuneaton Borough	Runcorn	Scarborough	Telford United	Trowbridge Town	Wealdstone	Weymouth	Worcester City	Yeovil Town
Altrincham	X	2-1	3-2	2-0	3-0	4-0	1-3	1-0	5-0	1-1	0-1	1-0	1-1	0-1	1-3	2-0	1-1	4-0	1-0	2-1	3-4	2-1
Bangor City	1-3	X	0-1	1-0	0-0	2-4	2-1	4-1	3-3	3-1	1-2	0-2	0-1	1-2	2-3	1-1	4-0	4-0	0-0	1-3	2-4	3-0
Barnet	1-2	3-1	X	1-2	1-2	3-1	2-1	3-2	0-1	0-3	0-2	0-4	2-1	1-2	2-0	0-1	0-0	2-1	1-1	1-1	2-0	2-0
Bath City	0-0	5-1	0-1	X	4-2	0-1	3-2	1-0	1-1	1-1	3-0	1-2	2-0	0-1	1-1	4-1	1-1	2-1	0-0	1-0	0-0	3-1
Boston United	2-2	3-2	0-0	0-0	X	3-0	3-2	2-2	0-4	3-1	2-3	1-0	3-1	3-0	1-2	1-1	2-3	2-0	1-1	4-3	0-1	3-2
Dagenham	0-2	3-1	3-1	3-1	2-0	X	1-4	1-1	1-2	2-0	0-0	0-1	3-1	4-2	0-2	1-1	1-2	6-2	1-0	1-2	0-1	1-0
Enfield	0-1	3-1	0-1	2-0	1-0	3-0	X	3-3	0-3	2-2	0-1	0-3	1-2	0-1	0-1	2-1	3-1	2-1	0-2	0-1	2-2	3-0
Frickley Athletic	3-1	2-0	3-1	1-2	7-1	4-0	1-1	X	4-1	1-1	0-2	2-0	4-1	1-3	2-1	2-1	1-1	2-0	2-5	1-2	3-1	3-0
Gateshead	0-1	2-1	2-3	3-1	5-5	1-1	1-1	2-0	X	1-2	1-0	0-2	1-3	1-1	1-1	1-1	2-1	2-2	1-1	3-0	1-1	4-2
Kettering Town	1-1	1-3	0-1	0-0	2-1	2-2	1-0	0-1	3-0	X	4-2	1-0	3-4	1-1	2-3	4-1	3-2	1-2	0-2	0-1	2-3	0-1
Kidderminster Harriers	0-2	2-1	4-4	1-1	1-1	4-2	1-1	1-1	1-0	3-1	X	0-0	2-2	3-3	0-2	1-3	1-0	1-1	3-1	0-1	2-1	1-2
Maidstone United	1-0	2-0	1-1	1-1	2-2	2-0	3-1	1-0	1-0	3-1	1-1	X	0-1	1-0	1-1	1-1	6-0	4-1	2-1	2-2	1-1	4-0
Northwich Victoria	1-1	2-1	0-0	3-2	3-1	3-1	3-1	1-1	3-1	4-0	4-2	1-1	X	1-0	0-1	3-1	1-0	0-2	1-1	1-0	1-0	0-0
Nuneaton Borough	0-1	3-0	2-2	5-2	4-0	1-1	4-0	1-0	3-2	1-0	2-1	2-2	1-0	X	2-2	3-0	1-1	2-1	1-1	3-0	1-0	2-1
Runcorn	0-0	0-2	2-0	2-1	3-1	1-0	0-0	2-1	4-2	4-1	1-0	0-0	0-1	0-0	X	2-0	0-0	2-0	4-2	1-1	2-1	4-4
Scarborough	3-1	3-0	1-0	0-0	2-0	0-0	0-4	3-1	1-1	0-0	2-0	1-1	1-1	1-0	2-1	X	3-0	0-0	1-1	1-1	4-4	3-0
Telford United	2-1	2-1	0-0	3-2	3-2	3-1	0-3	0-1	4-0	1-0	3-0	3-1	0-2	1-0	1-1	1-0	X	1-0	0-1	1-0	2-0	2-2
Trowbridge Town	0-0	1-2	0-4	1-2	0-2	1-4	0-0	0-1	0-2	1-2	1-2	1-2	1-1	0-2	0-1	1-0	2-2	X	1-2	1-2	2-1	1-0
Wealdstone	3-1	5-0	3-0	0-3	1-1	1-0	2-1	0-0	4-2	4-2	2-0	1-2	1-0	0-0	4-2	1-1	4-0	6-0	X	2-0	3-1	1-0
Weymouth	0-1	5-0	2-2	2-1	1-3	0-2	1-1	1-1	0-0	1-3	1-1	0-1	1-3	1-1	0-1	2-1	6-1	2-3	0-4	X	0-2	1-3
Worcester City	0-1	0-0	2-0	2-4	2-2	2-2	1-3	0-0	3-1	0-3	1-1	3-0	2-0	1-1	3-0	3-0	0-1	5-2	1-1	1-0	X	4-0
Yeovil Town	1-2	1-1	2-4	0-2	4-2	0-2	3-2	3-0	0-0	2-0	1-1	1-3	2-0	1-0	0-1	1-2	1-0	3-1	0-0	6-3	2-2	X

FINAL TABLE

		Home					Away					Total						
	P	W	D	L	F	A	W	D	L	F	A	W	D	L	F	A	Pts	
Maidstone United	42	12	8	1	40	15	11	5	5	31	19	23	13	6	71	34	70	
Nuneaton Borough	42	14	6	1	44	17	10	5	6	26	23	24	11	7	70	40	69	
Altrincham	42	13	3	5	40	20	10	6	5	24	19	23	9	10	64	39	65	
Wealdstone	42	15	4	2	48	14	6	10	5	27	22	21	14	7	75	36	62	
Runcorn	42	11	8	2	34	18	9	5	7	27	27	20	13	9	61	45	62	
Bath City	42	10	7	4	33	17	7	5	9	27	31	17	12	13	60	48	53	
Northwich Victoria	42	11	8	2	35	18	5	6	10	19	29	16	14	12	54	47	51	
Worcester City	42	9	7	5	36	22	6	6	9	28	33	15	13	14	64	55	49	
Barnet	42	9	3	9	27	28	7	7	7	28	30	16	10	16	55	58	49	
Kidderminster Harriers	42	7	9	5	32	30	7	5	9	22	31	14	14	14	54	61	49	
Telford United	42	13	3	5	32	19	4	8	9	18	39	17	11	14	50	58	49	
Frickley Athletic	42	13	3	5	49	25	4	7	10	19	31	17	10	15	68	56	48	
Scarborough	42	10	10	1	32	16	4	6	11	20	39	14	16	12	52	55	48	
Enfield	42	8	3	10	27	27	6	6	9	34	31	14	9	19	61	58	43	
Weymouth	42	5	4	12	28	33	8	4	9	26	32	13	8	21	54	65	42	
Gateshead	42	7	9	5	35	30	5	4	12	24	43	12	13	17	59	73	42	
Boston United	42	10	6	5	39	30	3	6	12	27	50	13	12	17	66	80	41	
Dagenham	42	10	3	8	34	26	4	5	12	23	43	14	8	20	57	69	40	
Kettering Town	42	8	3	10	31	31	4	6	11	22	36	12	9	21	53	67	37	
Yeovil Town	42	9	5	7	34	28	3	3	15	21	49	12	8	22	55	77	35	
Bangor City	42	7	4	10	35	32	3	2	16	19	50	10	6	26	54	82	29	R
Trowbridge Town	42	3	4	14	15	34	2	3	16	18	53	5	7	30	33	87	19	R

(2pts = Home win, 3pts = Away win, 1pt draw)

Barrow promoted from N.P.L., Dartford from Southern League.

F.A.Cup

First Qualifying Round		
Seaham Red Star	Gateshead	1-3
Bootle	Bangor City	0-1
Ashton Utd	Runcorn	0-1
Hednesford Town	Frickley Ath	1-2
Nuneaton Borough	Oldbury Utd	1-2
Barton Rovers	Kidderminster Harriers	0-1
Cambridge City	Wealdstone	1-2
Clandown	Trowbridge Town	4-2
Bath City	Shepton Mallet Town	4-0
Second Qualifying Round		
Accrington Stanley	Gateshead	1-1
Chorley	Bangor City	2-4
Hyde Utd	Runcorn	3-0
Bilston	Frickley Ath	1-1
Bedworth Utd	Kidderminster Harriers	2-1
Aveley	Wealdstone	1-1
Bath City	Merthyr Tydfil	0-1
replay		
Gateshead	Accrington Stanley	1-2
Frickley Ath	Bilston	2-0
Wealdstone	Aveley	2-0
Third Qualifying Round		
Bangor City	South Liverpool	1-0
Glossop	Frickley Ath	2-3
Wealdstone	Basildon Utd	3-1
Fourth Qualifying Round		
Bangor City	Scarborough	2-1
Basingstoke Town	Worcester City	1-1
Boston United	Stafford Rangers	3-1
Folkestone	Dagenham	1-1
Frickley Ath	North Shields	1-0
Harlow Town	Barnet	1-1
Kettering Town	Sutton Coldfield Town	3-2
Maidstone United	Sutton United	1-1
Wealdstone	Bishops Stortford	1-0
Weymouth	Farnborough Town	1-1
Yeovil Town	Minehead	2-2
replay		
Barnet	Harlow Town	5-1
Dagenham	Folkestone	3-0
Farnborough Town	Weymouth	3-2
Minehead	Yeovil Town	2-4
Sutton United	Maidstone United	1-3
Worcester City	Basingstoke Town	3-1
First Round		
Aldershot	Worcester City	1-1
Barnet	Bristol Rovers	0-0
Boston United	Bury	0-3
Dagenham	Brentford	2-2
Exeter City	Maidstone United	1-1
Frickley Ath	Altrincham	0-1
Kettering Town	Swindon Town	0-7
Northwich Victoria	Bangor City	1-1
Telford United	Stockport County	3-0
Wealdstone	Enfield	1-1
Yeovil Town	Harrow Borough	0-1
replay		
Bangor City	Northwich Victoria	1-0
Brentford	Dagenham	2-1
Bristol Rovers	Barnet	3-1
Enfield	Wealdstone	2-2
Maidstone United	Exeter City	2-1
Worcester City	Aldershot	2-1
second replay		
Wealdstone	Enfield	2-0

F.A.Cup

Second Round		
Bangor City	Blackpool	1-1
Colchester Utd	Wealdstone	4-0
Darlington	Altrincham	0-0
Maidstone United	Worcester City	3-2
Northampton Town	Telford United	1-1
replay		
Altrincham	Darlington	0-2
Blackpool	Bangor City	2-1
Telford United	Northampton Town	3-2
Third Round		
Darlington	Maidstone United	4-1
Rochdale	Telford United	1-4
Fourth Round		
Derby County	Telford United	3-2

League Cup
(All Rounds two legs)

First Round		
Trowbridge Town	Barnet	1-1
Barnet	Trowbridge Town	10-0
Kettering Town	Nuneaton Borough	4-2
Nuneaton Borough	Kettering Town	1-1
Dagenham	Yeovil Town	0-0
Yeovil Town	Dagenham	1-0
Worcester City	Kidderminster Harriers	1-3
Kidderminster Harriers	Worcester City	4-5
Gateshead	Bangor City	1-1
Bangor City	Gateshead	2-3
Altrincham	Frickley Athletic	3-1
Frickley Athletic	Altrincham	4-0
Second Round		
Wealdstone	Barnet	1-3
Barnet	Wealdstone	2-3
Enfield	Maidstone United	1-1
Maidstone United	Enfield	2-4
Runcorn	Kettering Town	4-0
Kettering Town	Runcorn	1-1
Telford United	Northwich Victoria	1-1
Northwich Victoria	Telford United	2-4
Yeovil Town	Bath City	2-0
Bath City	Yeovil Town	1-1
Kidderminster Harriers	Weymouth	2-1
Weymouth	Kidderminster Harriers	0-2
Frickley Athletic	Gateshead	3-0
Gateshead	Frickley Athletic	4-2
Scarborough	Boston United	1-0
Boston United	Scarborough	0-1
Third Round		
Barnet	Enfield	1-1
Enfield	Barnet	1-3
Runcorn	Telford United	3-0
Telford United	Runcorn	4-0
Kidderminster Harriers	Yeovil Town	1-2
Yeovil Town	Kidderminster Harriers	3-1
Scarborough	Frickley Athletic	1-0
Frickley Athletic	Scarborough	1-3
Semi Final		
Barnet	Telford United	5-0
Telford United	Barnet	2-3
Yeovil Town	Scarborough	0-2
Scarborough	Yeovil Town	5-2
Final		
Scarborough	Barnet	2-0
Barnet	Scarborough	1-0

Challenge Shield

Enfield	Runcorn	4-1

Third Qualifying Round		
Frickley Athletic	Worksop Town	1-0
Dulwich Hamlet	Kettering Town	4-3
Hayes	Barnet	1-3
Trowbridge Town	Poole	4-2
Yeovil Town	Cheltenham Town	5-2
First Round		
Bangor City	Spennymoor Utd	3-1
Croydon	Bath City	0-0
Gateshead	Horden CW	1-1
Weymouth	Hendon	2-3
Hampton	Maidstone United	0-2
Worcester City	Nuneaton Borough	0-0
Dagenham	Fareham Town	0-0
Yeovil Town	Wealdstone	4-3
Leytonstone & Ilford	Trowbridge Town	0-0
Sutton Town	Frickley Athletic	1-4
Mossley	Telford United	1-2
Runcorn	Matlock Town	1-0
Marine	Scarborough	2-1
Barnet	Dartford	3-0
Merthyr Tydfil	Enfield	2-0
Altrincham	Kidderminster Harriers	0-2
Boston United	Northwich Victoria	1-1
replay		
Horden CW	Gateshead	1-3
Nuneaton Borough	Worcester City	2-0
Fareham Town	Dagenham	2-3
Trowbridge Town	Leytonstone & Ilford	1-2
Northwich Victoria	Boston United	5-1
Bath City	Croydon	6-0
Second Round		
Bangor City	Bath City	1-0
Carshalton Ath	Gateshead	1-2
Maidstone United	Nuneaton Borough	2-2
Dagenham	Yeovil Town	1-1
Frickley Athletic	Barrow	5-2
Telford United	Runcorn	2-1
Barnet	North Shields	4-1
Merthyr Tydfil	Kidderminster Harriers	0-1
Aylesbury United	Northwich Victoria	0-1
replay		
Nuneaton Borough	Maidstone United	1-0
Yeovil Town	Dagenham	1-4
Third Round		
Gateshead	Bangor City	2-2
Nuneaton Borough	Dagenham	2-2
Whitby Town	Frickley Athletic	2-0
Telford United	Bromsgrove Rovers	2-0
Barnet	Kidderminster Harriers	2-1
Dulwich Hamlet	Northwich Victoria	0-0
replay		
Bangor City	Gateshead	2-0
Dagenham	Nuneaton Borough	1-0
Northwich Victoria	Dulwich Hamlet	0-0

Third Round - second replay		
Northwich Victoria	Dulwich Hamlet	1-0
(Played at Nuneaton Borough)		
Fourth Round		
AP Leamington	Bangor City	1-6
Dagenham	Whitby Town	2-2
Telford United	Marine	3-3
Northwich Victoria	Barnet	1-0
replay		
Whitby Town	Dagenham	0-3
Marine	Telford United	2-0
Semi Final		
Bangor City	Dagenham	1-0
Dagenham	Bangor City	2-2
Northwich Victoria	Marine	1-1
Marine	Northwich Victoria	0-2
Final *(@ Wembley)*		
Northwich Victoria	Bangor City	1-1
replay *(@ Stoke City)*		
Northwich Victoria	Bangor City	2-1

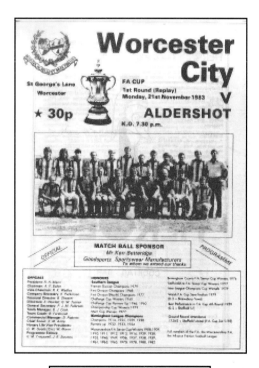

WORCESTER CITY 2
ALDERSHOT 1
Worcester claim a rare giant-killing, at the second attempt

25

Wealdstone were the first **1984/85** team to win the newly titled 'Gola League' and F.A.Trophy 'double', a feat that would suggest that they dominated the season. Yet the league table showed that the title was won with the lowest number of victories recorded by a champion club (20), the highest number of defeats (12) and a goal difference of only plus 10.

This was possibly the most evenly balanced season on record. Yeovil and Gateshead were cast adrift early and never regained the lost ground, but apart from them, the difference between top and bottom was relatively small, as shown by the fact that only thirteen points separated the teams in second and seventeenth places. Wealdstone took the early lead and were undefeated for nine matches, yet they then won only one of the next nine while losing in both the F.A.Cup and Bob Lord Trophy. At this time (the beginning of December), Altrincham were top with Enfield, Wealdstone and Boston just three points behind, but over the Christmas and New Year period the lead opened up to six points, albeit that Wealdstone had two games in hand, while the others dropped back.

Poor weather in January and February caused several postponements, and with progress being made in the F.A.Trophy and County Cup, Wealdstone did not play a league fixture for eight weeks, yet when they resumed on March 2nd they were still only six points off the lead with five games in hand, Altrincham having lost three on the trot.

The only team to make headway was Nuneaton. They were undefeated after 23rd February, which coincided with the restoration of Trevor Morley as a forward partner for Paul Culpin. In the last 14 games, 44 goals were scored, Culpin netting 23 including five against Barrow, and Nuneaton rose from sixteenth to second by the end of the season. Meanwhile Wealdstone caught up on their games in hand and five wins in nine days at the end of March saw them take top spot. Altrincham, Scarborough and Dartford shared the lead with the Stones, with two weeks to go, but despite only picking up 11 points from the last ten games, the North London club held off all challengers and were able to field a weakened side against Barnet in the last fixture, thereby resting players for the forthcoming Trophy final. It must be one of the few occasions when fans could celebrate after a 7-0 defeat!

The haul of silverware was completed the following season, when the Middlesex Senior Cup was won on August Bank Holiday Monday, the final against Enfield being held over due to the backlog of fixtures.

	Alt	Bar	Brw	Bth	Bos	Dag	Dar	Enf	Fri	Gat	Ket	Kid	Mai	Nor	Nun	Run	Sca	Tel	Wea	Wey	Wor	Yeo
Altrincham	X	0-2	2-0	0-0	7-2	3-1	2-1	3-2	3-4	2-0	2-1	2-1	2-0	1-2	1-0	0-1	3-0	0-1	1-2	2-0	1-1	2-0
Barnet	1-0	X	4-0	2-1	1-0	0-0	0-1	3-2	1-2	1-1	4-2	2-4	0-0	1-1	1-1	1-1	1-2	0-1	7-0	0-0	2-0	4-1
Barrow	0-2	1-0	X	0-1	1-1	3-1	0-0	1-1	6-0	0-1	0-1	1-3	0-2	0-0	0-0	1-1	1-1	2-1	2-1	3-3	1-0	2-2
Bath City	1-0	2-1	1-2	X	2-1	2-0	1-0	1-0	3-0	1-1	1-6	0-2	1-0	0-3	1-0	0-1	2-1	2-1	3-1	2-1	3-1	1-0
Boston United	0-0	2-1	1-3	1-2	X	4-1	2-0	3-2	2-1	1-1	3-1	2-3	1-0	3-4	2-3	2-0	3-3	1-3	1-1	2-2	4-1	3-0
Dagenham	1-1	0-0	1-1	0-0	1-2	X	0-1	0-3	4-1	0-2	2-1	2-2	4-1	2-1	2-1	2-1	0-2	1-0	1-2	2-2	1-3	2-0
Dartford	1-0	2-0	2-0	1-3	1-1	3-0	X	1-2	0-2	1-2	0-1	2-1	1-1	1-0	2-2	1-1	3-1	0-0	2-3	1-1	2-3	1-1
Enfield	3-3	3-3	0-0	1-1	1-1	3-2	0-1	X	1-0	3-1	5-3	5-2	1-2	3-2	1-0	1-1	3-4	0-0	2-0	2-1	6-0	4-0
Frickley Athletic	2-1	3-1	2-2	2-0	2-1	0-2	2-4	1-0	X	1-0	3-0	3-0	1-3	4-0	1-1	1-1	2-3	1-2	0-2	2-0	2-1	3-1
Gateshead	0-1	0-2	1-2	1-1	1-2	2-1	0-0	0-5	3-2	X	1-4	4-1	2-1	2-6	0-3	0-3	3-1	1-1	1-2	2-2	2-2	1-1
Kettering Town	1-2	4-0	0-0	1-2	2-1	0-1	0-2	4-3	5-0	1-1	X	2-2	2-0	2-1	3-0	0-1	4-2	0-1	1-1	1-0	1-0	3-0
Kidderminster Harriers	0-2	1-4	0-1	2-2	2-0	5-1	1-1	1-3	2-4	3-0	2-2	X	2-1	3-1	3-4	0-1	3-2	0-3	3-3	4-1	3-0	3-0
Maidstone United	3-0	1-0	2-0	2-0	2-2	0-1	2-1	2-2	1-1	1-0	3-0	1-4	X	1-0	2-2	5-1	2-2	0-0	0-1	1-4	3-0	3-3
Northwich Victoria	1-2	2-0	1-0	3-1	1-0	0-1	0-1	1-1	3-0	2-0	1-2	0-2	0-0	X	1-0	0-1	1-1	1-0	0-2	0-3	2-2	2-0
Nuneaton Borough	4-1	1-1	5-2	0-0	4-2	2-2	5-1	2-2	0-0	3-0	1-1	1-1	3-2	2-2	X	2-1	5-2	2-1	1-0	4-2	3-0	5-0
Runcorn	1-2	1-2	0-0	2-0	1-2	3-0	1-1	1-1	0-0	1-1	2-2	1-2	1-4	0-0	1-0	X	1-1	3-0	2-0	3-1	1-2	3-0
Scarborough	2-1	1-1	1-1	2-0	1-0	5-0	1-3	2-3	1-2	5-1	0-0	2-1	1-0	0-0	3-2	0-0	X	4-1	1-1	0-0	1-2	2-1
Telford United	0-2	1-0	3-1	3-1	1-1	1-1	1-2	2-0	5-3	1-1	3-2	0-0	0-1	2-1	3-1	1-2	2-1	X	4-2	0-0	1-1	3-1
Wealdstone	1-0	1-2	2-2	0-1	0-1	0-0	0-0	1-2	1-1	4-2	1-1	5-2	1-1	1-1	3-1	1-0	1-0	2-2	X	3-2	3-3	0-3
Weymouth	2-1	3-0	3-1	2-2	2-1	1-0	1-2	4-2	2-1	5-4	3-0	0-2	0-1	1-0	1-3	0-2	1-2	3-2	0-3	X	3-1	4-2
Worcester City	1-1	1-2	3-2	1-2	2-1	1-3	2-5	1-0	4-1	1-2	1-2	0-1	1-4	0-1	4-1	0-0	0-4	1-1	0-1	1-1	X	0-2
Yeovil Town	1-2	2-1	1-2	3-2	2-4	2-1	2-2	0-0	1-2	0-4	1-1	0-0	3-0	1-0	1-2	1-3	2-2	3-3	0-2	0-0	1-2	X

		Home					Away					Total					
	P	W	D	L	F	A	W	D	L	F	A	W	D	L	F	A	Pts	
Wealdstone	42	8	8	5	31	26	12	2	7	33	28	20	10	12	64	54	62	
Nuneaton Borough	42	13	8	0	55	23	6	6	9	30	30	19	14	9	85	53	58	
Dartford	42	7	7	7	28	25	10	6	5	29	23	17	13	12	57	48	57	
Bath City	42	15	1	5	30	22	6	8	7	22	27	21	9	12	52	49	57	
Altrincham	42	13	2	6	39	21	8	4	9	24	26	21	6	15	63	47	56	
Scarborough	42	10	7	4	35	20	7	6	8	34	42	17	13	12	69	62	54	
Enfield	42	11	7	3	48	27	6	6	9	36	34	17	13	12	84	61	53	
Kidderminster Harriers	42	8	4	9	40	38	9	4	8	39	39	17	8	17	79	77	51	
Northwich Victoria	42	9	4	8	22	19	7	7	7	28	27	16	11	15	50	46	50	
Telford United	42	10	7	4	36	24	5	7	9	23	30	15	14	13	59	54	49	
Frickley Athletic	42	12	3	6	38	25	6	4	11	27	46	18	7	17	65	71	49	
Kettering Town	42	9	6	6	37	22	6	6	9	31	37	15	12	15	68	59	48	
Maidstone United	42	10	7	4	38	24	5	6	10	20	27	15	13	14	58	51	48	
Runcorn	42	6	9	6	27	21	7	6	8	21	26	13	15	14	48	47	48	
Barnet	42	9	7	5	36	20	6	4	11	23	32	15	11	16	59	52	47	
Weymouth	42	13	1	7	41	32	2	12	7	29	34	15	13	14	70	66	45	
Boston United	42	10	5	6	43	32	5	5	11	26	37	15	10	17	69	69	45	
Barrow	42	6	9	6	25	22	5	7	9	22	35	11	16	15	47	57	43	
Dagenham	42	8	6	7	28	27	5	4	12	19	40	13	10	19	47	67	41	
Worcester City	42	7	4	10	29	36	5	5	11	26	48	12	9	21	55	84	38	R
Gateshead *	42	5	6	10	27	42	4	6	11	24	40	9	12	21	51	82	33	R
Yeovil Town	42	4	7	10	26	36	2	4	15	18	51	6	11	25	44	87	25	R

FINAL TABLE

*Gateshead one point deducted

Home win = 2pts, Away win = 3pts, draw = 1pt

Stafford Rangers promoted from N.P.L., Cheltenham Town from Southern League, Wycombe Wanderers from Isthmian League

F.A.Cup

First Qualifying Round		
Barrow	Colwyn Bay	4-0
Leek Town	Runcorn	2-1
Bath City	Barnstaple Town	4-1
Frickley Ath	Caernarfon Town	3-0
Consett	Gateshead	0-2
Rushall Olympic	Kidderminster Harriers	1-2
Wisbech Town	Nuneaton Borough	2-6
Hounslow	Wealdstone	2-5
Second Qualifying Round		
Marine	Barrow	3-0
Minehead	Bath City	0-0
Rhyl	Frickley Ath	0-2
Crook Town	Gateshead	1-2
Rothwell Town	Kidderminster Harriers	1-4
Irthlingborough Diamonds	Nuneaton Borough	0-5
Wealdstone	Dunstable	6-0
replay		
Bath City	Minehead	3-0
Third Qualifying Round		
Frome Town	Bath City	3-1
Oswestry Town	Frickley Ath	1-1
Gateshead	Newcastle Blue Star	1-1
Kidderminster Harriers	Bridgnorth Town	3-2
Nuneaton Borough	Gainsborough Trinity	2-0
Grays Ath	Wealdstone	2-1
replay		
Frickley Ath	Oswestry Town	2-0
Newcastle Blue Star	Gateshead	3-1
Fourth Qualifying Round		
Aveley	Dagenham	0-1
Barnet	Boston United	3-1
Grays Ath	Dartford	1-3
Canterbury City	Enfield	0-1
Frickley Ath	Moor Green	5-0
Kettering Town	Harrow Borough	1-1
Kidderminster Harriers	King's Lynn	1-1
Bishop's Stortford	Maidstone United	1-0
Hednesford Town	Nuneaton Borough	0-4
Tow Law Town	Scarborough	1-0
Weymouth	Worcester City	3-1
Yeovil Town	Witney Town	3-1
replay		
Harrow Borough	Kettering Town	0-2
King's Lynn	Kidderminster Harriers	1-0
First Round		
Blackpool	Altrincham	0-1
Plymouth Argyle	Barnet	3-0
Dagenham	Swindon Town	0-0
Metropolitan Police	Dartford	0-3
Exeter City	Enfield	2-2
Frickley Ath	Stalybridge Celtic	2-1
Kettering Town	Bournemouth	0-0
Northwich Victoria	Crewe Alexandra	3-1
Nuneaton Borough	Scunthorpe Utd	1-1
Lincoln City	Telford United	1-1
Weymouth	Millwall	0-3
Torquay Utd	Yeovil Town	2-0
replay		
Swindon Town	Dagenham	1-2
Enfield	Exeter City	3-0
Bournemouth	Kettering Town	3-2
Scunthorpe Utd	Nuneaton Borough	2-1
Telford United	Lincoln City	2-1

F.A.Cup

Second Round		
Altrincham	Doncaster Rovers	1-3
Dagenham	Peterborough Utd	1-0
Dartford	Bournemouth	1-1
Millwall	Enfield	1-0
Darlington	Frickley Ath	1-0
Wigan Ath	Northwich Victoria	2-1
Preston North End	Telford United	1-4
replay		
Bournemouth	Dartford	4-1
Third Round		
Carlisle Utd	Dagenham	1-0
Telford United	Bradford City	2-1
Fourth Round		
Darlington	Telford United	1-1
replay		
Telford United	Darlington	3-0
Fifth Round		
Everton	Telford United	3-0

League Cup

First Round (two legs)		
Boston United	Kettering Town	0-4
Kettering Town	Boston United	3-2
Dagenham	Weymouth	1-1
Weymouth	Dagenham	3-1
Dartford	Yeovil Town	1-3
Yeovil Town	Dartford	0-1
Frickley Ath	Barrow	1-1
Barrow	Frickley Ath	3-1
Gateshead	Scarborough	1-1
Scarborough	Gateshead	2-1
Telford United	Enfield	2-2
Enfield	Telford United	5-2
Second Round		
Altrincham	Scarborough	2-1
Runcorn	Barrow	2-0
Bath City	Weymouth	1-1
(Weymouth won on away goals)		
Kettering Town	Northwich Victoria	1-0
Kidderminster Harriers	Nuneaton Borough	2-1
Barnet	Maidstone United	0-3
Wealdstone	Enfield	1-2
Yeovil Town	Worcester City	3-2
Third Round		
Maidstone United	Yeovil Town	3-1
Enfield	Weymouth	5-2
Kettering Town	Altrincham	1-2
Runcorn	Kidderminster Harriers	4-3
Semi Final		
Enfield	Maidstone United	0-1
Runcorn	Altrincham	2-1
Final (two legs)		
Maidstone United	Runcorn	0-2
Runcorn	Maidstone United	1-0

Challenge Shield

Maidstone United	Scarborough	3-1

Third Qualifying Round		
Macclesfield Town	Kettering Town	0-2
Alvechurch	Boston United	1-2
Gloucester City	Yeovil Town	2-0
Weymouth	Forest Green Rovers	6-1
First Round		
Morecambe	Altrincham	0-2
Scarborough	Chorley	1-0
Gateshead	Stalybridge Celtic	2-1
Frickley Athletic	Barrow	5-1
Burton Albion	Kettering Town	2-1
Boston United	Blyth Spartans	5-4
Gretna	Kidderminster Harriers	3-2
Grantham	Runcorn	0-0
Northwich Victoria	Telford United	0-4
Stafford Rangers	Nuneaton Borough	2-0
Wycombe Wanderers	Dartford	6-1
Worthing	Worcester City	3-2
Enfield	Stourbridge	5-1
Bath City	Bishops Stortford	0-0
Dagenham	Barnet	3-3
Weymouth	Cheltenham Town	2-3
Harlow Town	Wealdstone	0-0
Gloucester City	Maidstone United	0-2
replay		
Runcorn	Grantham	3-2
Bishops Stortford	Bath City	2-2
Barnet	Dagenham	3-2
Wealdstone	Harlow Town	5-0
Second replay		
Bishops Stortford	Bath City	1-2
Second Round		
Marine	Enfield	0-3
Maidstone United	Worthing	0-0
Runcorn	Scarborough	1-0
Barnet	Gretna	1-0
Bath City	Cheltenham Town	2-1
Boston United	Frome Town	4-0
Telford United	Fisher Athletic	1-2
Wealdstone	Wycombe Wanderers	2-1
Burton Albion	Altrincham	1-2
Frickley Athletic	Gateshead	4-1
replay		
Worthing	Maidstone United	0-2
Third Round		
Runcorn	Barnet	0-0
Fisher Athletic	Frickley Athletic	0-3
Boston United	Wokingham Town	1-0
Harrow Borough	Enfield	1-6
Maidstone United	Bath City	1-1
Wealdstone	Welling United	3-1
Altrincham	Bishop Auckland	2-1
replay		
Barnet	Runcorn	1-1
Bath City	Maidstone United	0-1

Third Round - second replay		
Barnet	Runcorn	0-0
third replay		
Runcorn	Barnet	4-0
Fourth Round		
Boston United	Runcorn	3-0
Maidstone United	Enfield	0-1
Altrincham	Stafford Rangers	4-1
Wealdstone	Frickley Athletic	3-1
Semi Final *(two legs)*		
Enfield	Wealdstone	0-2
Wealdstone	Enfield	0-1
Altrincham	Boston United	0-0
Boston United	Altrincham	3-2
Final *(@ Wembley)*		
Wealdstone	Boston United	2-1

WEALDSTONE 0
ENFIELD 1
Even a home defeat in the Trophy can't stop Wealdstone's progress to the 'Double'.

1985/86

After the 1984-5 season had promised so much, but ultimately delivered only disappointments, Enfield were able to draw on these experiences to ensure that this time their endeavours would not be in vain. No one team started in blistering form, and despite only winning five of their first nine games Enfield topped the league on 21st September. However, defeat at Wycombe the following Saturday marked the start of a sixteen match unbeaten run which was only ended in late January, when Wycombe again proved a stumbling block. On this occasion, the Buckinghamshire club scored twice in injury time to secure three points. In contrast to their league form, Enfield had disappointed in other matches, having lost in the F.A.Cup, the Bob Lord Trophy and the Middlesex Senior Cup, all within eleven days in November.

The main threat to the 'E' came from Weymouth and Altrincham, while Runcorn were off the pace, but with a game in hand. The top three managed to maintain their advantage until the Christmas/New Year period when Weymouth's form declined, with just one win in eight games. Meanwhile Altrincham were so embroiled in cup competitions that they played only two league matches between January 12th and March 14th. and consequently fell behind. But the cup-ties were rewarding as they became the first 'Gola League' team to beat First Division (top flight) opposition, when Birmingham City were overcome 2-1 at St.Andrews. After York City ended their F.A.Cup run in Round 4, they progressed to Wembley via the F.A.Trophy, where they beat Cheshire neighbours Runcorn by a single goal.

The best late season form was shown by Frickley and Kidderminster. The Harriers were fifteenth on December 14th, but a run of fifteen wins and two draws in the next seventeen games saw them rise to second place. They were eventually pipped for the runners-up spot by Frickley, who with just three defeats in their last twenty-six matches, managed to secure their best league position with a winning goal seven minutes from time in their final fixture. But no one was going to deprive Enfield, who were in top spot from the first Saturday in December, and they eventually won the title by seven points.

Heading in the opposite direction were Wycombe Wanderers. Fixture congestion meant that twenty-three league and cup games were played by the Buckinghamshire side in the final nine weeks of the season, with only one win and three draws being secured in their last fourteen league matches. A point in their final match, at home to Kettering, appeared sufficient for safety, but Dagenham had a 'double-header' in Cheshire on the final weekend. Three points were gained at Northwich on the Saturday and the following day, Dagenham 'keeper John Jacobs scored after forty-five seconds at Runcorn, with a wind-assisted punt upfield. Despite a second half equaliser from the homesters, the Daggers resilient defending brought them the point they needed and condemned Wycombe to their first ever relegation.

1985/86 Season Results Grid

	Altrincham	Barnet	Barrow	Bath City	Boston United	Cheltenham Town	Dagenham	Dartford	Enfield	Frickley Athletic	Kettering Town	Kidderminster Harriers	Maidstone United	Northwich Victoria	Nuneaton Borough	Runcorn	Scarborough	Stafford Rangers	Telford United	Wealdstone	Weymouth	Wycombe Wanderers
Altrincham	X	2-0	2-0	1-2	1-3	4-1	3-1	0-0	1-4	1-0	2-2	2-1	1-0	2-1	7-4	1-1	2-0	1-3	1-0	1-0	3-1	4-3
Barnet	2-2	X	4-1	1-0	3-0	2-2	4-1	2-0	0-1	1-2	3-0	0-1	3-3	1-0	0-1	1-2	1-0	0-2	1-2	1-0	2-2	0-1
Barrow	0-1	0-1	X	1-1	2-1	2-2	1-0	1-2	1-2	2-2	1-0	3-4	1-1	1-2	2-0	0-4	2-4	0-1	1-0	1-1	3-4	1-1
Bath City	0-2	1-1	6-0	X	2-0	1-1	1-1	2-0	0-2	1-2	1-1	2-4	1-1	0-0	0-2	0-1	0-0	0-1	3-0	2-3	2-2	3-1
Boston United	1-3	1-2	2-1	1-1	X	1-2	3-0	3-0	1-2	0-3	4-1	2-1	2-2	3-0	3-2	2-1	2-1	1-1	2-2	1-0	5-0	1-1
Cheltenham Town	2-0	2-1	2-0	1-2	2-1	X	2-2	3-1	2-0	1-1	5-1	2-6	2-1	2-0	5-3	1-1	5-1	2-0	1-1	1-2	0-1	4-2
Dagenham	1-3	2-1	3-0	0-1	2-2	1-3	X	2-1	0-2	0-0	1-0	0-1	0-0	1-0	3-2	2-3	0-0	1-1	1-4	0-2	2-2	1-1
Dartford	3-2	5-3	3-2	1-2	0-1	3-3	1-1	X	2-3	1-2	0-2	5-1	1-1	2-0	0-1	0-1	1-1	3-3	2-1	1-2	1-1	1-0
Enfield	1-1	1-0	4-0	3-1	3-0	1-0	3-1	1-0	X	3-1	1-1	2-2	1-3	1-0	3-2	2-0	4-0	3-1	4-0	1-0	4-4	2-3
Frickley Athletic	0-0	3-3	2-0	2-1	5-1	2-1	3-2	1-0	1-4	X	3-0	3-1	2-0	1-0	2-2	3-1	2-1	3-0	3-1	2-1	1-0	2-2
Kettering Town	2-2	1-1	4-2	2-0	3-1	2-1	0-2	2-2	2-1	2-0	X	2-2	2-0	2-1	1-4	0-0	0-0	0-1	4-0	2-1	0-2	4-1
Kidderminster Harriers	0-2	0-2	2-1	3-1	3-2	5-1	2-0	4-1	1-2	1-1	0-0	X	3-1	2-2	2-1	2-4	5-1	1-1	3-0	3-1	1-2	8-2
Maidstone United	1-2	2-2	0-0	3-2	1-2	1-0	2-1	3-0	3-3	3-2	0-0	2-1	X	0-1	5-1	1-1	1-1	2-4	4-4	0-1	0-0	1-1
Northwich Victoria	1-2	0-1	0-1	1-2	3-4	3-1	0-1	2-0	2-2	2-3	2-0	0-0	1-0	X	0-3	1-1	0-0	2-0	0-1	2-2	0-1	4-0
Nuneaton Borough	0-0	4-1	0-1	2-3	0-1	0-1	1-2	3-1	1-5	0-1	0-3	0-3	1-0	1-3	X	1-0	3-1	3-0	1-1	0-0	3-0	3-0
Runcorn	2-1	0-0	3-1	2-0	3-0	5-0	1-1	5-0	1-1	2-2	0-1	0-2	3-0	2-3	3-1	X	0-0	3-0	1-0	1-1	1-2	2-1
Scarborough	1-0	3-1	3-1	2-1	2-1	1-0	2-1	1-1	1-3	2-3	2-3	3-5	2-0	0-0	2-1	1-1	X	2-4	3-1	0-1	1-1	1-2
Stafford Rangers	1-1	0-0	1-0	1-0	2-1	2-0	3-1	5-1	1-1	0-0	0-0	3-2	2-1	1-2	2-0	1-1	0-3	X	0-3	2-1	2-3	1-1
Telford United	2-1	2-2	3-1	1-0	2-1	3-0	2-1	2-1	2-2	2-1	2-0	0-1	2-4	4-0	1-1	2-3	1-0	0-0	X	2-1	4-1	3-1
Wealdstone	2-2	2-0	4-0	0-1	7-2	0-0	0-4	2-1	2-4	2-0	3-1	0-3	3-2	0-0	1-0	1-0	0-3	2-3	1-1	X	1-0	2-0
Weymouth	0-0	4-2	3-2	0-0	0-0	0-0	2-1	2-1	2-2	2-3	1-0	1-2	2-0	2-2	2-0	5-2	4-1	1-1	5-2	4-2	X	1-1
Wycombe Wanderers	0-1	2-0	1-1	1-4	4-1	3-3	1-1	3-2	1-0	1-3	0-0	2-5	2-2	1-1	2-0	0-1	2-1	2-4	1-2	1-0	0-3	X

Final Table

	P	Home					Away					Total					
		W	D	L	F	A	W	D	L	F	A	W	D	L	F	A	Pts
Enfield	42	15	4	2	48	20	12	6	3	46	27	27	10	5	94	47	76
Frickley Athletic	42	16	4	1	46	21	9	6	6	32	29	25	10	7	78	50	69
Kidderminster Harriers	42	12	4	5	51	28	12	3	6	48	34	24	7	11	99	62	67
Altrincham	42	14	3	4	42	27	8	8	5	28	22	22	11	9	70	49	63
Weymouth	42	11	8	2	43	24	8	7	6	32	36	19	15	8	75	60	61
Runcorn	42	11	6	4	40	17	8	8	5	30	27	19	14	9	70	44	60
Stafford Rangers	42	10	7	4	30	22	9	6	6	31	32	19	13	10	61	54	60
Telford United	42	13	5	3	42	24	5	5	11	26	42	18	10	14	68	66	51
Kettering Town	42	11	6	4	37	24	4	9	8	18	29	15	15	12	55	53	49
Wealdstone	42	10	5	6	35	28	6	4	11	22	28	16	9	17	57	56	47
Cheltenham Town	42	13	4	4	47	27	3	7	11	22	42	16	11	15	69	69	46
Bath City	42	5	8	8	28	25	8	3	10	25	29	13	11	18	53	54	45
Boston United	42	11	5	5	41	26	5	2	14	25	50	16	7	19	66	76	44
Barnet	42	9	4	8	32	23	4	7	10	24	37	13	11	18	56	60	41
Scarborough	42	10	4	7	35	31	3	7	11	19	35	13	11	18	54	66	40
Northwich Victoria	42	5	6	10	24	25	5	6	10	18	29	10	12	20	42	54	37
Maidstone United	42	7	9	5	35	29	2	7	12	22	37	9	16	17	57	66	36
Nuneaton Borough	42	8	3	10	27	27	5	2	14	31	46	13	5	24	58	73	36
Dagenham	42	6	7	8	23	29	4	5	12	25	37	10	12	20	48	66	36
Wycombe Wanderers	42	7	6	8	30	35	3	7	11	25	49	10	13	19	55	84	36 R
Dartford	42	7	6	8	36	33	1	3	17	15	49	8	9	25	51	82	26 R
Barrow	42	5	6	10	26	34	2	2	17	15	52	7	8	27	41	86	24 R

Home win = 2pts, Away win = 3pts, draw = 1pt

Gateshead promoted from N.P.L., Welling United from Southern League, Sutton United from Isthmian League

CUP COMPETITIONS

F.A. Cup

First Qualifying Round		
Brandon United	Barrow	5-0
Bath City	Taunton Town	4-1
Minehead	Cheltenham Town	1-1
Stevenage Borough	Kidderminster Harriers	0-2
Hemel Hempstead	Nuneaton Borough	1-3
Prescot Cables	Runcorn	1-2
Bridlington Town	Scarborough	0-1
Lye Town	Stafford Rangers	1-3
replay		
Cheltenham Town	Minehead	1-2
Second Qualifying Round		
Bath City	Clevedon Town	1-0
Hednesford Town	Kidderminster Harriers	1-5
Moor Green	Nuneaton Borough	1-4
Accrington Stanley	Runcorn	1-1
Crook Town	Scarborough	0-1
Halesowen Town	Stafford Rangers	3-2
replay		
Runcorn	Accrington Stanley	9-1
Third Qualifying Round		
Bath City	Exmouth Town	2-0
Kidderminster Harriers	Tamworth	4-3
Nuneaton Borough	Hinckley Ath	0-0
Mossley	Runcorn	0-2
Blyth Spartans	Scarborough	1-1
replay		
Hinckley Ath	Nuneaton Borough	0-1
Scarborough	Blyth Spartans	3-1
Fourth Qualifying Round		
Barnet	Enfield	0-7
Bath City	Croydon	4-1
Dagenham	Atherstone Utd	5-1
Dartford	Worcester City	2-0
Frickley Ath	Northwich Victoria	2-1
Chelmsford City	Kettering Town	1-0
Kidderminster Harriers	Bishops Stortford	3-4
Bromley	Maidstone United	0-2
Dunstable	Nuneaton Borough	0-2
Rhyl	Runcorn	0-2
Scarborough	Bishop Auckland	4-1
Ton Pentre	Weymouth	1-3
Wycombe Wanderers	Burton Albion	1-0
First Round		
Chorley	Altrincham	0-2
Farnborough Town	Bath City	0-4
Dagenham	Cambridge Utd	2-1
Bournemouth	Dartford	0-0
Enfield	Bognor Regis Town	0-2
Frickley Ath	Halesowen Town	1-1
Fareham Town	Maidstone United	0-3
Nuneaton Borough	Burnley	2-3
Runcorn	Boston United	2-2
Notts County	Scarborough	6-1
Stockport County	Telford United	0-1
Reading	Wealdstone	1-0
Chelmsford City	Weymouth	1-0
Wycombe Wanderers	Colchester Utd	2-0
replay		
Boston United	Runcorn	1-1
Dartford	Bournemouth	0-2
Halesowen Town	Frickley Ath	1-3
second replay		
Runcorn	Boston United	4-1

F.A. Cup

Second Round		
Blackpool	Altrincham	1-2
Peterborough Utd	Bath City	1-0
Bournemouth	Dagenham	4-1
Hartlepool Utd	Frickley Ath	0-1
Plymouth Argyle	Maidstone United	3-0
Runcorn	Wigan Ath	1-1
Derby County	Telford United	6-1
Wycombe Wanderers	Chelmsford City	2-0
replay		
Wigan Ath	Runcorn	4-0
Third Round		
Birmingham City	Altrincham	1-2
Frickley Ath	Rotherham Utd	1-3
York City	Wycombe Wanderers	2-0
Fourth Round		
York City	Altrincham	2-0

League Cup

First Round (two legs)		
Barnet	Dagenham	3-2
Dagenham	Barnet	0-0
Frickley Ath	Northwich Victoria	0-1
Northwich Victoria	Frickley Ath	0-4
Barrow	Stafford Rangers	0-1
Stafford Rangers	Barrow	1-0
Kettering Town	Cheltenham Town	0-1
Cheltenham Town	Kettering Town	5-1
Boston United	Telford United	1-1
Telford United	Boston United	3-2
Wycombe Wanderers	Weymouth	1-3
Weymouth	Wycombe Wanderers	4-2
Second Round (two legs)		
Barnet	Bath City	1-1
Bath City	Barnet	0-1
Cheltenham Town	Maidstone United	2-3
Maidstone United	Cheltenham Town	1-0
Enfield	Dartford	1-2
Dartford	Enfield	1-1
Kidderminster Harriers	Runcorn	1-4
Runcorn	Kidderminster Harriers	8-3
Scarborough	Altrincham	3-2
Altrincham	Scarborough	2-0
Nuneaton Borough	Stafford Rangers	1-1
Stafford Rangers	Nuneaton Borough	2-1
Frickley Ath	Telford United	4-0
Telford United	Frickley Ath	1-0
Wealdstone	Weymouth	1-1
Weymouth	Wealdstone	3-2
Third Round		
Altrincham	Stafford Rangers	0-2
Runcorn	Frickley Ath	6-2
Weymouth	Dartford	8-1
Barnet	Maidstone United	2-0
Semi Final		
Runcorn	Stafford Rangers	0-0
Weymouth	Barnet	0-1
replay		
Stafford Rangers	Runcorn	2-1
Final (two legs)		
Stafford Rangers	Barnet	2-1
Barnet	Stafford Rangers	0-1

Challenge Shield

Wealdstone	Runcorn	2-2
(Runcorn won 5-3 on pens)		

Third Qualifying Round		
Barrow	Mossley	0-0
Dorchester Town	Weymouth	3-5
replay		
Mossley	Barrow	2-4
First Round		
Ryhope CA	Altrincham	1-3
Stafford Rangers	Nuneaton Borough	1-0
Dagenham	Sheppey Utd	3-0
Cheltenham Town	Fisher Athletic	3-0
Northwich Victoria	Workington	1-0
Wealdstone	Welling United	1-0
Bedworth Utd	Frickley Athletic	1-1
Saltash Utd	Dartford	1-2
Enfield	Waterlooville	3-0
Maidstone United	Weymouth	3-0
Chelmsford City	Bath City	2-1
Sutton United	Kettering Town	0-1
Barnet	Wycombe Wanderers	0-1
Scarborough	Barrow	2-1
Telford United	Southport	2-4
Kidderminster Harriers	Boston United	5-2
Runcorn	Marine	2-0
replay		
Frickley Athletic	Bedworth Utd	5-0
Second Round		
Altrincham	Bangor City	6-1
Stafford Rangers	Bishop Auckland	0-1
Dagenham	Cheltenham Town	0-1
Bishops Stortford	Northwich Victoria	2-0
Wealdstone	Frickley Athletic	2-1
Dartford	South Bank	1-3
Enfield	Maidstone United	3-2
Slough Town	Kettering Town	1-2
Crawley Town	Wycombe Wanderers	0-2
Scarborough	Southport	0-0
Corby Town	Kidderminster Harriers	0-4
Windsor & Eton	Runcorn	0-1
replay		
Southport	Scarborough	1-1
second replay		
Southport	Scarborough	1-0
Third Round		
Altrincham	Bishop Auckland	1-0
Cheltenham Town	Bishops Stortford	0-0
Wealdstone	South Bank	0-0
Enfield	Chelmsford City	5-3
Worthing	Kettering Town	0-0
Wycombe Wanderers	Leek Town	2-2
Southport	Kidderminster Harriers	1-1
Runcorn	Burton Albion	2-0

Third Round - replay		
Bishops Stortford	Cheltenham Town	1-3
South Bank	Wealdstone	2-1
Kettering Town	Worthing	2-1
Leek Town	Wycombe Wanderers	5-5
Kidderminster Harriers	Southport	6-1
second replay		
Wycombe Wanderers	Leek Town	1-1
(Played at Worcester City)		
third replay		
Wycombe Wanderers	Leek Town	1-0
(Played at Worcester City)		
Fourth Round		
Cheltenham Town	Altrincham	0-2
South Bank	Enfield	0-2
Kettering Town	Wycombe Wanderers	2-1
Kidderminster Harriers	Runcorn	1-2
Semi Final *(two legs)*		
Enfield	Altrincham	1-1
Altrincham	Enfield	2-0
Runcorn	Kettering Town	0-0
Kettering Town	Runcorn	0-2
Final *(@ Wembley)*		
Altrincham	Runcorn	1-0

WELCOME TO WESTFIELD LANE

Gola League

FRICKLEY ATHLETIC F.C.

Official Souvenir Programme

Football Association Challenge Cup (3rd Round)

Frickley Athletic
v
Rotherham United

Saturday 4th January 1986
Kick Off 2 p.m.

50p

FRICKLEY ATHLETIC 1
ROTHERHAM UNITED 3
Frickley's one and only appearance in the F.A.Cup 3rd round.

1986/87

For the Conference mem- bers the promised land was on the horizon. Subject to fulfilling the necessary criteria, the Champions would find themselves in Division Four within nine months. All the usual suspects were in the frame, but at 50-1 outsiders, Scarborough got very few mentions.

Having finished 15th the previous season, the Yorkshire side appointed Neil Warnock as manager, and during the close season he signed a dozen new players. A 3-0 opening day defeat was disappointing but with a team loaded with Football League experience, a solid, dependable unit soon evolved. They stood 10th when Cheltenham beat them at the end of October, but seven weeks later they were top. The team embarked upon a twenty-two match unbeaten run, a Conference record. Maidstone, Enfield and Altrincham saw their challenges fade and by mid January the title had become a two horse race. Ironically, Scarborough's unbeaten run coincided with the signing of goalkeeper Kevin Blackwell from Barnet, their main rivals. Blackwell continued to train with Barnet until the last few weeks of the season when the arrangement was considered inappropriate. Scarborough won their last 13 away games, conceding only six goals in the process and on the final day of the season, the largest Conference crowd thus far, of 5,640, was able to celebrate the teams success.

Unfortunately, Scarborough's season was not without sadness. Club President and lifelong supporter, David Jenkinson, passed away in November. The following month, crowd trouble at the F.A.Trophy match with Morecambe saw Chairman Barry Adamson trying to restore the peace. During the scuffle he was hit several times and suffered a fatal heart attack minutes later as he was giving a statement to the police in the club offices.

Weymouth became the first Conference team to move to a new ground. A new stadium was built on the site of the old Wessex speedway stadium on the outskirts of the town and to mark the last game at the Recreation Ground, supporters were given free admittance. A crowd of 1,700 saw the Terras end their 75 years tenure of the ground with a 2-2 draw with Sutton United.

For Nuneaton, their stay in the Alliance was brought to an end by off-field problems. In April their stand was closed when it failed structural, electrical and fire safety tests. Major works, a new stand or an alternative ground were needed for the next season and with a battle for boardroom control going through the courts the pressure was on. A groundshare with Coventry City was sought, but could not be finalised in time and offers of assistance from Northampton Town and Stafford Rangers were deemed unsuitable by the league's authorities.

1986/87 Season Results Grid

	Altrincham	Barnet	Bath City	Boston United	Cheltenham Town	Dagenham	Enfield	Frickley Athletic	Gateshead	Kettering Town	Kidderminster Harriers	Maidstone United	Northwich Victoria	Nuneaton Borough	Runcorn	Scarborough	Stafford Rangers	Sutton United	Telford United	Wealdstone	Welling United	Weymouth
Altrincham	X	2-0	1-1	3-1	2-0	0-2	0-1	1-1	1-1	4-1	3-1	4-0	1-1	2-2	0-0	1-0	2-0	2-1	2-1	1-2	1-1	2-1
Barnet	1-0	X	2-1	5-1	0-1	1-0	1-0	3-0	3-1	1-2	5-2	3-1	4-0	4-1	3-0	2-2	1-2	1-2	2-2	2-1	1-1	2-2
Bath City	1-1	0-1	X	4-2	0-0	2-0	1-3	4-2	1-1	1-2	3-2	1-0	1-1	2-3	1-2	0-3	4-2	1-3	3-1	2-0	1-1	2-1
Boston United	4-2	0-3	1-2	X	1-1	1-0	5-1	2-2	6-0	2-1	2-1	0-3	0-1	2-1	2-0	1-3	2-0	0-0	2-3	2-0	4-3	1-1
Cheltenham Town	1-1	1-2	1-1	1-3	X	6-1	2-0	2-0	4-2	3-1	1-2	2-0	5-2	1-1	1-1	2-3	2-1	1-2	3-1	0-1	2-0	2-0
Dagenham	3-1	1-3	1-2	3-2	1-1	X	0-3	0-1	0-0	1-2	3-1	0-2	3-3	3-1	3-2	0-2	1-0	2-1	3-1	1-0	1-1	2-0
Enfield	0-2	0-3	1-0	2-3	2-2	1-0	X	0-0	1-1	0-0	3-0	0-1	1-2	3-1	5-0	0-1	2-0	0-0	3-1	4-2	0-2	4-0
Frickley Athletic	2-2	0-3	2-2	0-1	0-2	1-3	1-4	X	3-1	2-2	0-1	0-2	1-1	1-1	0-2	0-2	2-1	1-1	4-2	3-1	3-1	2-2
Gateshead	1-3	1-5	1-2	1-3	1-1	3-2	1-2	2-0	X	1-1	2-4	1-4	1-1	3-2	1-3	0-1	2-2	1-1	0-2	1-1	1-1	1-4
Kettering Town	0-2	1-1	2-0	1-2	0-0	3-1	2-0	1-2	5-1	X	1-2	1-0	2-2	1-1	1-2	2-2	1-4	3-1	0-2	5-1	3-0	
Kidderminster Harriers	3-0	0-3	2-4	1-2	5-1	4-2	3-4	4-1	3-1	2-1	X	2-2	3-0	3-0	0-1	1-1	0-0	0-4	5-2	3-0		1-1
Maidstone United	3-0	1-0	0-0	2-2	1-1	2-1	0-2	1-1	3-0	3-0	5-0	X	5-2	2-0	3-2	2-1	2-3	0-1	0-0	1-0	4-0	3-1
Northwich Victoria	1-1	1-2	1-1	4-0	1-0	2-3	2-0	1-1	1-2	0-0	1-2	1-1	X	1-2	0-1	1-1	1-0	1-0	2-1	2-1	1-1	
Nuneaton Borough	2-2	1-3	1-0	1-5	0-0	3-3	2-0	2-1	1-1	0-0	1-2	2-0	0-1	X	1-0	3-0	0-0	1-1	0-2	1-1	1-2	0-4
Runcorn	1-1	1-1	0-1	3-1	1-0	4-0	1-1	1-0	4-0	1-0	4-3	3-2	7-3	1-1	X	0-2	3-1	3-2	3-0	1-1	2-2	1-1
Scarborough	2-2	0-0	1-1	0-0	1-3	2-1	1-1	4-2	3-2	1-0	2-1	0-0	2-1	1-0	1-2	X	2-0	2-1	0-0	2-1	2-0	2-1
Stafford Rangers	2-3	0-3	0-1	0-1	0-1	1-1	0-3	2-0	1-0	2-2	4-1	2-3	4-1	3-1	2-0	0-0	X	4-2	1-1	1-0	3-1	0-0
Sutton United	2-3	3-1	7-2	3-1	0-0	1-0	0-1	3-0	3-0	8-0	3-1	3-1	2-1	2-3	1-1	0-2	3-0	X	2-2	2-2	2-0	2-3
Telford United	4-0	0-1	4-2	5-2	3-1	0-2	2-1	4-1	2-1	2-0	2-1	1-1	1-0	1-1	2-0	0-0	0-0	0-2	X	1-3	2-1	5-1
Wealdstone	0-2	0-0	1-2	0-4	1-0	2-2	0-3	2-2	2-1	0-3	0-0	1-1	6-0	0-3	1-3	0-3	2-1	0-1		X	3-1	3-1
Welling United	0-1	1-1	1-1	4-2	1-3	1-0	2-3	3-2	3-4	0-3	1-0	2-2	3-2	1-2	3-0	1-3	2-4	3-1	1-3	1-1	X	5-0
Weymouth	2-2	3-3	1-2	3-4	4-3	3-0	0-1	3-2	0-1	2-0	2-1	4-1	2-2	1-0	1-1	0-1	1-3	2-2	3-0	3-2	3-2	X

Final Table

	P	Home					Away					Total						
		W	D	L	F	A	W	D	L	F	A	W	D	L	F	A	Pts	
Scarborough	42	12	7	2	31	19	15	3	3	33	14	27	10	5	64	33	91	P
Barnet	42	13	4	4	47	22	12	6	3	39	17	25	10	7	86	39	85	
Maidstone United	42	14	4	3	43	16	7	6	8	28	32	21	10	11	71	48	73	
Enfield	42	9	5	7	32	21	12	2	7	34	26	21	7	14	66	47	70	
Altrincham	42	11	7	3	35	18	7	8	6	31	35	18	15	9	66	53	69	
Boston United	42	11	4	6	40	28	10	2	9	42	46	21	6	15	82	74	69	
Sutton United	42	12	4	5	52	24	7	7	7	29	27	19	11	12	81	51	68	
Runcorn	42	12	7	2	45	23	6	6	9	26	35	18	13	11	71	58	67	
Telford United	42	12	5	4	41	23	6	5	10	28	36	18	10	14	69	59	64	
Bath City	42	9	5	7	35	31	8	7	6	28	31	17	12	13	63	62	63	
Cheltenham Town	42	11	4	6	43	25	5	9	7	21	25	16	13	13	64	50	61	
Kidderminster Harriers	42	10	4	7	46	34	7	0	14	31	47	17	4	21	77	81	55	
Stafford Rangers	42	9	5	7	32	25	5	6	10	26	35	14	11	17	58	60	53	
Weymouth	42	10	5	6	43	33	3	7	11	25	44	13	12	17	68	77	51	
Dagenham	42	10	4	7	32	29	4	3	14	24	43	14	7	21	56	72	49	
Kettering Town	42	8	5	8	35	28	4	6	11	19	38	12	11	19	54	66	47	
Northwich Victoria	42	6	7	8	25	23	4	7	10	28	46	10	14	18	53	69	44	
Nuneaton Borough	42	6	8	7	23	28	4	6	11	25	45	10	14	18	48	73	44	R
Wealdstone	42	7	5	9	26	34	4	5	12	24	36	11	10	21	50	70	43	
Welling United	42	8	4	9	39	38	2	6	13	22	46	10	10	22	61	84	40	
Frickley Athletic	42	5	7	9	28	37	2	4	15	19	45	7	11	24	47	82	32	R
Gateshead	42	3	7	11	26	45	3	6	12	22	50	6	13	23	48	95	31	R

(New points scoring, win = 3pts, draw = 1pt)

Macclesfield Town promoted from N.P.L., Fisher Athletic from Southern League, Wycombe Wanderers from Isthmian League.

CUP COMPETITIONS

F.A.Cup

First Qualifying Round

Bishop Auckland	Gateshead	2-0
Long Eaton Utd	Northwich Victoria	1-4
Goole Town	Scarborough	2-1
Hinckley Ath	Kidderminster Harriers	0-1
Shepshed Charterhouse	Stafford Rangers	0-1
Kettering Town	Lowestoft Town	2-1
Sutton United	Hounslow	2-0
Welling United	Darenth Heathside	6-0
Barnet	Dulwich Hamlet	0-2
Cheltenham Town	Bideford	3-4

Second Qualifying Round

Worksop Town	Northwich Victoria	0-2
Wigston Fields	Kidderminster Harriers	0-5
Atherstone United	Stafford Rangers	2-4
Tiptree Utd	Kettering Town	0-3
Yeading	Sutton United	4-1
Welling United	Bracknell Town	2-1

Third Qualifying Round

Skelmersdale Utd	Northwich Victoria	2-3
Malvern Town	Kidderminster Harriers	0-2
Wolverton Town	Stafford Rangers	1-4
Kettering Town	Corby Town	2-0
Hendon	Welling United	0-1

Fourth Qualifying Round

Bath City	Yeovil Town	2-1
Boston United	Gainsborough Trinity	6-0
Chelmsford City	Kidderminster Harriers	2-1
Dagenham	Wealdstone	0-3
Enfield	Bury Town	1-1
Goole Town	Nuneaton Borough	1-2
Kettering Town	Windsor & Eton	1-0
Northwich Victoria	Stafford Rangers	0-1
Southwick	Maidstone United	1-1
Wembley	Welling United	2-3
Woking	Weymouth	1-0

replay

Bury Town	Enfield	0-1
Maidstone United	Southwick	1-1

second replay

Maidstone United	Southwick	2-2

third replay

Southwick	Maidstone United	1-5

First Round

Bath City	Aylesbury United	3-2
Dartford	Enfield	1-1
Frickley Athletic	Altrincham	0-0
Kettering Town	Gillingham	0-3
Nuneaton Borough	Rochdale	0-3
Port Vale	Stafford Rangers	1-0
Runcorn	Boston United	1-1
Telford United	Burnley	3-0
Wealdstone	Swansea City	1-1
Welling United	Maidstone United	1-1

replay

Altrincham	Frickley Athletic	4-0
Boston United	Runcorn	1-2
Enfield	Dartford	3-0
Maidstone United	Welling United	4-1
Swansea City	Wealdstone	2-1

(abandoned 54 mins, waterlogged pitch)

Swansea City	Wealdstone	4-1

Second Round

Bristol City	Bath City	1-1
Maidstone United	Cambridge Utd	1-0
Scunthorpe Utd	Runcorn	1-0
Swindon Town	Enfield	3-0
Telford United	Altrincham	1-0

replay

Bath City	Bristol City	0-3

(Played at Bristol City)

Third Round

Telford United	Leeds Utd	1-2
Watford	Maidstone United	3-1

League Cup

First Round

Altrincham	Matlock Town	3-1
Aylesbury United	Kidderminster Harriers	3-2
Bishop Stortford	Welling United	2-1
Burton Albion	Nuneaton Borough	1-1
Crawley Town	Maidstone United	0-1
Croydon	Enfield	2-1
Dagenham	Tooting & Mitcham	1-1
Dulwich Hamlet	Barnet	3-1
Frickley Athletic	Buxton	1-2
Gateshead	Southport	2-1
Fareham Town	Bath City	0-1
Horwich RMI	Runcorn	0-2
Kettering Town	Telford United	0-0
Scarborough	Hyde Utd	2-1
Slough Town	Cheltenham Town	2-2
Stafford Rangers	Kings Lynn	1-1
Wealdstone	Sutton United	2-4
Windsor & Eton	Weymouth	0-2
Worcester City	Boston United	3-4
Workington	Northwich Victoria	0-3

replay

Tooting & Mitcham	Dagenham	2-2

(Dagenham won on away goals)

Nuneaton Borough	Burton Albion	0-1
Telford United	Kettering Town	0-2
Cheltenham Town	Slough Town	0-1
Kings Lynn	Stafford Rangers	1-2

Second Round

Witton Albion	Altrincham	1-1
Bath City	Weymouth	1-1
Chelmsford City	Dagenham	1-1
Kettering Town	Boston United	3-2
Harrow Borough	Maidstone United	2-3
Buxton	Northwich Victoria	4-0
South Liverpool	Runcorn	0-1
Scarborough	Gateshead	1-0
Stafford Rangers	Morecambe	2-2
Sutton United	Dulwich Hamlet	3-2

replay

Altrincham	Witton Albion	3-0
Dagenham	Chelmsford City	4-1
Morecambe	Stafford Rangers	1-1

(Morecambe won on away goals)

Weymouth	Bath City	1-2

Third Round

Altrincham	Kettering Town	2-2
Dagenham	Hendon	1-1
Maidstone United	Yeovil Town	5-1
Runcorn	Alvechurch	3-1
Buxton	Scarborough	0-2
Sutton United	Bath City	4-0

replay

Hendon	Dagenham	2-1
Kettering Town	Altrincham	2-0

Fourth Round

Aylesbury Utd	Maidstone United	0-0
Runcorn	Kettering Town	1-2
Burton Albion	Scarborough	1-0
Sutton United	Hendon	0-2

replay

Maidstone United	Aylesbury Utd	0-3

Semi final

Aylesbury Utd	Kettering Town	0-2

Final

Kettering Town	Hendon	3-1

Challenge Shield

Enfield	Stafford Rangers	0-1

36

Third Qualifying Round

Kings Lynn	Nuneaton Borough	1-1

replay

Nuneaton Borough	Kings Lynn	1-0

First Round

Northwich Victoria	Burton Albion	0-2
Telford United	Nuneaton Borough	1-4
Newcastle Blue Star	Stafford Rangers	2-1
Southport	Gateshead	1-2
Scarborough	Morecambe	1-0
Bishop Auckland	Runcorn	2-3
Kidderminster Harriers	Mossley	0-0
Altrincham	Crook Town	1-0
Boston United	Frickley Athletic	4-3
Crawley Town	Bath City	1-2
Barnet	Wokingham Town	6-0
Wealdstone	Maidstone United	1-1
Barking	Weymouth	2-2
Enfield	Aylesbury United	0-2
Cheltenham Town	Dulwich Hamlet	1-0
Chelmsford City	Sutton United	1-2
Kettering Town	Yeovil Town	2-3
Welling United	St Albans City	6-0
Dagenham	Harrow Borough	2-0

replay

Mossley	Kidderminster Harriers	0-1
Maidstone United	Wealdstone	2-1
Weymouth	Barking	3-1

Second Round

Blyth Spartans	Bath City	2-2
Barnet	Hitchin Town	1-1
Nuneaton Borough	Gateshead	3-2
Kidderminster Harriers	Worthing	2-0
Dagenham	Marine	2-1
Maidstone United	Altrincham	2-0
Scarborough	Sutton United	2-2
Corby Town	Welling United	3-0
Yeovil Town	Runcorn	0-0
Cambridge City	Boston United	0-1
Bishops Stortford	Cheltenham Town	0-1
Burton Albion	Weymouth	3-0

replay

Bath City	Blyth Spartans	0-1
Hitchin Town	Barnet	0-5
Sutton United	Scarborough	0-2
Runcorn	Yeovil Town	2-1

Third Round

Runcorn	Dartford	1-1
Scarborough	Fareham Town	0-2
Cheltenham Town	Kidderminster Harriers	2-3
Corby Town	Maidstone United	0-3
Dagenham	Aylesbury United	0-0
Barnet	Boston United	1-1
Nuneaton Borough	Blyth Spartans	2-2

replay

Dartford	Runcorn	2-1
Aylesbury United	Dagenham	1-2
Boston United	Barnet	3-3
Blyth Spartans	Nuneaton Borough	2-2

second replay

Barnet	Boston United	3-0

(Played at Cambridge Utd)

Blyth Spartans	Nuneaton Borough	2-2

third replay

Nuneaton Borough	Blyth Spartans	1-0

Fourth Round

Maidstone United	Burton Albion	1-1
Nuneaton Borough	Dartford	1-3
Dagenham	Kidderminster Harriers	1-3
Barnet	Fareham Town	0-1

replay

Burton Albion	Maidstone United	1-0

Semi Final *(two legs)*

Kidderminster Harriers	Fareham Town	0-0
Fareham Town	Kidderminster Harriers	0-2

(Played at Southampton)

Final *(@ Wembley)*

Kidderminster Harriers	Burton Albion	0-0

replay *(@ West Bromwich Albion)*

Kidderminster Harriers	Burton Albion	2-1

Saturday, 2nd May, 1987

Scarborough Football Club welcomes Weymouth

GM Vauxhall Conference

Scarborough Football Club

Members of the
GM/Vauxhall Conference League 1986/87

MAJOR SPONSOR—SCARBOROUGH BUILDING SOCIETY

The BORO celebrates Its Diamond Jubilee Year as a Professional Club 1926 — 1986

Today's Match Ball Sponsor is:-
BRITISH RAIL PROVINCIAL (Eastern)
who are also sponsoring the Match

30p

SCARBOROUGH 2
WEYMOUTH 1
A Conference record gate
celebrates Scarborough's promotion.

1987/88

Lincoln City created an unwanted piece of football history when they became the first team to suffer automatic relegation to the Conference. Thrown into unknown territory, the club decided to remain full-time, sold several players, and invested a substantial amount - in non-League terms - on experienced Football League players. For the fans expecting an easy ride, an opening day 4-2 defeat at Barnet followed by a 3-0 reversal at Weymouth provided a rude awakening. However, the side soon adjusted to its new surroundings and by the end of September they were seventh. At this point the transition was complete and Lincoln suffered only one defeat in the next twenty-five games. Yet even this form was not enough to shake off the opposition and coming to the final run-in, the championship was still a three horse race involving also Barnet and Kettering.

Barnet had held top spot since November and possessed tremendous goalscoring potential, but they faltered badly winning only two of their last nine games. Despite winning the final game of the season at Welling, the destination of the Championship Trophy was out of their hands, having lost the lead two days earlier. Kettering were the form team, being undefeated since the New Year and after beating Lincoln with three games to go, this boost gave them the chance of ultimate victory. It was not to be, as three defeats followed, and it was Lincoln who secured the championship against Wycombe in front of a Conference record crowd of 9,432.

It was the third time in the season that Lincoln had set a league attendance best, firstly with a figure of 5,822 in their Boxing Day local derby at Boston, then this figure was increased to 7,542 in the return fixture on Easter Monday.

It was a far cry from the start of the season when it appeared that Weymouth would be the team to catch. The Dorset team started their competitive fixtures at the Wessex Stadium with their 3-0 win over Lincoln, and won their first five matches. The key component was a miserly defence which conceded only six goals in their first 18 games. Instrumental in this was goalkeeper Peter Guthrie, whose performances earned him a £100,000 transfer to Tottenham Hotspur. At this point Weymouth's form slumped, not helped by drainage problems with the new pitch which prevented them from playing a match at home from Boxing Day until March 5th. By now well off the pace, they still managed to turn their new ground into a fortress until the final day of the season, when Enfield were the first team to take three points away from Dorset.

1987/88 Season Results Grid

	Altrincham	Barnet	Bath City	Boston Utd	Cheltenham Town	Dagenham	Enfield	Fisher Ath	Kettering Town	Kidderminster Harriers	Lincoln City	Macclesfield Town	Maidstone United	Northwich Victoria	Runcorn	Stafford Rangers	Sutton Utd	Telford United	Wealdstone	Welling United	Weymouth	Wycombe Wanderers
Altrincham	X	1-1	2-0	4-1	1-1	6-0	5-1	2-3	2-2	2-3	0-0	1-3	0-0	2-0	2-0	2-0	0-1	0-3	1-0	1-0	3-0	4-2
Barnet	3-1	X	4-0	1-0	1-1	3-2	3-0	2-0	4-0	1-1	4-2	2-1	2-0	4-1	1-2	2-2	6-2	0-2	5-1	5-2	3-2	1-1
Bath City	2-0	0-1	X	2-1	1-1	4-2	0-1	1-3	2-0	3-3	2-1	3-4	1-3	0-0	0-1	0-3	0-4	1-2	0-0	0-0	3-1	2-1
Boston Utd	2-2	2-1	2-0	X	4-1	1-0	2-3	2-1	0-2	1-0	1-2	0-2	3-3	0-1	2-2	4-1	0-0	1-1	0-1	1-2	1-0	4-0
Cheltenham Town	1-0	0-2	3-3	1-5	X	5-1	1-1	2-0	1-2	2-2	3-3	1-0	2-2	1-1	0-0	2-3	1-1	3-0	1-1	2-2	2-1	2-2
Dagenham	3-2	0-0	1-1	4-2	1-3	X	1-2	1-5	0-5	1-2	0-3	0-0	0-3	1-0	1-4	2-4	0-1	0-1	1-2	1-2	0-3	2-1
Enfield	1-1	2-0	1-3	3-2	0-1	2-2	X	0-0	2-0	5-2	0-0	1-2	2-4	0-1	1-3	0-0	2-3	1-4	5-2	1-0	3-2	3-2
Fisher Ath	3-2	2-2	2-0	0-0	1-0	5-1	2-3	X	1-1	3-1	1-1	1-2	0-3	0-0	0-2	1-2	1-1	0-1	3-1	1-0	1-0	0-0
Kettering Town	1-2	1-1	1-1	3-0	1-1	3-0	2-1	2-1	X	1-1	2-0	3-0	0-2	3-1	0-3	1-0	2-2	1-0	3-2	1-0	3-0	3-0
Kidderminster Harriers	4-1	1-1	3-2	1-0	3-2	1-1	4-0	1-1	2-1	X	3-3	3-2	2-1	1-1	1-1	0-0	2-2	2-4	2-1	5-2	1-0	0-2
Lincoln City	5-0	2-1	3-0	5-1	5-1	3-0	4-0	3-0	0-1	5-3	X	3-0	1-1	3-2	1-0	2-1	1-1	0-0	3-0	2-1	0-0	2-0
Macclesfield Town	1-0	2-2	0-2	2-1	1-0	3-1	0-3	2-4	0-0	1-2	2-0	X	1-0	5-0	4-0	2-3	1-1	1-1	3-2	3-2	1-2	1-1
Maidstone United	2-2	2-1	3-0	1-2	2-2	2-0	3-2	2-2	2-3	1-2	1-2	2-0	X	1-1	3-0	4-2	2-4	2-4	1-1	0-1	2-1	0-1
Northwich Victoria	1-2	2-1	2-1	6-0	0-0	1-0	1-1	1-2	0-1	1-1	2-3	2-1	2-3	X	2-0	1-1	1-4	1-2	0-0	0-0	1-1	1-1
Runcorn	1-1	0-1	2-1	3-0	2-2	2-1	2-2	5-1	1-0	2-0	4-1	1-2	3-2	2-1	X	1-1	1-0	2-1	1-0	4-0	2-1	1-2
Stafford Rangers	3-0	1-1	1-0	3-4	2-2	4-0	3-1	3-2	2-1	0-2	1-4	0-1	2-3	3-0	2-1	X	2-0	1-1	5-2	2-0	0-0	3-0
Sutton Utd	2-1	0-1	3-1	1-2	3-0	1-1	3-3	2-0	2-2	2-0	4-1	2-3	5-1	1-1	2-2	2-0	X	2-1	1-1	1-1	0-1	2-2
Telford United	1-0	2-4	3-1	2-1	0-1	1-0	4-0	2-1	2-3	4-3	0-1	0-0	1-0	1-1	2-1	1-2	3-3	X	1-1	2-0	1-0	0-0
Wealdstone	0-0	0-6	1-1	1-1	1-4	2-3	1-0	1-1	0-0	1-1	0-0	1-1	1-3	2-2	0-1	4-2	0-0	2-2	X	1-1	0-2	0-0
Welling United	0-1	0-2	2-1	3-1	0-1	6-1	1-1	1-1	3-1	1-2	1-4	3-1	0-1	1-1	1-1	0-5	1-4	4-1	4-0	X	0-2	1-0
Weymouth	1-0	2-0	3-1	3-1	1-1	1-0	1-3	1-1	2-1	1-1	3-0	1-1	2-1	0-0	0-0	2-0	2-1	1-0	2-1	4-0	X	0-0
Wycombe Wanderers	1-0	0-7	2-2	1-2	5-3	2-1	1-5	1-1	0-3	0-1	1-2	5-0	1-5	1-1	2-2	0-4	1-1	2-1	1-0	3-1	2-1	X

FINAL TABLE

	P	Home W	Home D	Home L	Home F	Home A	Away W	Away D	Away L	Away F	Away A	Total W	Total D	Total L	Total F	Total A	Pts	
Lincoln City	42	16	4	1	53	13	8	6	7	33	35	24	10	8	86	48	82	P
Barnet	42	15	4	2	57	23	8	7	6	36	22	23	11	8	93	45	80	
Kettering Town	42	13	5	3	37	20	9	4	8	31	28	22	9	11	68	48	75	
Runcorn	42	14	4	3	42	20	7	7	7	26	27	21	11	10	68	47	74	
Telford United	42	11	5	5	33	23	9	5	7	32	27	20	10	12	65	50	70	
Stafford Rangers	42	12	4	5	43	25	8	5	8	36	33	20	9	13	79	58	69	
Kidderminster Harriers	42	11	8	2	42	28	7	7	7	33	38	18	15	9	75	66	69	
Sutton United	42	9	8	4	41	25	7	10	4	36	29	16	18	8	77	54	66	
Maidstone United	42	8	5	8	38	33	10	4	7	41	31	18	9	15	79	64	63	
Weymouth	42	13	7	1	33	13	5	2	14	20	30	18	9	15	53	43	63	
Macclesfield Town	42	10	5	6	36	27	8	4	9	28	35	18	9	15	64	62	63	
Enfield	42	8	5	8	35	34	7	5	9	33	44	15	10	17	68	78	55	
Cheltenham Town	42	6	11	4	36	32	5	9	7	28	35	11	20	11	64	67	53	
Altrincham	42	11	5	5	41	21	3	5	13	18	38	14	10	18	59	59	52	
Fisher Athletic	42	8	7	6	28	23	5	6	10	30	38	13	13	16	58	61	52	
Boston United	42	9	5	7	33	25	5	2	14	27	50	14	7	21	60	75	49	
Northwich Victoria	42	8	6	7	30	25	2	11	8	16	32	10	17	15	46	57	47	
Wycombe Wanderers	42	8	5	8	32	43	3	8	10	18	33	11	13	18	50	76	46	
Welling United	42	8	4	9	33	32	3	5	13	17	40	11	9	22	50	72	42	
Bath City	42	7	5	9	27	32	2	5	14	21	44	9	10	23	48	76	37	R
Wealdstone	42	3	11	7	20	33	2	6	13	19	43	5	17	20	39	76	32	R
Dagenham	42	4	3	14	20	46	1	3	17	17	58	5	6	31	37	104	21	R

F
I
N
A
L

T
A
B
L
E

Chorley promoted from N.P.L., Aylesbury United from Southern League, Yeovil Town from Isthmian League.

F.A.Cup

First Qualifying Round

Warrington Town	Northwich Victoria	1-1
Stalybridge Celtic	Macclesfield Town	1-1
Walsall Wood	Stafford Rangers	0-3
Wisbech Town	Kettering Town	2-0
Witney Town	Barnet	0-3
Cheltenham Town	Dorchester Town	4-1
Aylesbury United	Wycombe Wanderers	2-0
Camberley Town	Welling United	0-2
Dorking	Fisher Athletic	0-2
Wivenhoe Town	Sutton United	0-3
Frome Town	Weymouth	2-2
replay		
Macclesfield Town	Stalybridge Celtic	5-1
Northwich Victoria	Warrington Town	5-1
Weymouth	Frome Town	3-0

Second Qualifying Round

Northwich Victoria	Droylsden	2-1
Macclesfield Town	Chadderton	5-0
Stafford Rangers	Moor Green	2-3
Irthlingborough Diamonds	Barnet	0-4
Welling United	Walton & Hersham	2-1
Mangotsfield U	Cheltenham T	1-1
Chatham Town	Fisher Athletic	0-3
Sutton United	Redhill	3-1
Weymouth	Radstock Town	3-0
replay		
Cheltenham Town	Mangotsfield U	2-0

Third Qualifying Round

Northwich Victoria	St Helens Town	3-2
Macclesfield Town	Marine	0-0
Berkhamsted Town	Barnet	0-3
Welling United	Burnham	3-1
Weston -Super-Mare	Cheltenham T	1-2
Hayes	Fisher Athletic	2-0
Sutton United	Bromley	0-0
Weymouth	Fareham Town	2-2
replay		
Marine	Macclesfield Town	1-2
Bromley	Sutton United	1-2
Fareham Town	Weymouth	1-2

Fourth Qualifying Round

Bath City	Slough Town	3-1
Boston United	Welling United	1-1
Cheltenham Town	Bracknell Town	2-1
Enfield	Aylesbury United	1-2
Great Yarmouth Town	Dagenham	0-2
Brigg Town	Lincoln City	1-4
(Played at Lincoln City)		
Macclesfield Town	Whitby Town	3-1
Maidstone United	Dartford	2-0
Northwich Victoria	Easington Colliery	3-0
Runcorn	Barrow	2-1
Sutton United	Basingstoke Town	3-0
Tamworth	Wealdstone	2-0
Weymouth	Yeovil Town	1-3
Willenhall Town	Barnet	0-6
replay		
Welling United	Boston United	3-2

First Round

Altrincham	Wigan Ath	0-2
Barnet	Hereford United	0-1
Chelmsford City	Bath City	1-2
Chester City	Runcorn	0-1
Dagenham	Maidstone United	0-2
Halesowen Town	Kidderminster Harriers	2-2
Lincoln City	Crewe Alexandra	2-1
Macclesfield Town	Carlisle United	4-2
Northwich Victoria	Colwyn Bay	1-0
Sutton United	Aldershot	3-0
Telford United	Stockport County	1-1
Welling United	Carshalton Ath	3-2
Wolverhampton Wanderers	Cheltenham Town	5-1
replay		
Kidderminster Harriers	Halesowen Town	4-0
Stockport County	Telford United	2-0

Second Round

Macclesfield Town	Rotherham Utd	4-0
Maidstone United	Kidderminster Harriers	1-1
Mansfield Town	Lincoln City	4-3
Northwich Victoria	Blackpool	0-2
Peterborough Utd	Sutton United	1-3
Runcorn	Stockport County	0-1
Welling United	Bath City	0-1
replay		
Kidderminster Harriers	Maidstone United	2-2

F.A.Cup

Second Round - second replay

Kidderminster Harriers	Maidstone United	0-0
third replay		
Maidstone United	Kidderminster Harriers	2-1

Third Round

Mansfield Town	Bath City	4-0
Sheffield Utd	Maidstone United	1-0
Sutton United	Middlesborough	1-1
Port Vale	Macclesfield Town	1-0
replay		
Middlesborough	Sutton United	1-0

League Cup

(Conference clubs only)

First Round

Altrincham	Runcorn	1-0
Carshalton Ath	Barnet	1-2
Gosport Borough	Bath City	0-1
Leicester Utd	Boston Utd	0-1
Cheltenham Town	Slough Town	1-2
Dagenham	Hayes	1-0
Enfield	Ashford Town	4-1
Fisher Ath	Bromley	1-4
Kettering Town	VS Rugby	1-0
Bromsgrove Rovers	Kidderminster H	1-0
Lincoln City	Matlock Town	2-1
Hyde Utd	Macclesfield Town	3-4
Maidstone Utd	Wealdstone	4-1
Northwich Victoria	Worksop Town	4-2
Cambridge City	Stafford Rangers	1-3
Chelmsford City	Sutton Utd	1-3
Nuneaton Borough	Telford Utd	1-3
Croydon	Welling Utd	0-1
Dorchester Town	Weymouth	1-1
Wycombe Wand	Bognor Regis Town	0-1
replay		
Weymouth	Dorchester Town	2-1

Second Round

Dartford	Barnet	1-3
Bath City	Weymouth	1-5
Boston Utd	Bromsgrove Rovers	0-2
Dagenham	Harrow Borough	1-1
Lincoln City	Bedworth Utd	4-1
Macclesfield Town	Altrincham	0-1
Maidstone Utd	Enfield	0-2
Northwich Victoria	Rhyl	1-0
Stafford Rangers	Kettering Town	0-1
Sutton Utd	Leytonstone-Ilford	2-0
Telford Utd	Worcester City	4-1
Welling Utd	Bromley	0-0
replay		
Harrow Borough	Dagenham	1-0
Bromley	Welling Utd	1-2

Third Round

Altrincham	Horwich RMI	1-2
Enfield	Barnet	2-1
Kettering Town	Northwich Victoria	2-3
Sutton Utd	Bognor Regis Town	2-1
Telford Utd	Lincoln City	2-1
Welling Utd	Yeovil Town	1-0
Weymouth	Harrow Borough	2-0

Fourth Round

Enfield	Sutton Utd	1-1
Northwich Victoria	Horwich RMI	1-1
Morecambe	Telford Utd	1-1
Welling Utd	Weymouth	0-2
replay		
Horwich RMI	Northwich Victoria	3-2
Sutton Utd	Enfield	1-3
Telford Utd	Morecambe	0-2

Semi Final

Horwich RMI	Enfield	3-1
Morecambe	Weymouth	1-2

Final

Horwich RMI	Weymouth	2-0

Challenge Shield

Scarborough	Kidderminster Harriers	1-2

Third Qualifying Round

Redditch Utd	Northwich Victoria	1-1
Grays Ath	Welling Utd	0-2
replay		
Northwich Victoria	Redditch Utd	4-1

First Round

Kidderminster Harriers	Frickley Athletic	1-1
Bangor City	Boston United	2-2
Caernarfon Town	Stafford Rangers	1-1
Hyde Utd	Altrincham	0-1
Buxton	Telford United	2-4
Runcorn	Northwich Victoria	2-0
Macclesfield Town	Bishop Auckland	2-1
Welling United	Leyton-Wingate	1-6
Fisher Athletic	Marlow	2-0
Enfield	Worthing	4-2
Slough Town	Dagenham	3-1
Windsor & Eton	Barnet	1-1
Sutton United	Bishops Stortford	0-2
Aylesbury United	Kettering Town	1-1
Banbury Utd	Wealdstone	2-2
Bath City	Merthyr Tydfil	2-1
Harrow Borough	Weymouth	1-1
Maidstone United	Dartford	5-1
Wycombe Wanderers	Cheltenham Town	2-3
South Liverpool	Lincoln City	1-1
replay		
Frickley Athletic	Kidderminster Harriers	1-3
Boston United	Bangor City	0-0
Stafford Rangers	Caernarfon Town	1-0
Barnet	Windsor & Eton	2-1
Kettering Town	Aylesbury United	5-1
Wealdstone	Banbury United	1-0
Weymouth	Harrow Borough	1-2
Lincoln City	South Liverpool	2-2
second replay		
Boston United	Bangor City	2-1
Lincoln City	South Liverpool	3-1

Second Round

Kidderminster Harriers	Runcorn	0-2
Lincoln City	Cambridge City	2-1
Rhyl	Macclesfield Town	0-2
Cheltenham Town	Crawley Town	2-0
Fisher Athletic	Slough Town	2-1
Enfield	Bishops Stortford	3-1
Leyton-Wingate	Boston United	5-2
Bath City	Stafford Rangers	0-2
Marine	Maidstone United	0-4
Wealdstone	Telford United	0-3
Barnet	Bromsgrove Rovers	0-0
Altrincham	Kettering Town	1-1
replay		
Bromsgrove Rovers	Barnet	3-1
Kettering Town	Altrincham	2-3

Third Round

Altrincham	Fisher Athletic	1-1
Runcorn	Barrow	0-1
Cheltenham Town	Bromsgrove Rovers	2-1
Leyton-Wingate	Macclesfield Town	1-2
Lincoln City	Maidstone United	2-1
Witton Albion	Enfield	1-2
Telford United	Stafford Rangers	1-1

Third Round - replay

Fisher Athletic	Altrincham	0-0
Stafford Rangers	Telford United	2-3
second replay		
Fisher Athletic	Altrincham	1-1
third replay		
Altrincham	Fisher Athletic	1-0

Fourth Round

Enfield	Lincoln City	1-0
Wokingham Town	Macclesfield Town	2-0
Cheltenham Town	Telford United	2-4
Altrincham	Barrow	0-0
replay		
Barrow	Altrincham	2-1

Semi Final *(two legs)*

Barrow	Enfield	1-2
Enfield	Barrow	0-1
Telford United	Wokingham Town	2-0
Wokingham Town	Telford United	0-1
replay		
Enfield	Barrow	1-1
(Played at Kidderminster)		
second replay		
Enfield	Barrow	1-0
(Played at Stafford Rangers)		

Final *(@ Wembley)*

Enfield	Telford United	0-0
replay *(@ West Bromwich Albion)*		
Enfield	Telford United	3-2

MAIDSTONE UNITED 4
STAFFORD RANGERS 2
Maidstone bid farewell to the
London Road Ground.

1988/89

Now based at Dartford's Watling Street ground, Maidstone United reacted favourably to a change of scenery. The forward partnership of Butler and Gall flourished with a total of 52 goals and shrewd summer signings, including Ashford, Berry and Golley gave the team a formidable look. Sixteen points in their first six matches saw the Stones top the table before a run of just two points from seven games saw them slump to eighth place. They were also the first side to lose to Newport County during this period. However, their good form returned, and they suffered only two more defeats after October 8th.

The championship was secured on May 1st when their closest rivals Kettering lost to Enfield, while Maidstone were beating Welling Utd to secure the Kent Senior Cup. The eight point winning margin was the largest by any side thus far.

For others, new surroundings proved less rewarding, Newport County, fresh from Division 4 languished in the bottom four through to March, when their financial crisis finally caught up with them. After sanctioning three postponements, the league reluctantly announced County's expulsion when they failed to fulfil a league fixture with Enfield on March 18th. County's record of four wins and seven draws from twenty-nine fixtures was expunged. However, they did go out with a bang, losing a Clubcall Cup-tie by the odd goal in eleven to Kidderminster in their final fixture – despite taking the lead on five occasions.

Barnet had a record-breaking season, but unfortunately this was not due to on the field performances. Two transfer records were set for non-League players when Nicky Bissett was sold to Brighton for £115.000, followed swiftly by Lee Payne's departure to Newcastle in exchange for £125.000. A record deal between non-League clubs was also set when Gary Abbott moved across North London to Enfield for £40.000.

The most publicised aspect of the season was Sutton's F.A.Cup run. After overcoming non-League opposition in the first and second rounds, the home draw against 1987 cup winners, Coventry City attracted much interest and brought the B.B.C. cameras to Gander Green Lane. A 2-1 victory, courtesy of goals by Rains and Hanlan, led to a fourth round tie away at Norwich City, and ultimate defeat by 8 goals to nil. This overshadowed Kettering's endeavours, as they beat Bristol Rovers and Halifax Town in reaching the fourth round, before succumbing 2-1 to First Division Charlton Athletic.

	Alt	Ayl	Bar	Bos	Che	Cho	Enf	Fis	Ket	Kid	Mac	Mai	Nor	Run	Sta	Sut	Tel	Wel	Wey	Wyc	Yeo	New
Altrincham	X	1-0	1-1	0-0	0-1	1-2	0-0	1-1	1-2	3-1	1-3	0-1	2-2	1-2	2-1	1-0	0-0	3-1	2-1	2-2	2-2	1-0
Aylesbury United	1-2	X	1-3	1-2	0-0	4-3	2-1	1-1	0-1	1-5	1-2	1-2	2-0	1-2	1-1	1-0	2-0	0-0	4-1	0-2	3-2	n/p
Barnet	3-0	1-0	X	0-0	3-1	2-4	2-1	2-3	3-2	0-2	1-4	2-1	2-0	3-2	1-2	1-1	1-3	2-3	4-1	1-0	2-0	4-1
Boston United	3-1	2-0	5-0	X	1-1	2-0	3-2	2-4	1-1	0-2	3-2	1-4	2-1	0-6	2-1	3-1	1-0	2-0	2-0	0-1	1-1	1-1
Cheltenham Town	2-1	0-0	1-2	3-1	X	2-2	3-2	2-2	2-1	4-1	3-0	0-4	2-2	2-1	1-2	2-3	0-1	1-1	1-1	0-1	1-1	3-2
Chorley	1-0	1-1	2-3	0-1	1-4	X	1-2	1-1	0-1	1-3	0-1	1-3	3-1	1-3	3-1	2-1	2-0	1-1	0-0	3-2	2-3	0-2
Enfield	2-1	2-1	4-0	1-2	3-4	1-2	X	2-1	1-1	1-3	2-1	1-1	1-2	0-3	4-2	1-1	0-1	0-1	3-0	3-4	1-1	3-0
Fisher Athletic	1-1	0-2	1-2	1-3	2-0	4-0	1-2	X	3-0	2-0	2-2	0-2	2-4	0-1	0-1	1-0	0-1	1-3	3-2	3-3	4-2	3-2
Kettering Town	0-1	5-2	3-1	1-2	2-0	3-0	0-1	2-1	X	2-1	1-0	3-3	2-1	2-0	1-0	1-0	1-0	2-1	1-0	2-1	1-0	n/p
Kidderminster Harriers	2-3	4-3	1-0	0-2	3-2	0-2	1-3	2-1	1-1	X	0-1	3-6	1-1	2-1	3-2	1-0	1-1	1-0	2-0	2-2		1-1
Macclesfield Town	1-0	3-1	1-0	0-1	0-0	3-2	1-1	2-2	0-1	1-1	X	4-3	0-2	3-2	1-3	2-1	3-0	2-0	0-1	2-3		3-0
Maidstone United	7-2	1-1	3-2	3-0	2-0	2-0	3-1	1-0	0-0	0-3	3-3	X	4-1	2-2	3-0	1-1	1-3	3-0	3-0	1-3	5-0	2-1
Northwich Victoria	4-3	1-1	1-1	0-1	1-0	0-4	2-2	3-0	1-1	2-4	3-2	2-0	X	0-1	1-1	4-2	0-2	2-0	2-0	1-3		3-1
Runcorn	3-0	5-0	3-0	1-2	2-1	3-0	1-2	1-1	2-1	1-3	2-2	0-1	3-1	X	4-1	1-2	0-0	1-2	2-3	2-1		0-0
Stafford Rangers	0-2	3-1	1-2	4-1	1-1	3-2	3-1	0-1	2-1	0-1	1-1	0-2	0-1	0-4	X	1-1	1-3	3-0	1-0	1-1	2-6	3-0
Sutton United	3-2	5-2	5-1	0-0	1-1	1-2	3-1	2-0	0-2	1-1	1-2	1-1	3-3	3-1	2-0	X	1-2	0-1	3-1	3-0	5-2	1-1
Telford United	0-1	0-1	0-3	0-1	2-0	2-1	3-0	0-1	0-1	1-0	1-3	1-2	1-4	1-1	2-2	0-0	X	0-0	1-0	1-2	0-1	3-1
Welling United	0-0	5-0	1-1	3-2	0-2	1-0	0-0	3-1	2-1	0-1	2-0	0-0	0-0	4-0	1-3	1-1	0-1	X	4-0	0-1	0-2	n/p
Weymouth	1-3	0-0	1-1	2-2	3-2	2-3	2-3	1-0	3-0	3-1	1-2	1-3	2-2	1-1	1-0	2-2	0-0	1-0	X	0-3	0-2	n/p
Wycombe Wanderers	2-1	1-0	2-3	2-1	1-0	1-1	3-2	3-0	0-1	1-0	1-1	2-3	1-4	3-3	6-1	2-1	1-0	1-1	0-0	X	1-1	5-0
Yeovil Town	2-3	1-0	2-1	1-1	1-3	2-1	1-2	1-2	2-2	1-3	2-0	1-2	2-1	2-2	2-0	0-0	4-3	4-0	2-3	1-1	X	n/p
Newport County	n/p	2-2	1-7	1-1	0-1	2-0	n/p	n/p	1-2	1-2	n/p	2-1	n/p	n/p	n/p	n/p	0-3	0-1	4-0	3-5	1-1	X

	P	Home					Away					Total						
		W	D	L	F	A	W	D	L	F	A	W	D	L	F	A	Pts	
Maidstone United	40	12	5	3	48	22	13	4	3	44	24	25	9	6	92	46	84	P
Kettering Town	40	16	1	3	35	15	7	6	7	21	24	23	7	10	56	39	76	
Boston United	40	12	3	5	36	28	10	5	5	25	23	22	8	10	61	51	74	
Wycombe Wanderers	40	9	7	4	34	25	11	4	5	34	27	20	11	9	68	52	71	
Kidderminster Harriers	40	10	4	6	32	32	11	2	7	36	25	21	6	13	68	57	69	
Runcorn	40	11	3	6	39	22	8	5	7	38	31	19	8	13	77	53	65	
Macclesfield Town	40	9	5	6	31	26	8	5	7	32	31	17	10	13	63	57	61	
Barnet	40	11	2	7	36	30	7	5	8	28	39	18	7	15	64	69	61	
Yeovil Town	40	8	5	7	34	30	7	6	7	34	37	15	11	14	68	67	56	
Northwich Victoria	40	8	5	7	31	30	6	6	8	33	35	14	11	15	64	65	53	
Welling United	40	8	6	6	27	16	6	5	9	18	30	14	11	15	45	46	53	
Sutton United	40	10	5	5	43	26	2	10	8	21	28	12	15	13	64	54	51	
Enfield	40	7	4	9	33	32	7	4	9	29	35	14	8	18	62	67	50	
Altrincham	40	6	8	6	24	23	7	2	11	27	38	13	10	17	51	61	49	
Cheltenham Town	40	7	7	6	32	29	5	5	10	23	29	12	12	16	55	58	48	
Telford United	40	5	5	10	17	24	8	4	8	20	19	13	9	18	37	43	48	
Chorley	40	6	4	10	26	32	7	2	11	31	39	13	6	21	57	71	45	
Fisher Athletic	40	6	4	10	31	32	4	7	9	24	33	10	11	19	55	65	41	
Stafford Rangers	40	7	4	9	27	32	4	3	13	22	42	11	7	22	49	74	40	
Aylesbury United	40	7	4	9	27	30	2	5	13	16	41	9	9	22	43	71	36	R
Weymouth	40	6	7	7	27	30	1	3	16	10	40	7	10	23	37	70	31	R

FINAL TABLE

Newport County   29   3   3   7   18   26   1   4   11   13   36   4   7   18   31   62   19
(Newport County expelled, record deleted)

Barrow promoted from N.P.L., Merthyr Tydfil from Southern League, Farnborough Town from Isthmian League.

CUP COMPETITIONS

F.A.Cup

First Qualifying Round		
Northwich Victoria	Arnold	5-0
Boston United	Coventry Sporting	8-1
Stafford Rangers	Halesowen Harriers	2-0
Ware	Kettering Town	0-3
Barnet	Epsom & Ewell	7-0
Wycombe Wanderers	Haverhill Rovers	4-1
Ramsgate	Fisher Athletic	0-2
Trowbridge Town	Weymouth	1-2
Radstock Town	Cheltenham Town	0-2
Second Qualifying Round		
Eastwood Hanley	Northwich Victoria	0-1
Boston United	Mile Oak Rovers & Youth	5-0
Stafford Rangers	Rushall Olympic	1-0
Great Yarmouth Town	Kettering Town	0-3
Thanet United	Fisher Athletic	1-3
Barnet	Leatherhead	4-3
Finchley	Wycombe Wanderers	0-3
Weston-super-Mare	Weymouth	0-1
Gloucester City	Cheltenham Town	3-0
Third Qualifying Round		
Hyde Utd	Northwich Victoria	1-1
Boston United	Hinckley Town	3-4
Stafford Rangers	Leicester Utd	1-1
Kettering Town	Boreham Wood	4-0
Barnet	Grays Ath	0-1
Staines Town	Wycombe Wanderers	0-1
Fisher Athletic	Kingstonian	1-1
Weymouth	Forest Green Rovers	3-0
replay		
Northwich Victoria	Hyde Utd	3-0
Leicester Utd	Stafford Rangers	2-3
Kingstonian	Fisher Athletic	1-4
Fourth Qualifying Round		
Aylesbury United	Sudbury Town	1-1
Fisher Athletic	Dulwich Hamlet	3-3
Fleetwood Town	Runcorn	1-3
Frickley Athletic	Chorley	1-1
Macclesfield Town	Altrincham	0-0
Newport County	Weymouth	2-1
Northwich Victoria	Billingham Synthonia	2-0
Stafford Rangers	Kidderminster Harriers	2-1
Sutton United	Walton & Hersham	1-1
Welling United	Hinckley Town	1-1
Worcester City	Yeovil Town	1-2
Wycombe Wanderers	Kettering Town	1-2
replay		
Altrincham	Macclesfield Town	4-0
Chorley	Frickley Athletic	0-1
Dulwich Hamlet	Fisher Athletic	0-3
Hinckley Town	Welling United	0-3
Sudbury Town	Aylesbury United	0-1
Walton & Hersham	Sutton United	0-3
First Round		
Altrincham	Lincoln City	3-2
Bristol Rovers	Fisher Athletic	3-0
Dagenham	Sutton United	0-4
Enfield	Leyton Orient	1-1
Frickley Athletic	Northwich Victoria	0-2
Kettering Town	Dartford	2-1
Newport County	Maidstone United	1-2
Runcorn	Wrexham	2-2
Stafford Rangers	Crewe Alexandra	2-2
Telford United	Carlisle United	1-1
Waterlooville	Aylesbury United	1-4
Welling United	Bromsgrove Rovers	3-0
Yeovil Town	Merthyr Tydfil	3-2
replay		
Carlisle United	Telford United	4-1
Crewe Alexandra	Stafford Rangers	3-2
Leyton Orient	Enfield	2-2
Wrexham	Runcorn	2-3
second replay		
Leyton Orient	Enfield	0-1
Second Round		
Altrincham	Halifax Town	0-3
Aylesbury United	Sutton United	0-1
Bath City	Welling United	0-0
Enfield	Cardiff City	1-4
Kettering Town	Bristol Rovers	2-1
Northwich Victoria	Tranmere Rovers	1-2
Reading	Maidstone United	1-1
Runcorn	Crewe Alexandra	0-3
Yeovil Town	Torquay Utd	1-1

F.A.Cup

Second Round - replay		
Maidstone United	Reading	1-2
Torquay Utd	Yeovil Town	1-0
Welling United	Bath City	3-2
Third Round		
Kettering Town	Halifax Town	1-1
Sutton United	Coventry City	2-1
Welling United	Blackburn Rovers	0-1
replay		
Halifax Town	Kettering Town	2-3
Fourth Round		
Norwich City	Sutton United	8-0
Charlton Ath	Kettering Town	2-1

League Cup (Conference clubs only)

First Round		
Bangor City	Altrincham	4-0
Bromsgrove Rovers	Boston Utd	2-1
Dorchester Town	Cheltenham Town	0-3
Enfield	Bishops Stortford	3-4
Kidderminster Harriers	Telford Utd	2-0
Leytonstone & Ilford	Welling United	1-0
Maidstone Utd	Fisher Athletic	2-0
Runcorn	Barrow	1-0
Morecambe	Chorley	0-0
Stafford Rangers	Northwich Victoria	2-1
Wealdstone	Aylesbury United	2-0
Weymouth	Fareham Town	1-1
Windsor & Eton	Barnet	1-4
Witton Albion	Macclesfield Town	2-0
Wokingham Town	Wycombe Wanderers	1-2
Worksop Town	Kettering Town	0-3
Yeovil Town	Newport County	4-5
Dartford	Sutton United	1-2
replay		
Chorley	Morecambe	2-2
(Morecambe won on away goals)		
Second Round		
Bromsgrove Rovers	Barnet	1-2
Buxton	Newport County	3-4
Kidderminster Harriers	Wycombe Wanderers	4-1
Leytonstone & Ilford	Kettering Town	3-0
Maidstone United	Crawley Town	3-0
Runcorn	Caernarfon Town	3-0
Stafford Rangers	Cheltenham Town	1-0
Sutton United	Croydon	2-0
Wealdstone	Hayes	3-2
Weymouth	Leyton Wingate	0-1
Third Round		
Barnet	Dover Athletic	5-1
Leytonstone & Ilford	Maidstone United	1-3
Newport County	Kidderminster Harriers	5-6
Runcorn	Morecambe	5-3
Stafford Rangers	Worcester City	2-1
Wealdstone	Sutton United	0-4
Fourth Round		
Bishops Stortford	Sutton United	4-3
Hyde Utd	Stafford Rangers	1-0
Kidderminster Harriers	Runcorn	0-1
Maidstone United	Barnet	1-2
Semi Final		
Bishops Stortford	Barnet	1-1
Hyde Utd	Runcorn	2-1
replay		
Barnet	Bishops Stortford	4-1
Final		
Barnet	Hyde Utd	3-3
(Barnet won 5-3 pens)	(@ Telford United)	

Challenge Shield

Lincoln City	Enfield	3-1

44

F.A. Trophy

Third Qualifying Round

Northwich Victoria	Goole Town	2-0
Leyton-Wingate	Welling United	2-2
Wycombe Wanderers	Cambridge City	2-0
replay		
Welling United	Leyton-Wingate	3-1

First Round

Barnet	Gravesend & Northfleet	1-1
Basingstoke Town	Kettering Town	1-1
Bath City	Wycombe Wanderers	0-0
Boston United	Stafford Rangers	2-0
Bromley	Wealdstone	1-2
Burton Albion	Chorley	4-1
Buxton	Altrincham	0-2
Dagenham	Aylesbury United	2-2
Enfield	Hendon	4-1
Fareham Town	Yeovil Town	1-2
Fisher Athletic	Cheltenham Town	0-1
Kidderminster Harriers	Maidstone United	2-1
Marine	Macclesfield Town	2-2
Matlock Town	Northwich Victoria	2-6
Runcorn	Gretna	2-3
Sutton United	Kingstonian	1-0
Telford United	Witton Albion	3-0
Welling United	Slough Town	4-0
Weymouth	Newport County	2-1
replay		
Gravesend & Northfleet	Barnet	2-1
Kettering Town	Basingstoke Town	5-3
Wycombe Wanderers	Bath City	4-0
Aylesbury United	Dagenham	4-0
Macclesfield Town	Marine	4-1

Second Round

Boston United	Northwich Victoria	3-2
Gravesend & Northfleet	Kettering Town	1-1
Kidderminster Harriers	Burton Albion	1-1
Aylesbury United	Merthyr Tydfil	1-3
Sutton United	Bishop Auckland	1-1
Wealdstone	Wycombe Wanderers	0-1
Cheltenham Town	Barrow	0-0
Altrincham	Carshalton Ath	2-0
Windsor & Eton	Enfield	1-0
Woking	Weymouth	2-1
South Bank	Macclesfield Town	0-3
Yeovil Town	Telford United	1-4
Leicester Utd	Welling United	1-3
replay		
Kettering Town	Gravesend & Northfleet	1-2
Burton Albion	Kidderminster Harriers	0-1
Bishop Auckland	Sutton United	2-1
Barrow	Cheltenham Town	0-0
second replay		
Barrow	Cheltenham Town	1-0

Third Round

Kidderminster Harriers	Telford United	1-1
Welling United	Boston United	0-0
Wycombe Wanderers	Merthyr Tydfil	2-0
Altrincham	Barrow	5-3
Macclesfield Town	Gravesend & Northfleet	2-0
replay		
Telford United	Kidderminster Harriers	2-0
Boston United	Welling United	0-1

Fourth Round

Macclesfield Town	Welling United	1-0
Newcastle Blue Star	Telford United	1-4
Hyde Utd	Wycombe Wanderers	1-0
Dartford	Altrincham	1-0

Semi Final *(two legs)*

Dartford	Macclesfield Town	0-0
Macclesfield Town	Dartford	4-1
Hyde Utd	Telford United	0-1
Telford United	Hyde Utd	3-0

Final *(@ Wembley)*

Telford United	Macclesfield Town	1-0

NEWPORT COUNTY
88-89

AMBERSCENE

CLUBCALL CUP
Third Round

Kidderminster Harriers

Tuesday, 21st February 1989
Kick-off 7.30 p.m.

Official Programme 40p

NEWPORT COUNTY 5
KIDDERMINSTER HARRIERS 6
An eleven goal thriller, but this was the
last ever game for Newport County

1989/90

Darlington became the second team in three years to bounce straight back into the Football League when they pipped Barnet to the title on the last day of the season. The climax to the season would have been difficult to predict in view of Darlo's excellent start to the campaign which saw them lead from the opening day until Boxing Day. When their first loss occurred, in early November, Barnet were the opponents and the campaign developed into a two horse race, apart from a spell around the New Year when Macclesfield took the lead. Darlington's defence proved to be decisive, conceding only 25 goals. It was well marshalled on the field by a ex-Scotland international Frank Gray ably assisted by Corner, Smith and McJannet, who each possessed considerable Football League experience. When the final day arrived, only a point was needed at Welling, provided that Barnet did not win by 13 clear goals, and when Gary Coatsworth scored the only goal of the game three minutes from time, no one could deny that the Quakers were worthy champions.

After almost 30 years of unbroken success, Enfield finished bottom of the table and suffered relegation for the first time in their 96 year history. After an average start to the season, long term injuries and three changes of manager saw their fortunes plummet. A run of twelve matches without victory saw them fall below Fisher, with the low point being a Conference record 9-0 defeat at Runcorn, a result which was not helped by the late arrival of their England semi-professional international defenders Pape and Howell, who had travelled independently of the team. Even a late season spending spree could not avoid the inevitable.

The 'great escape' was performed by Fisher Athletic, who had kept Enfield company in the depths for so long. After Malcolm Allison's resignation in November, manager Mike Bailey had looked to be fighting a losing battle. However, the last four matches were won, fourteen goals were scored, and Chorley were overtaken on the last day,. The main saviour was recent signing Hughie Mann, who scored nine goals in the last five games, including all four on the final day against Merthyr.

The end of the season saw the demise of two of non-League football's most famous grounds, when Yeovil bade farewell to the Huish with a single goal victory over Telford, whilst Wycombe left Loakes Park after a crowd of 4,000 saw them lose 9-4 to a star-studded International X1, which included George Best. Meanwhile Northwich Victoria waved goodbye to a familiar face, Dave Ryan, who had missed only six league matches since the Alliance Premier League was formed, and had played 183 consecutive Conference matches when a shoulder injury brought the run to an end. When he was dropped later in the season, he left the club after 727 appearances.

	Altrincham	Barnet	Barrow	Boston United	Cheltenham Town	Chorley	Darlington	Enfield	Farnborough Town	Fisher Athletic	Kettering Town	Kidderminster Harriers	Macclesfield Town	Merthyr Tydfil	Northwich Victoria	Runcorn	Stafford Rangers	Sutton United	Telford United	Welling United	Wycombe Wanderers	Yeovil Town
Altrincham	X	2-1	1-1	0-0	5-0	1-0	0-1	3-0	2-3	1-1	1-1	0-1	0-1	4-1	0-2	1-2	3-1	0-0	0-1	4-0	1-2	2-1
Barnet	1-0	X	1-0	1-2	4-0	5-0	0-2	2-0	4-1	4-1	4-1	2-1	0-0	4-0	1-0	2-2	1-1	4-1	2-1	1-1	2-0	1-0
Barrow	1-1	1-1	X	2-1	2-1	3-1	1-1	2-2	3-1	1-1	1-0	2-1	1-1	1-5	1-0	2-2	2-1	1-0	3-0	1-1	0-3	2-1
Boston United	2-3	1-2	2-1	X	2-1	0-1	1-3	1-0	2-2	2-0	1-2	2-3	3-0	2-2	1-3	3-2	2-0	3-1	2-2	2-1	2-0	0-1
Cheltenham Town	0-0	2-0	1-0	0-0	X	2-0	0-1	3-1	4-0	0-0	1-1	2-1	1-2	0-2	2-3	2-2	1-3	2-0	1-2	3-2	1-1	2-1
Chorley	2-1	1-4	0-1	0-0	0-2	X	0-3	2-2	1-0	2-0	2-2	1-0	0-0	1-2	0-2	1-1	3-2	1-2	4-0	1-0		3-2
Darlington	2-0	1-2	0-0	6-1	5-1	3-0	X	2-1	1-1	5-0	2-1	3-0	1-1	0-0	4-0	1-1	2-1	2-0	1-1	1-0	0-1	1-0
Enfield	2-1	1-3	3-0	0-1	4-2	2-0	0-3	X	0-0	1-2	0-3	2-1	1-1	2-0	2-0	3-2	4-1	2-3	1-2	2-3	3-5	1-1
Farnborough Town	0-0	0-1	3-0	1-0	4-0	1-3	1-0	2-3	X	1-1	1-1	0-1	1-2	0-1	0-1	6-3	3-3	1-3	2-1	3-1	1-1	2-4
Fisher Athletic	3-0	1-2	4-0	1-0	2-5	2-0	0-2	3-2	4-2	X	3-1	1-1	1-3	1-2	1-0	0-1	0-2	1-2	1-3	1-3	3-1	1-2
Kettering Town	3-0	3-2	2-0	5-0	1-0	2-1	1-3	3-2	1-1	3-0	X	0-2	0-0	2-0	3-1	1-1	0-0	2-0	1-1	0-1	1-0	1-0
Kidderminster Harriers	1-2	0-1	2-2	1-3	1-2	3-1	3-2	2-0	3-1	1-1	2-3	X	2-2	1-2	4-0	0-0	3-0	2-2	2-4	1-1	0-2	3-2
Macclesfield Town	1-0	0-1	2-1	0-0	3-0	0-0	0-0	4-0	0-0	0-1	3-1	1-2	X	3-2	3-1	4-0	2-2	1-1	3-0	3-2	1-0	1-1
Merthyr Tydfil	0-0	2-1	3-3	1-0	1-1	1-0	1-1	5-1	1-1	1-4	3-2	3-1	2-3	X	1-1	3-2	4-3	2-3	0-0	4-0	1-1	2-2
Northwich Victoria	2-3	0-2	1-0	1-0	0-0	0-1	1-0	1-0	0-2	2-1	2-2	1-2	2-0	3-1	X	1-1	4-3	2-3	0-2	2-3	3-0	1-4
Runcorn	0-0	2-2	4-3	3-1	2-4	3-2	2-1	9-0	3-2	4-0	3-1	2-1	2-0	1-0	2-1	X	3-0	1-0	3-0	0-1	2-0	1-1
Stafford Rangers	3-1	1-1	1-1	0-0	0-1	0-4	1-0	3-2	1-3	1-1	0-1	4-2	1-1	1-0	1-1	3-1	X	3-1	2-0	0-2	1-0	0-1
Sutton United	2-1	1-3	3-3	2-0	0-2	3-0	2-1	2-0	2-3	2-1	2-1	1-2	2-1	1-1	2-1	3-0	1-0	X	6-1	1-0	1-2	3-1
Telford United	1-3	1-3	3-0	4-2	0-0	0-4	0-1	1-1	4-2	3-1	1-3	1-1	1-0	1-1	2-1	2-1	0-2	1-1	X	0-0	4-1	1-1
Welling United	1-1	3-1	0-0	6-0	1-1	3-1	0-1	3-0	4-3	2-0	3-0	4-1	0-1	0-3	2-0	1-1	1-0	1-0	1-1	X	0-0	0-1
Wycombe Wanderers	1-1	1-0	4-0	1-0	0-4	4-0	0-1	1-0	1-0	6-1	2-2	3-3	1-1	1-2	3-3	5-0	2-1	3-2	1-1	1-0	X	1-2
Yeovil Town	0-0	3-2	2-2	2-1	1-1	2-1	0-2	3-1	0-0	2-2	0-2	1-1	0-0	4-0	1-2	1-1	0-0	3-1	1-0	0-4	4-2	X

		Home						Away						Total						
	P	W	D	L	F	A	W	D	L	F	A	W	D	L	F	A	Pts	
Darlington	42	13	6	2	43	12	13	3	5	33	13	26	9	7	76	25	87	P
Barnet	42	15	4	2	46	14	11	3	7	35	27	26	7	9	81	41	85	
Runcorn	42	16	3	2	52	20	3	10	8	27	42	19	13	10	79	62	70	
Macclesfield Town	42	11	6	4	35	16	6	9	6	21	25	17	15	10	56	41	66	
Kettering Town	42	13	5	3	35	15	5	7	9	31	38	18	12	12	66	53	66	
Welling United	42	11	6	4	36	16	7	4	10	26	34	18	10	14	62	50	64	
Yeovil Town	42	9	8	4	32	25	8	4	9	30	29	17	12	13	62	54	63	
Sutton United	42	14	2	5	42	24	5	4	12	26	40	19	6	17	68	64	63	
Merthyr Tydfil	42	9	9	3	41	30	7	5	9	26	33	16	14	12	67	63	62	
Wycombe Wanderers	42	11	6	4	42	24	6	4	11	22	32	17	10	15	64	56	61	
Cheltenham Town	42	9	6	6	30	22	7	5	9	28	38	16	11	15	58	60	59	
Telford United	42	8	7	6	31	29	7	6	8	25	34	15	13	14	56	63	58	
Kidderminster Harriers	42	7	6	8	37	33	8	3	10	27	34	15	9	18	64	67	54	
Barrow	42	11	8	2	33	25	1	8	12	18	42	12	16	14	51	67	52	
Northwich Victoria	42	9	3	9	29	30	6	2	13	22	37	15	5	22	51	67	50	
Altrincham	42	8	5	8	31	20	4	8	9	18	28	12	13	17	49	48	49	
Stafford Rangers	42	9	6	6	25	23	3	6	12	25	39	12	12	18	50	62	48	
Boston United	42	10	3	8	36	30	3	5	13	12	37	13	8	21	48	67	47	
Fisher Athletic	42	9	1	11	34	34	4	6	11	21	44	13	7	22	55	78	46	
Chorley	42	9	5	7	26	26	4	1	16	16	41	13	6	23	42	67	45	R
Farnborough Town	42	7	5	9	33	30	3	7	11	27	43	10	12	20	60	73	42	R
Enfield	42	9	3	9	36	34	1	3	17	16	55	10	6	26	52	89	36	R

F I N A L   T A B L E

Gateshead promoted from N.P.L., Bath City from Southern League, Slough Town from Isthmian League.

CUP COMPETITIONS

F.A.Cup

First Qualifying Round		
Cleator Moor Celtic	Barrow	1-4
Boston United	Leek Town	3-3
Stafford Rangers	Hinckley Town	1-0
Bishops Stortford	Barnet	0-1
Baldock Town	Wycombe Wanderers	0-2
Hampton	Fisher Athletic	3-1
Cheltenham Town	Saltash Utd	1-0
replay		
Leek Town	Boston United	0-3
Second Qualifying Round		
Barrow	Alnwick Town	3-1
Boston United	Alfreton Town	1-0
Stafford Rangers	Milton Keynes/Wolverton T	2-0
Barnet	Newmarket Town	4-2
Wycombe Wanderers	Boreham Wood	3-1
Cheltenham Town	Weston-super-Mare	7-0
Third Qualifying Round		
Barrow	Whitley Bay	2-2
Matlock Town	Boston United	1-1
Lye Town	Stafford Rangers	1-2
Cambridge City	Barnet	3-4
Wycombe Wanderers	Gravesend & Northfleet	1-1
Dorchester Town	Cheltenham Town	2-1
replay		
Whitley Bay	Barrow	3-1
Boston United	Matlock Town	0-1
Gravesend & Northfleet	Wycombe Wanderers	1-1
second replay		
Gravesend & Northfleet	Wycombe Wanderers	0-3
Fourth Qualifying Round		
Burton Albion	Barnet	2-2
Chorley	Marine	1-1
Darlington	Runcorn	4-2
Dulwich Hamlet	Merthyr Tydfil	1-1
(Played at Fisher Ath)		
Exmouth Town	Farnborough Town	1-4
Kidderminster Harriers	Chelmsford City	2-2
Matlock Town	Enfield	3-1
Northwich Victoria	Goole Town	2-0
Stafford Rangers	Wycombe Wanderers	4-1
Staines Town	Yeovil Town	0-3
Tow Law Town	Altrincham	2-0
Welling United	Bromley	5-2
replay		
Barnet	Burton Albion	1-0
Chelmsford City	Kidderminster Harriers	1-3
Marine	Chorley	0-0
Merthyr Tydfil	Dulwich Hamlet	4-2
second replay		
Marine	Chorley	3-0
First Round		
Bristol City	Barnet	2-0
Darlington	Northwich Victoria	6-2
Farnborough Town	Hereford United	0-1
Gillingham	Welling United	0-0
Kettering Town	Northampton Town	0-1
Kidderminster Harriers	Swansea City	2-3
Macclesfield Town	Chester City	1-1
Maidstone United	Yeovil Town	2-1
Redditch United	Merthyr Tydfil	1-3
Stafford Rangers	Halifax Town	2-3
Sutton United	Torquay Utd	1-1
Telford United	Walsall	0-3
replay		
Chester City	Macclesfield Town	3-2
Torquay Utd	Sutton United	4-0
Welling United	Gillingham	1-0

F.A.Cup

Second Round		
Darlington	Halifax Town	3-0
Hereford United	Merthyr Tydfil	3-2
Reading	Welling United	0-0
replay		
Welling United	Reading	1-1
second replay		
Reading	Welling United	0-0
third replay		
Welling United	Reading	1-2
Third Round		
Cambridge Utd	Darlington	0-0
replay		
Darlington	Cambridge Utd	1-3

League Cup

First Round (two legs)			
Cheltenham Town	Telford Utd		1-0
Telford Utd	Cheltenham Town		3-1
Chorley	Barrow		0-1
Barrow	Chorley		2-0
Enfield	Fisher Athletic		2-3
Fisher Ath	Enfield		1-0
Farnborough Town	Merthyr Tydfil		1-2
Merthyr Tydfil	Farnborough Town		0-0
Stafford Rangers	Altrincham		1-1
Altrincham	Stafford Rangers		2-0
Sutton United	Welling Utd		3-2
Welling Utd	Sutton United	aet	4-2
Second Round			
Barnet	Kettering Town		3-2
Boston Utd	Fisher Athletic		3-0
Darlington	Macclesfield Town		5-2
Kidderminster Harriers	Runcorn		3-3
Northwich Victoria	Barrow		3-1
Telford Utd	Altrincham		3-2
Welling Utd	Yeovil Town		1-2
Wycombe Wanderers	Merthyr Tydfil		2-0
replay			
Runcorn	Kidderminster Harriers		1-3
Third Round			
Boston Utd	Wycombe Wanderers	aet	0-2
Kidderminster Harriers	Darlington		3-1
Telford Utd	Northwich Victoria		0-1
Yeovil Town	Barnet		3-2
Semi final (two legs)			
Northwich Victoria	Kidderminster Harriers		1-1
Kidderminster Harriers	Northwich Victoria	aet	6-1
Yeovil Town	Wycombe Wanderers		2-1
Wycombe Wanderers	Yeovil Town		3-2
(Yeovil Town won on away goals)			
Final (two legs)			
Yeovil Town	Kidderminster Harriers		3-0
Kidderminster Harriers	Yeovil Town		1-1

Challenge Shield

Maidstone United	Telford United	2-0

Third Qualifying Round

Chorley	Blyth Spartans	1-3
Rhyl	Stafford Rangers	0-0

replay

Stafford Rangers	Rhyl	2-1

First Round

Colne Dynamoes	Altrincham	5-0
Billingham Synthonia	Darlington	2-2

(Played at Darlington)

Stafford Rangers	Billingham Town	2-1
Telford United	Burton Albion	2-1
Northwich Victoria	Bishop Auckland	1-1
Barrow	Bangor City	1-0
Newcastle Blue Star	Runcorn	0-0
Boston United	Macclesfield Town	0-0
Welling United	Fisher Athletic	2-0
Kettering Town	Wokingham Town	0-2
Wycombe Wanderers	Metropolitan Police	1-3
Leyton-Wingate	Kidderminster Harriers	0-3
Enfield	Merthyr Tydfil	3-2
Sutton United	Dover Athletic	0-1
Dartford	Yeovil Town	1-2
Farnborough Town	Staines Town	1-0
Weymouth	Barnet	2-0
Cheltenham Town	Gravesend & Northfleet	5-1

replay

Darlington	Billingham Synthonia	3-1
Bishop Auckland	Northwich Victoria	2-3
Runcorn	Newcastle Blue Star	4-1
Macclesfield Town	Boston United	3-0

Second Round

Wokingham Town	Stafford Rangers	0-0
Darlington	Macclesfield Town	1-0
Barrow	Metropolitan Police	1-0
Witton Albion	Kidderminster Harriers	0-0
Cheltenham Town	Enfield	3-1
Farnborough Town	Windsor & Eton	2-1
Wivenhoe Town	Runcorn	1-1
Telford United	Welling United	0-0
Colne Dynamoes	Northwich Victoria	1-0
Yeovil Town	Aylesbury United	2-0

replay

Stafford Rangers	Wokingham Town	3-1
Kidderminster Harriers	Witton Albion	2-1
Runcorn	Wivenhoe	3-2
Welling United	Telford United	0-2

Third Round

Colne Dynamoes	Farnborough Town	2-1
Darlington	Runcorn	1-0
Kidderminster Harriers	Dover Athletic	3-0
Kingstonian	Cheltenham Town	3-3
Stafford Rangers	Redbridge Forest	1-1
Telford United	Leek Town	0-0
Yeovil Town	Barrow	1-1

Third Round - replay

Cheltenham Town	Kingstonian	0-3
Redbridge Forest	Stafford Rangers	1-2
Leek Town	Telford United	3-0
Barrow	Yeovil Town	2-1

Fourth Round

Bath City	Stafford Rangers	0-2
Kidderminster Harriers	Colne Dynamoes	0-0
Kingstonian	Barrow	2-2
Leek Town	Darlington	1-0

replay

Colne Dynamoes	Kidderminster Harriers	2-1
Barrow	Kingstonian	1-0

Semi Final *(two legs)*

Colne Dynamoes	Barrow	0-1
Barrow	Colne Dynamoes	1-1
Stafford Rangers	Leek Town	0-0
Leek Town	Stafford Rangers	1-0

Final *(@ Wembley)*

Barrow	Leek Town	3-0

RUNCORN 9
ENFIELD 0
Enfield's season hits
rock bottom in Cheshire.

1990/91

One of the best champion-ship races saw Barnet win promotion to the Football League on the last day of the season, pipping Colchester, Altrincham and Kettering. Kettering had been the early pace-setters with a record unbeaten start to the season. Their first defeat was registered on 3rd November, losing 5-1 at Wycombe, in their sixteenth game, having kept 11 clean sheets in the previous fifteen. At one stage in December they held a 10 point lead over Colchester and fifteen over Barnet, although they had played more matches.

However, the major challenge was being mounted by Altrincham. Having lost 2-1 at home to Kidderminster on 2nd October, they did not suffer a league defeat again until 24th April, when Barrow won 1-0 at Holker Street, a run of 28 games unbeaten. At this stage Alty were top of the table, but a fixture pile up caused by a run to the F.A.Trophy and Cheshire Senior Cup semi-finals, led to matches being played every other day, and their last five games yielded only two points and eventual third place.

Colchester United, fresh from relegation from Division Four, were in the top three in September and held their place until the season's end. They came the closest of the challengers to taking promotion away from Barnet, and on the final day they recorded a 2-0 home win over Kidderminster. With 30 minutes to go and Barnet trailing 1-2 at bottom of the table Fisher Athletic, the Championship was theirs. However three goals, two in the last four minutes, secured top spot for Barnet, in front of 4,283, Fisher's all-time record attendance.

As always, Barry Fry sent his team out to play open, attractive, football and it was shown by the fact that Barnet scored fifty goals, both home and away. Only Gary Phillips, in goal, was ever-present, but twelve other players appeared in at least half the matches. There was the usual wheeler-dealing by the Bees on the transfer market. Phil Gridelet was sold to Barnsley for a Conference record £175,000, this record being beaten five months later when Andy Clarke left for Division 1 Wimbledon in exchange for £250,000. The money was spent wisely and the arrival over the season of the late Kevin Durham, Paul Richardson, Nicky Evans, Kenny Lowe and Mark Carter strengthened the Barnet squad considerably. Their success was celebrated with a match at Underhill against Division 1 champions, Arsenal, which the visitors won 4-2.

1990/91 Season Results Grid

	Altrincham	Barnet	Barrow	Bath City	Boston United	Cheltenham Town	Colchester United	Fisher Athletic	Gateshead	Kettering Town	Kidderminster Harriers	Macclesfield Town	Merthyr Tydfil	Northwich Victoria	Runcorn	Slough Town	Stafford Rangers	Sutton United	Telford United	Welling United	Wycombe Wanderers	Yeovil Town
Altrincham	X	4-1	1-1	2-0	1-1	3-0	2-2	0-0	4-1	3-2	1-2	5-3	9-2	0-2	1-0	3-0	0-0	4-1	2-1	0-1	1-0	2-2
Barnet	0-0	X	3-1	2-0	5-0	2-1	1-3	8-1	1-1	0-1	2-3	3-1	2-3	1-1	2-0	6-1	2-0	1-0	0-0	3-2	3-2	3-2
Barrow	1-0	4-2	X	1-1	1-1	0-0	2-2	3-1	3-1	0-1	1-3	1-1	0-2	2-2	2-1	2-1	2-0	3-1	2-1	1-1	2-2	1-0
Bath City	2-3	1-4	1-1	X	1-0	2-0	1-2	0-1	3-0	3-3	4-1	0-2	0-0	4-1	6-1	4-0	0-1	2-2	0-1	2-1	1-2	2-1
Boston United	2-6	1-3	0-2	3-0	X	2-1	1-3	4-1	5-1	1-2	3-1	1-1	3-0	4-1	2-2	0-1	0-2	2-2	2-1	0-0	0-1	4-0
Cheltenham Town	1-4	1-4	3-1	0-0	5-0	X	1-2	0-0	1-0	2-2	0-0	2-2	0-1	1-1	1-3	2-0	1-2	3-2	0-1	3-0	1-0	1-0
Colchester United	1-1	0-0	1-0	2-0	3-1	3-1	X	2-1	3-0	3-1	2-0	1-0	3-1	4-0	2-2	2-1	2-0	1-0	2-0	2-1	2-2	0-1
Fisher Athletic	0-0	2-4	1-2	0-3	1-2	1-1	0-0	X	0-2	0-0	1-1	1-2	0-0	5-2	0-1	1-1	1-3	1-1	2-0	1-1	2-3	2-1
Gateshead	0-3	1-3	5-1	2-0	0-1	3-3	1-2	1-0	X	1-2	2-1	1-1	1-0	0-4	3-1	1-0	2-1	0-9	5-1	0-3	2-1	1-1
Kettering Town	1-1	1-3	2-0	1-1	1-1	5-1	1-0	3-2	1-0	X	4-1	2-0	2-0	1-0	3-0	0-0	2-0	5-2	2-5	0-0	0-1	1-1
Kidderminster Harriers	0-1	0-3	3-1	3-2	3-3	2-0	0-0	3-3	2-3	3-0	X	0-0	1-2	3-1	3-1	1-2	2-1	1-0	1-3	1-2	1-2	0-0
Macclesfield Town	0-1	3-3	3-0	3-1	2-0	5-1	1-0	1-1	4-0	1-0	0-0	X	0-1	1-2	2-1	2-1	2-0	2-1	4-2	1-2	2-1	0-2
Merthyr Tydfil	0-2	1-1	0-2	0-0	2-0	3-0	3-0	7-0	3-1	1-3	1-2	0-2	X	3-2	0-0	3-0	1-1	3-0	2-3	1-0	2-4	1-1
Northwich Victoria	1-1	0-2	2-2	2-0	3-1	5-2	2-2	0-0	3-2	0-1	1-1	4-1	0-3	X	1-4	1-0	1-1	1-0	2-4	1-2	1-1	2-0
Runcorn	1-3	3-2	3-1	1-1	2-1	2-2	0-3	5-1	2-0	2-1	5-1	1-2	2-1	3-1	X	3-1	1-0	5-1	0-0	2-3	1-1	0-3
Slough Town	3-3	1-3	3-0	2-0	2-0	0-3	0-2	1-0	1-1	0-3	0-0	0-1	1-2	2-4	2-1	X	2-1	1-2	2-0	3-0	3-3	2-0
Stafford Rangers	2-1	2-2	2-2	2-1	1-2	2-2	0-2	2-0	0-1	0-0	3-1	2-2	2-0	0-0	1-1	3-4	X	1-2	1-1	1-0	2-1	1-1
Sutton United	1-2	0-1	2-1	1-1	0-0	2-3	0-1	3-1	3-3	1-2	1-2	3-1	1-1	2-2	1-3	5-2	0-3	X	0-3	1-1	1-1	1-0
Telford United	1-2	1-1	0-1	2-2	1-0	1-2	2-0	3-1	1-2	0-1	1-0	1-2	3-1	1-0	2-0	2-1	0-0	4-2	X	2-1	1-0	1-2
Welling United	2-2	1-4	4-2	2-1	0-0	0-0	1-1	1-1	6-0	0-1	1-0	0-0	2-1	4-5	2-2	2-0	2-1	1-2	1-1	X	1-1	0-3
Wycombe Wanderers	3-0	1-3	2-1	0-0	3-0	0-2	1-0	2-0	4-0	5-1	2-3	0-0	2-1	3-0	1-1	2-1	2-0	4-1	3-2	4-1	X	2-0
Yeovil Town	2-3	1-4	0-3	3-2	1-1	4-0	2-0	0-1	4-1	0-0	2-1	3-3	1-1	7-2	0-0	2-1	1-2	0-1	2-2	0-1	2-2	X

Final Table

	P	Home					Away					Total						
	P	W	D	L	F	A	W	D	L	F	A	W	D	L	F	A	Pts	
Barnet	42	13	4	4	50	23	13	5	3	53	29	26	9	7	103	52	87	P
Colchester United	42	16	4	1	41	14	9	6	6	27	22	25	10	7	68	35	85	
Altrincham	42	12	6	3	48	22	11	7	3	39	24	23	13	6	87	46	82	
Kettering Town	42	12	6	3	38	19	11	5	5	29	26	23	11	8	67	45	80	
Wycombe Wanderers	42	15	3	3	46	17	6	8	7	29	29	21	11	10	75	46	74	
Telford United	42	11	3	7	30	21	9	4	8	32	31	20	7	15	62	52	67	
Macclesfield Town	42	11	4	6	38	22	6	8	7	25	30	17	12	13	63	52	63	
Runcorn	42	12	4	5	44	29	4	6	11	25	38	16	10	16	69	67	58	
Merthyr Tydfil	42	9	5	7	37	24	7	4	10	25	37	16	9	17	62	61	57	
Barrow	42	10	8	3	34	24	5	4	12	25	41	15	12	15	59	65	57	
Welling United	42	7	10	4	33	27	6	5	10	22	30	13	15	14	55	57	54	
Northwich Victoria	42	8	7	6	33	30	5	6	10	32	45	13	13	16	65	75	52	
Kidderminster Harriers	42	8	5	8	33	30	6	5	10	23	37	14	10	18	56	67	52	
Yeovil Town	42	9	5	7	38	29	4	6	11	20	29	13	11	18	58	58	50	
Stafford Rangers	42	7	9	5	30	26	5	5	11	18	25	12	14	16	48	51	50	
Cheltenham Town	42	8	6	7	29	25	4	6	11	25	47	12	12	18	54	72	48	
Gateshead	42	10	3	8	32	38	4	3	14	20	54	14	6	22	52	92	48	
Boston United	42	9	4	8	40	31	3	7	11	15	38	12	11	19	55	69	47	
Slough Town	42	9	4	8	31	29	4	2	15	20	51	13	6	23	51	80	45	
Bath City	42	9	4	8	39	27	1	8	12	16	34	10	12	20	55	61	42	
Sutton United	42	6	6	9	29	33	4	3	14	33	49	10	9	23	62	82	39	R
Fisher Athletic	42	3	9	9	22	30	2	6	13	16	49	5	15	22	38	79	30	R

FINAL TABLE

Witton Albion promoted from N.P.L., Farnborough Town from Southern League, Redbridge Forest from Isthmian League.

F.A.Cup

First Qualifying Round

North Shields	Gateshead	1-1
Altrincham	Rhyl	3-2
Boston United	Lowestoft Town	7-0
Clapton	Barnet	0-2
(Played at Dagenham)		
Fisher Athletic	Harwich & Parkeston	0-0
Slough Town	Feltham	8-0
Wycombe Wanderers	Maidenhead Utd	3-0
Cheltenham Town	Exmouth Town	2-2

Replay

Gateshead	North Shields	0-1
Exmouth Town	Cheltenham Town	3-3
Harwich & Parkeston	Fisher Athletic	2-1

second replay

Cheltenham Town	Exmouth Town	3-0

Second Qualifying Round

Maine Road	Altrincham	0-1
Boston United	VS Rugby	3-1
Braintree Town	Barnet	0-2
Trowbridge Town	Wycombe Wanderers	0-0
Slough Town	Farnborough Town	2-3
Weston-Super-Mare	Cheltenham Town	0-2

Replay

Wycombe Wanderers	Trowbridge Town	2-1

Third Qualifying Round

Altrincham	Bangor City	3-0
Boreham Wood	Boston United	1-1
Cheltenham Town	Worcester City	4-2
Harlow Town	Barnet	1-3
Wycombe Wanderers	Wokingham Town	4-1

Replay

Boston United	Boreham Wood	4-0

Fourth Qualifying Round

Barnet	Heybridge Swifts	3-1
Bromsgrove Rovers	Kidderminster Harriers	1-2
Chelmsford City	Kettering Town	0-0
Dartford	Boston United	1-1
Dorking	Cheltenham Town	2-3
Dover Athletic	Merthyr Tydfil	0-0
Macclesfield Town	Altrincham	2-2
Marine	Stafford Rangers	1-1
Northwich Victoria	Spennymoor Utd	1-1
Runcorn	Newcastle Blue Star	1-0
Telford United	Egham Town	2-0
Welling United	Bashley	1-0
Woking	Bath City	2-1
Wycombe Wanderers	Basingstoke Town	6-0
Yeovil Town	Marlow	3-1

Replay

Altrincham	Macclesfield Town	3-0
Boston United	Dartford	2-1
Kettering Town	Chelmsford City	1-2
Merthyr Tydfil	Dover Athletic	2-0
Spennymoor Utd	Northwich Victoria	2-1
Stafford Rangers	Marine	2-1

First Round

Altrincham	Huddersfield Town	1-2
Barnet	Chelmsford City	2-2
Birmingham City	Cheltenham Town	1-0
Bishop Auckland	Barrow	0-1
Boston United	Wycombe Wanderers	1-1
Brentford	Yeovil Town	5-0
Colchester United	Reading	2-1
Merthyr Tydfil	Sutton United	1-1
Runcorn	Hartlepool Utd	0-3
Stafford Rangers	Burnley	1-3
Swansea City	Welling United	5-2
Telford United	Stoke City	0-0
Woking	Kidderminster Harriers	0-0

F.A.Cup

First Round - Replay

Chelmsford City	Barnet	0-2
Kidderminster Harriers	Woking	1-1
Stoke City	Telford United	1-0
Sutton United	Merthyr Tydfil	0-1
Wycombe Wanderers	Boston United	4-0

second replay

Kidderminster Harriers	Woking	1-2

Second Round

Barnet	Northampton Town	0-0
Colchester United	Leyton Orient	0-0
Whitley Bay	Barrow	0-1
Woking	Merthyr Tydfil	5-1
Wycombe Wanderers	Peterborough Utd	1-1

Replay

Leyton Orient	Colchester United	4-1
Northampton Town	Barnet	0-1
Peterborough Utd	Wycombe Wanderers	2-0

Third Round

Barnet	Portsmouth	0-5
Bolton Wanderers	Barrow	1-0

League Cup

First Round (two legs)

Altrincham	Barrow	2-2
Barrow	Altrincham	3-2
Bath City	Wycombe Wanderers	0-1
Wycombe Wanderers	Bath City	0-0
Northwich Victoria	Gateshead	3-0
Gateshead	Northwich Victoria	1-3
Slough Town	Fisher Athletic	2-4
Fisher Ath	Slough Town	2-1
Stafford Rangers	Boston Utd	1-0
Boston Utd	Stafford Rangers	3-3
Telford Utd	Cheltenham Town	5-2
Cheltenham Town	Telford Utd	4-2

Second Round

Barrow	Macclesfield Town	2-1
Fisher Ath	Colchester United aet	2-3
Kettering Town	Wycombe Wanderers	1-0
Kidderminster Harriers	Yeovil Town	3-2
Merthyr Tydfil	Sutton United	1-2
Northwich Victoria	Stafford Rangers	1-2
Telford Utd	Runcorn	0-2
Welling Utd	Barnet	1-0

Third Round

Barrow	Stafford Rangers	2-1
Kettering Town	Welling Utd	1-0
Runcorn	Kidderminster Harriers aet	1-2
Sutton United	Colchester United	2-0

Semi final (two legs)

Barrow	Kidderminster Harriers	2-0
Kidderminster Harriers	Barrow	2-4
Kettering Town	Sutton United	0-2
Sutton United	Kettering Town	4-1

Final (two legs)

Barrow	Sutton United	1-1
Sutton United	Barrow	5-0

Challenge Shield

Barrow	Darlington	0-4

Third Qualifying Round		
Boston United	Leicester Utd	3-2
Harrow Borough	Fisher Athletic	0-2
First Round		
Northwich Victoria	Tow Law Town	2-1
Runcorn	Boston United	2-0
Barrow	Chorley	2-0
Macclesfield Town	Gretna	0-2
Gateshead	Billingham Synthonia	2-2
Leek Town	Altrincham	0-4
Telford United	Emley	0-0
Barnet	Farnborough Town	2-3
Slough Town	Bath City	2-4
Kidderminster Harriers	Sutton United	4-2
Gloucester City	Yeovil Town	1-0
Gravesend & Northfleet	Cheltenham Town	2-2
Fisher Athletic	Redbridge Forest	1-2
Wycombe Wanderers	Wealdstone	1-0
Windsor & Eton	Colchester United	0-1
Molesey	Merthyr Tydfil	1-1
Welling United	Hayes	3-1
Kettering Town	Woking	2-0
Hyde Utd	Stafford Rangers	1-2
(Tie awarded to Hyde Utd, Stafford fielded ineligible player)		
replay		
Billingham Synthonia	Gateshead	0-3
Emley	Telford United	1-0
Cheltenham Town	Gravesend & Northfleet	5-1
Merthyr Tydfil	Molesey	1-0
Second Round		
Kidderminster Harriers	Dover Athletic	1-0
Farnborough Town	Bath City	1-3
Barrow	Kettering Town	0-0
Colchester United	Runcorn	2-0
Merthyr Tydfil	Gloucester City	1-3
Welling United	Aylesbury United	2-1
Altrincham	Gateshead	3-1
Northwich Victoria	Droylsden	4-1
Dartford	Cheltenham Town	0-2
VS Rugby	Wycombe Wanderers	0-1
replay		
Kettering Town	Barrow	2-1
Third Round		
Kidderminster Harriers	Bath City	3-1
Emley	Kettering Town	3-2
Colchester United	Wivenhoe Town	3-0
Welling United	Altrincham	1-2
Northwich Victoria	Stroud	2-0
Wycombe Wanderers	Cheltenham Town	2-1

Fourth Round		
Kidderminster Harriers	Emley	3-0
Colchester United	Witton Albion	0-2
Altrincham	Horwich RMI	5-0
Northwich Victoria	Wycombe Wanderers	2-3
Semi Final *(two legs)*		
Kidderminster Harriers	Witton Albion	1-0
Witton Albion	Kidderminster Harriers	4-3
Wycombe Wanderers	Altrincham	2-1
Altrincham	Wycombe Wanderers	0-2
replay		
Kidderminster Harriers	Witton Albion	2-1
(Played at Stafford Rangers)		
Final *(@ Wembley)*		
Wycombe Wanderers	Kidderminster Harriers	2-1

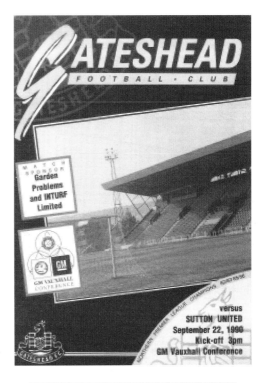

GATESHEAD 0
SUTTON UNITED 9
Despite a record away win in the Conference, Sutton are still relegated.

1991/92

Colchester became the third team in five years to regain their place in the Football League by winning the GM Vauxhall Conference, and only the second team to do the Conference and F.A. Trophy double. Their points total of 94 was a league record and was equalled by runners-up Wycombe.

The championship was virtually a two horse race from the turn of the year. Both Farnborough and Kettering could have bridged the gap as they had games in hand, due to extended F.A.Cup runs (4th Qualifying Round to 3rd Round replay and 1st Qualifying Round to 3rd Round respectively). However, this was never possible with the leaders maintaining their form throughout the season and Kettering could only finish a distant third, 21 points adrift of the top two.

Possibly the most crucial goal of the campaign was scored as early as September 28th, when Colchester won 2-1 away at Wycombe. A last minute punt from 'keeper Scott Barrett bounced once and flew past his opposite number, Paul Hyde, to secure the points. A double over Wycombe, together with 32 points from the final 12 matches, secured the title by nine goals. Wycombe gained some consolation by winning the Bob Lord Trophy.

Merthyr Tydfil finished a highly creditable fourth, particularly merited as they were embroiled in a lengthy battle with the Welsh F.A. With the League of Wales being established, the Welsh F.A. were keen to have Merthyr as members and revoked their permission to play within the English Pyramid. Unwilling to experience what would effectively be a drop of three divisions, The Martyrs launched an appeal, which was ultimately successful, and they were able to look forward to a secure future.

Finally, an entry from the file marked *"Every cloud has a silver lining"*, Merthyr's midfielder David D'Auria was driving to the home match with Runcorn when his car broke down some five miles from his destination. His only option was to run to the ground. He arrived resplendent in his blazer, carrying his kit bag with barely five minutes before the team sheets were handed in. Unfortunately his efforts were in vain as the run had created a large blister on his foot and he was unfit to play! Mark Tucker took his place in the starting line-up and scored both goals in the subsequent 2-0 victory.

	Altrincham	Barrow	Bath City	Boston United	Cheltenham Town	Colchester United	Farnborough Town	Gateshead	Kettering Town	Kidderminster Harriers	Macclesfield Town	Merthyr Tydfil	Northwich Victoria	Redbridge Forest	Runcorn	Slough Town	Stafford Rangers	Telford United	Welling United	Witton Albion	Wycombe Wanderers	Yeovil Town
Altrincham	X	1-1	4-0	2-4	2-1	1-2	1-1	1-1	1-1	1-1	3-1	1-1	0-1	0-3	2-2	3-7	3-0	2-3	1-2	2-2	0-4	2-1
Barrow	0-2	X	2-0	2-2	0-0	1-1	0-1	1-1	0-0	5-1	2-0	2-2	0-2	0-1	2-3	3-4	0-0	3-0	6-1	0-1	0-1	0-0
Bath City	3-2	2-1	X	2-0	5-1	0-0	1-2	0-1	1-1	0-1	1-1	0-0	2-0	0-0	3-1	2-1	0-1	1-2	0-3	0-2	1-1	3-1
Boston United	2-1	4-1	1-0	X	3-3	0-4	0-1	4-0	1-1	1-2	1-5	2-0	0-2	2-1	2-1	3-1	3-2	1-2	5-1	3-2	2-2	1-3
Cheltenham Town	0-2	0-0	1-2	1-1	X	1-1	4-3	3-2	0-3	1-2	2-3	1-2	1-0	0-7	4-1	1-0	0-0	2-1	3-2	0-1	2-1	1-1
Colchester United	3-3	5-0	5-0	1-0	4-0	X	2-3	2-0	3-1	3-0	2-0	2-0	1-0	1-0	2-1	4-0	2-0	2-0	3-1	3-2	3-0	4-0
Farnborough Town	3-0	5-0	1-2	5-0	1-1	0-2	X	3-1	1-3	2-1	4-2	0-0	2-4	1-0	0-2	2-1	1-1	2-2	1-1	1-1	1-3	0-0
Gateshead	4-0	1-1	0-1	2-1	2-1	0-2	0-2	X	0-0	0-3	2-0	0-1	2-0	0-1	1-1	2-1	0-0	0-2	1-1	2-1	2-3	1-0
Kettering Town	5-0	3-2	2-2	1-3	3-0	2-2	1-2	1-1	X	2-1	2-0	3-1	1-0	3-2	3-0	2-3	2-1	3-0	1-1	1-1	1-1	2-0
Kidderminster Harriers	1-0	1-2	0-1	1-3	2-1	2-2	1-1	5-3	2-3	X	1-1	2-2	3-0	5-1	1-3	3-3	2-1	1-2	1-3	0-1	1-0	1-1
Macclesfield Town	1-1	0-1	0-0	0-1	3-3	4-4	1-2	1-0	0-2	0-0	X	3-0	0-0	0-0	3-0	0-1	1-0	2-1	1-2	1-0	3-1	1-2
Merthyr Tydfil	3-1	2-1	1-1	2-0	3-1	2-0	1-0	1-4	4-1	2-1	3-2	X	2-1	2-2	2-0	1-2	2-2	2-1	1-0	1-2	2-2	2-2
Northwich Victoria	1-2	6-1	1-3	1-1	3-1	1-1	1-1	1-1	4-3	3-1	2-1	4-1	X	0-2	3-0	3-0	1-2	0-1	1-2	3-0	0-1	1-1
Redbridge Forest	0-1	2-2	3-1	1-4	1-2	2-1	2-0	2-1	4-0	5-0	0-0	1-1	4-3	X	1-2	4-0	4-3	1-0	2-0	3-1	0-5	0-0
Runcorn	2-2	2-2	0-2	2-2	2-1	1-3	1-1	1-1	0-0	4-1	0-0	1-1	3-1	1-0	X	1-0	0-0	0-2	2-2	0-1	1-2	2-2
Slough Town	2-3	1-0	2-2	3-1	1-3	2-4	0-5	2-0	0-2	3-1	0-3	0-0	0-1	4-0	1-0	X	2-2	0-3	0-3	0-1	0-1	1-4
Stafford Rangers	1-2	0-0	2-0	0-1	2-2	3-3	0-1	1-3	1-2	2-0	1-1	0-0	2-1	2-1	1-0	1-1	X	3-2	0-0	3-2	0-2	0-0
Telford United	2-1	4-2	0-2	0-2	2-1	0-3	1-2	1-1	1-1	3-1	0-1	1-2	1-4	3-3	1-0	2-2	4-1	X	2-1	2-1	1-0	1-0
Welling United	2-2	5-3	0-5	1-3	1-1	4-1	1-0	2-2	2-3	3-2	2-1	1-2	6-1	2-2	1-2	0-2	1-1	3-1	X	1-1	1-3	1-0
Witton Albion	2-0	0-1	2-2	1-0	4-2	2-2	4-1	0-3	1-0	2-1	1-1	3-2	1-1	2-0	2-1	6-0	1-1	2-2	1-1	X	1-2	3-1
Wycombe Wanderers	4-2	3-2	1-0	2-1	2-2	1-2	2-1	2-1	1-0	2-0	0-1	4-0	2-0	1-0	1-0	3-0	3-0	6-1	4-0	4-0	X	1-0
Yeovil Town	2-1	2-0	1-1	1-1	1-1	0-1	2-2	1-0	0-1	1-1	0-1	1-1	2-1	0-1	1-4	1-0	0-1	0-2	3-0	2-1	1-0	X

		Home					Away					Total						
	P	W	D	L	F	A	W	D	L	F	A	W	D	L	F	A	Pts	
Colchester United	42	19	1	1	57	11	9	9	3	41	29	28	10	4	98	40	94	P
Wycombe Wanderers	42	18	1	2	49	13	12	3	6	35	22	30	4	8	84	35	94	
Kettering Town	42	12	6	3	44	23	8	7	6	28	27	20	13	9	72	50	73	
Merthyr Tydfil	42	14	4	3	40	24	4	10	7	19	32	18	14	10	59	56	68	
Farnborough Town	42	8	7	6	36	27	10	5	6	32	26	18	12	12	68	53	66	
Telford United	42	10	4	7	32	31	9	3	9	30	35	19	7	16	62	66	64	
Redbridge Forest	42	12	4	5	42	27	6	5	10	27	29	18	9	15	69	56	63	
Boston United	42	10	4	7	40	35	8	5	8	31	31	18	9	15	71	66	63	
Bath City	42	8	6	7	27	22	8	6	7	27	29	16	12	14	54	51	60	
Witton Albion	42	11	6	4	41	26	5	4	12	22	34	16	10	16	63	60	58	
Northwich Victoria	42	10	4	7	40	25	6	2	13	23	33	16	6	20	63	58	54	
Welling United	42	8	6	7	40	38	6	6	9	29	41	14	12	16	69	79	54	
Macclesfield Town	42	7	7	7	25	21	6	6	9	25	29	13	13	13	50	50	52	
Gateshead	42	8	5	8	22	22	4	7	10	27	35	12	12	18	49	57	48	
Yeovil Town	42	8	6	7	22	21	3	8	10	18	28	11	14	17	40	49	47	
Runcorn	42	5	11	5	26	26	6	2	13	24	37	11	13	18	50	63	46	
Stafford Rangers	42	7	8	6	25	24	3	8	10	16	35	10	16	16	41	59	46	
Altrincham	42	5	8	8	33	39	6	4	11	28	43	11	12	19	61	82	45	
Kidderminster Harriers	42	8	6	7	35	32	4	3	14	21	45	12	9	21	56	77	45	
Slough Town	42	7	3	11	26	39	6	3	12	30	43	13	6	23	56	82	45	
Cheltenham Town	42	8	5	8	28	35	2	8	11	28	47	10	13	19	56	82	43	R
Barrow	42	5	8	8	29	23	3	6	12	23	49	8	14	20	52	72	38	R

FINAL TABLE

Stalybridge Celtic promoted from N.P.L., Bromsgrove Rovers from Southern League, Woking from Isthmian League.

F.A.Cup

First Qualifying Round		
Workington	Gateshead	0-1
Eastwood Hanley	Northwich Victoria	2-1
Skelmersdale Utd	Macclesfield Town	0-4
Blakenall	Boston United	1-2
Wisbech Town	Kettering Town	0-3
Redbridge Forest	Haringey Borough	5-0
Bridgend Town	Cheltenham Town	3-3
Slough Town	Croydon	2-2
Stroud	Bath City	1-3
replay		
Cheltenham Town	Bridgend Town	5-0
Croydon	Slough Town	0-3
Second Qualifying Round		
Gateshead	Alnwick Town	6-0
Macclesfield Town	Borrowash Victoria	1-2
Boston United	Tamworth	1-1
Kettering Town	Braintree Town	3-1
Grays Ath	Redbridge Forest	3-1
Yeading	Slough Town	0-0
Cheltenham Town	Taunton Town	8-0
Bath City	Maesteg Park Ath	5-2
replay		
Tamworth	Boston United	1-0
Slough Town	Yeading	1-0
Third Qualifying Round		
Gateshead	Netherfield	0-0
Kettering Town	Heybridge Swifts	3-0
Berkhamstead Town	Slough Town	1-4
Weymouth	Cheltenham Town	4-0
Bath City	Worcester City	1-2
replay		
Netherfield	Gateshead	0-3
Fourth Qualifying Round		
Barrow	Bridlington Town	0-1
Colchester United	Burton Albion	5-0
Kettering Town	Stafford Rangers	0-0
Merthyr Tydfil	Windsor & Eton	1-1
Runcorn	Gateshead	1-0
Salisbury	Farnborough Town	1-7
Slough Town	Kingstonian	2-1
Telford United	Knowsley Utd	1-0
Tonbridge	Yeovil Town	1-2
Welling United	Alvechurch	5-1
Whitley Bay	Witton Albion	1-4
Winsford Utd	Altrincham	3-2
replay		
Stafford Rangers	Kettering Town	0-2
Windsor & Eton	Merthyr Tydfil	1-0
First Round		
Colchester United	Exeter City	0-0
Halesowen Town	Farnborough Town	2-2
Kettering Town	Wycombe Wanderers	1-1
Kidderminster Harriers	Aylesbury United	0-1
Leyton Orient	Welling United	2-1
Slough Town	Reading	3-3
Stoke City	Telford United	0-0
Runcorn	Tranmere Rovers	0-3
(Played at Tranmere)		
Witton Albion	Halifax Town	1-1
Yeovil Town	Walsall	1-1
replay		
Exeter City	Colchester United	0-0
(Exeter City won 4-2 on pens)		
Farnborough Town	Halesowen Town	4-0
Halifax Town	Witton Albion	1-2
Reading	Slough Town	2-1
Telford United	Stoke City	2-1
Walsall	Yeovil Town	0-1
Wycombe Wanderers	Kettering Town	0-2

F.A.Cup

Second Round		
Maidstone Utd	Kettering Town	1-2
Preston North End	Witton Albion	5-1
Torquay Utd	Farnborough Town	1-1
Woking	Yeovil Town	3-0
Wrexham	Telford United	1-0
replay		
Farnborough Town	Torquay Utd	4-3
Third Round		
Blackburn Rovers	Kettering Town	4-1
Farnborough Town	West Ham United	1-1
(Played at West Ham)		
replay		
West Ham Utd	Farnborough Town	1-0

League Cup

First Round (two legs)		
Bath City	Slough Town	2-1
Slough Town	Bath City	2-0
Cheltenham Town	Kidderminster Harriers	4-2
Kidderminster Harriers	Cheltenham Town	3-1
(Kidderminster Harriers won on away goals)		
Farnborough Town	Yeovil Town	3-2
Yeovil Town	Farnborough Town	3-0
Gateshead	Witton Albion	3-0
Witton Albion	Gateshead	5-0
Northwich Victoria	Stafford Rangers	2-0
Stafford Rangers	Northwich Victoria	1-1
Redbridge Forest	Boston Utd	2-0
Boston Utd	Redbridge Forest	4-0
Second Round		
Altrincham	Barrow	2-1
Colchester United	Kettering Town	4-0
Merthyr Tydfil	Wycombe Wanderers	1-3
Northwich Victoria	Boston Utd	3-2
Runcorn	Witton Albion aet	2-2
Slough Town	Kidderminster Harriers	0-1
Telford Utd	Macclesfield Town aet	1-2
Yeovil Town	Welling Utd	2-0
replay		
Witton Albion	Runcorn	0-2
Third Round		
Colchester United	Wycombe Wanderers	2-6
Kidderminster Harriers	Yeovil Town	1-2
Macclesfield Town	Altrincham aet	1-1
Runcorn	Northwich Victoria	2-1
replay		
Altrincham	Macclesfield Town	3-1
Semi final (two legs)		
Runcorn	Altrincham	2-1
Altrincham	Runcorn	1-3
Yeovil Town	Wycombe Wanderers	0-0
Wycombe Wanderers	Yeovil Town	2-0
Final (two Legs)		
Runcorn	Wycombe Wanderers	1-0
Wycombe Wanderers	Runcorn	2-0

Challenge Shield

Wycombe Wanderers	Barnet	1-0

Third Qualifying Round

Moor Green	Boston United	1-3
Slough Town	Margate	0-0
replay		
Margate	Slough Town	1-2

First Round

Altrincham	Stalybridge Celtic	1-2
Whitby Town	Barrow	0-2
Sutton United	Bath City	1-2
Macclesfield Town	Boston United	0-0
Cheltenham Town	Wealdstone	3-2
Colchester Utd	Kingstonian	2-2
Sutton Coldfield Town	Farnborough Town	0-3
Blyth Spartans	Gateshead	0-0
VS Rugby	Kettering Town	0-1
Walton & Hersham	Kidderminster Harriers	0-2
Merthyr Tydfil	Dartford	1-1
Northwich Victoria	Hyde Utd	1-0
Redbridge Forest	Bromsgrove Rovers	1-1
Leek Town	Runcorn	3-3
Enfield	Slough Town	4-0
Stafford Rangers	Marine	0-1
Telford United	Guisborough Town	2-0
Welling United	Dover Athletic	3-2
Witton Albion	Billingham Synthonia	2-2
Wycombe Wanderers	Salisbury	2-0
Yeovil Town	Chesham Utd	3-1
replay		
Billingham Synthonia	Witton Albion	1-2
Boston United	Macclesfield Town	0-2
Gateshead	Blyth Spartans	3-0
(Played at Blyth Spartans)		
Runcorn	Leek Town	3-1
Bromsgrove Rovers	Redbridge Forest	0-1
Kingstonian	Colchester Utd	2-3
Dartford	Merthyr Tydfil	1-2

Second Round

Gateshead	Barrow	1-0
Bath City	Dorking	2-0
Farnborough Town	Southport	5-0
Bashley	Kettering Town	2-3
Macclesfield Town	Bangor City	1-0
Merthyr Tydfil	Colchester Utd	0-0
Morecambe	Welling United	2-1
Northwich Victoria	Cheltenham Town	4-2
Redbridge Forest	Enfield	2-0
Runcorn	Kidderminster Harriers	1-1
Telford United	Northallerton Town	3-0
Witton Albion	Aylesbury United	1-0
Wycombe Wanderers	Woking	1-0
Bromley	Yeovil Town	1-3
replay		
Colchester Utd	Merthyr Tydfil	1-0
Kidderminster Harriers	Runcorn	5-2

Third Round

Bath City	Wycombe Wanderers	1-1
Colchester Utd	Morecambe	3-1
Marine	Kettering Town	2-1
Northwich Victoria	Macclesfield Town	0-1
Redbridge Forest	Farnborough Town	3-2
Telford United	Gateshead	0-0
Witton Albion	Stalybridge Celtic	1-0
Yeovil Town	Kidderminster Harriers	3-1
replay		
Gateshead	Telford United	0-1
(Played at Blyth Spartans)		
Wycombe Wanderers	Bath City	2-0

Fourth Round

Colchester Utd	Telford United	4-0
Marine	Redbridge Forest	1-1
Wycombe Wanderers	Witton Albion	1-2
Yeovil Town	Macclesfield Town	1-2
replay		
Redbridge Forest	Marine	0-1

Semi Final (two legs)

Colchester Utd	Macclesfield Town	3-0
Macclesfield Town	Colchester Utd	1-1
Witton Albion	Marine	2-2
Marine	Witton Albion	1-4

Final (at Wembley)

Colchester Utd	Witton Albion	3-1

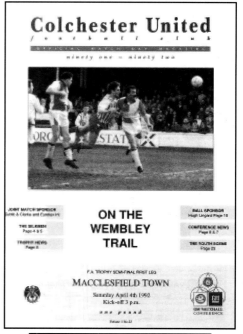

COLCHESTER UNITED 3
MACCLESFIELD TOWN 0
The 'U's' move another step
closer to the non-League 'Double'.

1992/93

With Colchester safely ensconced in the Football League Division 3 and with no club relegated from the Football League, the way was clear for Wycombe to achieve the goal that they had so narrowly missed out on the previous season. They emulated Colchester's achievement of a Conference and F.A.Trophy double, won the championship Shield, and were runners-up in the Drinkwise Cup, to Northwich Victoria, making it the most successful season for a single club in Conference history.

The Wanderers started the season with 28 points from the first 10 matches and topped the table from September onwards, finishing fifteen points clear of second-placed Bromsgrove Rovers. Their support, both home and away, was outstanding. Their average home gate was 4,602, the highest since the Conference was formed in 1979, and on their travels they recorded the highest league attendance at 15 of their 21 opponents grounds. The biggest gate of the season attended the local derby with Slough on March 23rd, when 7,230 saw the top two teams meet at Adams Park, with an estimated 2,000 locked out. Wycombe won through a solitary Keith Scott goal. For Slough, who had been the main challengers since December, it proved to be a damaging defeat, and with only six points accruing from their last eight games, they dropped away to finish in fifth place.

Other teams suffered from extreme fluctuations in their form. Witton Albion were the last team to lose their unbeaten record when Yeovil beat them 2-1 at Wincham Park on 10th October. From that point they went on a run of 13 matches without a win, until they beat Merthyr away on 23rd January. The slump in form saw them drop from second to sixteenth place, just two points above the relegation positions.

In the F.A.Cup, Yeovil grabbed the headlines as so often they had before, and have done since. They overcame Torquay United and Hereford United away from home, in the 1st and 2nd rounds proper, to set a record of sixteen victories over Football League opposition. In the third round, Huish Park played host to Arsenal and the record attendance of 8,612 witnessed an Ian Wright hat-trick to help the visitors to a victory, almost 22 years to the day since their previous visit to the town in the F.A.Cup, albeit at a different venue.

Another notable achievement was Clive Freeman of Altrincham winning the November BBC 'Goal of the Month' competition, for his 35 yard rocket in the F.A.Cup first round replay against Chester City, which secured a 2-0 victory. It was the first occasion that the prize had been won by a non-League player.

1992/93 Season Results Grid

	Altrincham	Bath City	Boston United	Bromsgrove Rovers	Dagenham & Redbridge	Farnborough Town	Gateshead	Kettering Town	Kidderminster Harriers	Macclesfield Town	Merthyr Tydfil	Northwich Victoria	Runcorn	Slough Town	Stafford Rangers	Stalybridge Celtic	Telford United	Welling United	Witton Albion	Woking	Wycombe Wanderers	Yeovil Town
Altrincham	X	1-0	1-1	2-2	1-0	2-2	0-1	3-0	2-2	1-0	0-1	0-0	0-2	1-1	1-5	0-0	0-3	2-0	2-1	1-0	0-2	1-2
Bath City	3-0	X	2-1	0-3	2-1	5-2	1-1	0-0	2-1	0-0	1-3	0-5	1-1	0-1	2-1	1-1	4-1	1-1	0-0	2-0	2-0	0-0
Boston United	1-2	1-2	X	1-2	3-1	0-0	0-2	0-1	0-3	3-1	2-0	3-5	0-0	0-0	0-1	1-1	2-2	2-1	2-2	1-2	0-3	1-0
Bromsgrove Rovers	4-1	1-1	2-1	X	1-2	2-2	3-0	1-1	2-2	3-0	1-2	1-2	0-0	0-1	2-3	4-0	0-0	2-2	3-2	1-0	1-0	1-0
Dagenham & Redbridge	2-2	2-1	1-0	1-1	X	5-1	3-1	1-2	3-2	1-2	6-1	4-1	5-1	4-4	0-1	1-2	0-2	1-0	1-1	5-1	1-2	1-1
Farnborough Town	2-5	2-1	4-0	1-1	1-4	X	6-1	3-2	2-2	0-0	2-1	0-3	2-3	1-1	1-1	1-2	0-1	3-2	1-1	0-3	0-2	2-1
Gateshead	2-0	0-4	2-2	0-0	1-1	1-0	X	1-1	1-0	1-0	4-0	0-2	4-1	1-0	0-1	0-0	0-1	1-2	3-1	1-1	0-1	4-1
Kettering Town	1-1	0-1	3-3	3-2	0-0	2-1	2-0	X	1-2	1-0	1-3	2-1	3-3	5-0	2-0	2-0	1-1	2-4	2-1	0-1	0-4	3-0
Kidderminster Harriers	0-1	1-0	0-2	1-0	0-1	1-5	3-3	0-0	X	2-1	1-0	5-3	2-0	1-1	2-1	2-1	2-1	0-0	1-3	1-3	1-3	1-3
Macclesfield Town	1-1	1-0	2-1	0-2	1-1	1-2	1-0	1-0	1-1	X	0-1	1-2	1-1	1-2	4-1	1-1	1-1	1-0	1-1	1-1	1-1	1-1
Merthyr Tydfil	2-2	1-1	0-3	1-1	0-2	1-3	1-1	2-1	4-3	1-2	X	3-0	0-3	1-1	0-0	1-1	4-0	1-1	0-1	1-5	1-4	1-1
Northwich Victoria	1-2	3-1	3-3	0-1	1-1	3-0	0-0	2-2	0-1	1-3	1-2	X	3-2	1-0	1-2	1-3	1-0	1-1	1-3	1-0	0-0	0-1
Runcorn	0-1	1-3	1-2	2-1	1-0	1-4	4-2	2-2	0-0	1-2	2-3	0-1	X	0-3	0-2	2-1	3-1	3-0	4-4	2-3	2-1	1-0
Slough Town	1-4	1-1	3-0	1-3	2-0	3-1	1-0	3-0	3-1	2-1	2-1	0-4	1-1	X	2-1	2-3	2-0	4-2	2-3	0-1	1-1	3-0
Stafford Rangers	0-0	3-2	0-0	3-4	0-1	2-2	2-1	2-4	0-1	1-0	0-1	0-1	1-0	0-1	X	0-0	2-1	4-3	1-1	0-0	0-1	1-1
Stalybridge Celtic	1-0	1-1	2-1	1-0	0-3	2-0	2-1	0-0	2-2	2-1	2-2	0-6	0-0	0-0	1-0	X	3-3	0-0	1-2	3-0	2-2	1-1
Telford United	2-1	0-0	0-1	0-1	0-1	6-3	1-0	3-1	3-1	5-0	1-0	2-1	1-1	0-0	0-2	0-0	X	0-1	0-3	3-3	2-3	1-0
Welling United	2-0	0-3	2-2	4-2	0-2	3-1	2-1	1-1	0-0	1-0	1-0	1-5	3-2	2-1	1-2	1-4	1-3	X	2-2	1-1	2-2	0-3
Witton Albion	1-1	0-0	2-0	1-1	2-2	1-1	1-3	4-2	2-2	1-1	1-3	0-3	1-1	2-5	2-0	2-1	0-1	1-2	X	1-2	2-2	1-2
Woking	0-2	0-1	3-0	0-1	1-1	4-1	1-4	3-2	1-5	4-0	0-1	4-0	1-2	0-3	2-1	3-2	1-0	1-2	0-1	X	0-3	0-0
Wycombe Wanderers	0-2	2-0	3-3	4-0	1-0	1-1	2-1	1-2	1-1	0-1	4-0	1-0	5-1	1-0	2-2	4-0	4-0	3-0	2-1	0-0	X	5-1
Yeovil Town	1-0	2-1	2-1	2-2	0-3	5-2	1-3	2-1	2-2	1-1	0-1	1-1	4-0	5-1	2-0	1-1	1-0	1-0	2-0	4-1	3-0	X

Final Table

	P	Home					Away					Total						
		W	D	L	F	A	W	D	L	F	A	W	D	L	F	A	Pts	
Wycombe Wanderers	42	13	5	3	46	16	11	6	4	38	21	24	11	7	84	37	83	P
Bromsgrove Rovers	42	9	7	5	35	22	9	7	5	32	27	18	14	10	67	49	68	
Dagenham & Redbridge *	42	10	5	6	48	29	9	6	6	27	18	19	11	12	75	47	67	
Yeovil Town	42	13	5	3	42	21	5	7	9	17	28	18	12	12	59	49	66	
Slough Town	42	12	3	6	39	28	6	8	7	21	27	18	11	13	60	55	65	
Stafford Rangers	42	7	6	8	22	24	11	4	6	33	23	18	10	14	55	47	64	
Bath City	42	9	8	4	29	23	6	6	9	24	23	15	14	13	53	46	59	
Woking	42	9	2	10	30	33	8	6	7	28	29	17	8	17	58	62	59	
Kidderminster Harriers	42	9	5	7	26	30	5	11	5	34	30	14	16	12	60	60	58	
Altrincham	42	7	7	7	21	25	8	6	7	28	27	15	13	14	49	52	58	
Northwich Victoria	42	5	6	10	24	29	11	2	8	44	26	16	8	18	68	55	56	
Stalybridge Celtic	42	7	10	4	25	26	6	7	8	23	29	13	17	12	48	55	56	
Kettering Town	42	10	5	6	36	28	4	8	9	25	35	14	13	15	61	63	55	
Gateshead	42	9	6	6	27	19	5	4	12	26	37	14	10	18	53	56	52	
Telford United	42	9	5	7	31	24	5	5	11	24	36	14	10	18	55	60	52	
Merthyr Tydfil	42	4	9	8	26	37	10	1	10	25	42	14	10	18	51	79	52	
Witton Albion	42	5	9	7	30	34	6	8	7	32	31	11	17	14	62	65	50	
Macclesfield Town	42	7	9	5	23	20	5	4	12	17	30	12	13	17	40	50	49	
Runcorn	42	8	3	10	32	36	5	7	9	26	40	13	10	19	58	76	49	
Welling United	42	8	6	6	34	37	4	6	11	23	35	12	12	18	57	72	48	
Farnborough Town	42	8	5	8	34	36	4	6	11	34	51	12	11	19	68	87	47	R
Boston United	42	5	6	10	23	31	4	7	10	27	38	9	13	20	50	69	40	R

FINAL TABLE

Dagenham & Redbridge one point deducted.

Southport promoted from N.P.L., Dover Athletic from Southern League.

CUP COMPETITIONS

F.A.Cup

First Qualifying Round		
Gateshead	Billingham Synthonia	3-1
Altrincham	Curzon Ashton	3-0
Glossop North End	Macclesfield Town	0-1
Alfreton Town	Stafford Rangers	0-0
Stocksbridge Park Steels	Stalybridge Celtic	0-4
Northwich Victoria	Winsford Utd	4-1
Boston United	Kings Lynn	2-1
Corinthian Casuals	Slough Town	1-1
Glastonbury	Bath City	0-4
Dagenham & Redbridge	Billericay Town	1-1
replay		
Stafford Rangers	Alfreton Town	3-0
Billericay Town	Dagenham & Redbridge	1-4
Slough Town	Corinthian Casuals	4-3
Second Qualifying Round		
Gateshead	Whitby Town	5-2
Altrincham	Sheffield	3-1
Hucknall Town	Macclesfield Town	1-1
Bedworth Utd	Stafford Rangers	1-1
Northwich Victoria	Raunds Town	0-2
Boston United	Aveley	1-2
Dagenham & Redbridge	Stowmarket Town	6-1
Warrington Town	Stalybridge Celtic	0-3
Metropolitan Police	Slough Town	0-1
Falmouth Town	Bath City	0-3
replay		
Macclesfield Town	Hucknall Town	3-1
Stafford Rangers	Bedworth Town	1-0
Third Qualifying Round		
Spennymoor Utd	Gateshead	0-7
Colwyn Bay	Altrincham	3-3
Stalybridge Celtic	Accrington Stanley	1-2
Macclesfield Town	Horwich RMI	1-0
Stafford Rangers	Frickley Ath	3-0
Wealdstone	Dagenham & Redbridge	1-6
Slough Town	Yeading	2-1
Bath City	Weymouth	2-0
replay		
Altrincham	Colwyn Bay	1-1
second replay		
Altrincham	Colwyn Bay	3-1
Fourth Qualifying Round		
Abingdon Town	Merthyr Tydfil	0-0
Ashford Town	Slough Town	1-2
Crawley Town	Yeovil Town	1-2
Farnborough Town	Dorking	1-1
Gainsborough Trinity	Altrincham	0-2
Gateshead	Whitley Bay	3-0
Hednesford Town	Dagenham & Redbridge	1-3
Kettering Town	Corby Town	2-1
Kidderminster Harriers	Atherstone Utd	2-0
Kingstonian	Welling United	2-1
Netherfield	Macclesfield Town	1-1
Runcorn	Marine	1-4
Stafford Rangers	Bromsgrove Rovers	3-0
Telford United	St Albans City	1-2
Tiverton Town	Bath City	0-0
replay		
Bath City	Tiverton Town	2-1
Dorking	Farnborough Town	2-0
Macclesfield Town	Netherfield	5-0
Merthyr Tydfil	Abingdon Town	2-1
First Round		
Accrington Stanley	Gateshead	3-2
Bury	Witton Albion	2-0
Cardiff City	Bath City	2-3
Chester City	Altrincham	1-1
Colchester United	Slough Town	4-0
Dagenham & Redbridge	Leyton Orient	4-5
Exeter City	Kidderminster Harriers	1-0
Gillingham	Kettering Town	3-2
Lincoln City	Stafford Rangers	0-0
Macclesfield Town	Chesterfield	0-0
Torquay Utd	Yeovil Town	2-5
Woking	Nuneaton Borough	3-2
Wycombe Wanderers	Merthyr Tydfil	3-1

F.A.Cup

replay		
Altrincham	Chester City	2-0
Chesterfield	Macclesfield Town	2-2
(Macclesfield Town won 3-2 on pens)		
Stafford Rangers	Lincoln City	2-1
Second Round		
Altrincham	Port Vale	1-4
Bath City	Northampton Town	2-2
Macclesfield Town	Stockport County	0-2
Marine	Stafford Rangers	3-2
Brighton & Hove Albion	Woking	1-1
Wycombe Wanderers	West Bromwich Albion	2-2
Yeovil Town	Hereford United	0-0
replay		
Hereford United	Yeovil Town	1-2
Northampton Town	Bath City	3-0
West Bromwich Albion	Wycombe Wanderers	1-0
Woking	Brighton & Hove Albion	1-2
Third Round		
Yeovil Town	Arsenal	1-3

League Cup

First Round (two legs)		
Altrincham	Macclesfield Town	1-3
Macclesfield Town	Altrincham	0-0
Northwich Victoria	Gateshead	2-1
Gateshead	Northwich Victoria	0-2
Stafford Rangers	Bromsgrove Rovers	4-2
Bromsgrove Rovers	Stafford Rangers	2-1
Stalybridge Celtic	Kidderminster Harriers	1-1
Kidderminster Harriers	Stalybridge Celtic	4-2
Woking	Welling Utd	1-2
Welling Utd	Woking	2-2
Yeovil Town	Slough Town	2-0
Slough Town	Yeovil Town	2-2
Second Round		
Bath City	Yeovil Town	0-0
Boston Utd	Dagenham & Redbridge	1-2
Kidderminster Harriers	Kettering Town	3-0
Merthyr Tydfil	Farnborough Town	4-2
Runcorn	Northwich Victoria	2-3
Stafford Rangers	Telford Utd	0-0
Welling Utd	Wycombe Wanderers	2-3
Witton Albion	Macclesfield Town	0-1
replay		
Yeovil Town	Bath City	1-0
Telford Utd	Stafford Rangers	5-2
Third Round		
Dagenham & Redbridge	Merthyr Tydfil	4-2
Macclesfield Town	Kidderminster Harriers	3-1
Northwich Victoria	Telford Utd	3-1
Yeovil Town	Wycombe Wanderers	0-1
Semi Final (two legs)		
Northwich Victoria	Macclesfield Town	2-0
Macclesfield Town	Northwich Victoria	1-1
Wycombe Wanderers	Dagenham & Redbridge	3-1
Dagenham & Redbridge	Wycombe Wanderers	0-0
Final (two legs)		
Northwich Victoria	Wycombe Wanderers	0-0
Wycombe Wanderers	Northwich Victoria	2-3

Challenge Shield

Wycombe Wanderers	Colchester United	3-0

Third Qualifying Round

Slough Town	Bromley	3-1
Stafford Rangers	Wembley	1-1
replay		
Wembley	Stafford Rangers	0-1

First Round

Spennymoor Utd	Boston United	1-2
Telford United	Northwich Victoria	2-1
Hyde Utd	Runcorn	1-2
Gateshead	Gretna	3-0
Winsford Utd	Altrincham	1-0
Stalybridge Celtic	Accrington Stanley	2-0
Macclesfield Town	Witton Albion	0-0
Sutton United	Woking	3-0
Yeading	Slough Town	1-1
Welling United	Aylesbury United	2-1
Grays Ath	Stafford Rangers	1-0
Merthyr Tydfil	Wivenhoe Town	3-0
Yeovil Town	Dagenham & Redbridge	0-0
Kidderminster Harriers	Enfield	1-3
Wycombe Wanderers	Cheltenham Town	3-1
Stevenage Borough	Bath City	2-0
Kettering Town	Bromsgrove Rovers	0-0
Farnborough Town	Abingdon Town	4-0
replay		
Witton Albion	Macclesfield Town	2-1
Slough Town	Yeading	2-1
Dagenham & Redbridge	Yeovil Town	2-1
Bromsgrove Rovers	Kettering Town	4-1

Second Round

Farnborough Town	Enfield	4-0
St Albans City	Witton Albion	0-2
Welling United	Boston United	1-2
Gateshead	Heybridge Swifts	3-0
Kingstonian	Telford United	1-2
Morecambe	Wycombe Wanderers	1-1
Sutton United	Slough Town	3-1
Bromsgrove Rovers	Dagenham & Redbridge	3-1
Gloucester City	Runcorn	3-3
Stalybridge Celtic	Merthyr Tydfil	1-1
replay		
Wycombe Wanderers	Morecambe	2-0
Runcorn	Gloucester City	2-2
Merthyr Tydfil	Stalybridge Celtic	1-0
second replay		
Gloucester City	Runcorn	0-0
third replay		
Runcorn	Gloucester City	4-1

Third Replay

Northallerton Town	Farnborough Town	1-3
Runcorn	Winsford Utd	1-0
Witton Albion	Marine	1-0
Wycombe Wanderers	Bromsgrove Rovers	2-0
Merthyr Tydfil	Warrington	1-1
Grays Ath	Gateshead	1-1
Telford United	Boston United	1-1

replay		
Warrington	Merthyr Tydfil	3-2
Gateshead	Grays Ath	3-0
Boston United	Telford United	4-0

Fourth Round

Wycombe Wanderers	Gateshead	1-0
Boston United	Runcorn	0-2
Witton Albion	Farnborough Town	3-2

Semi Final *(two legs)*

Wycombe Wanderers	Sutton United	2-3
Sutton United	Wycombe Wanderers	0-4
Runcorn	Witton Albion	2-0
Witton Albion	Runcorn	1-0

Final *(@ Wembley)*

Wycombe Wanderers	Runcorn	4-1

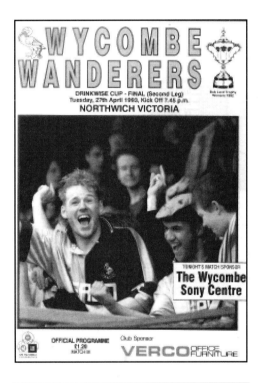

WYCOMBE WANDERERS 2
NORTHWICH VICTORIA 3
A rare disappointment for the all-conquering Wanderers in the Drinkwise Cup Final.

1993/94

Kidderminster gave very little indication of what the season would hold when they lost five of their opening seven matches, and scoring only two goals in the process. But from mid-September onwards, their league campaign took off in spectacular fashion. Their next reversal was at the end of November, and in total they lost only two matches in thirty. This alone would be noteworthy, but combined with a record-breaking F.A.Cup run, it was nothing short of remarkable.

Although they had appeared in the first round in five of the last six years, Kiddy had never ventured beyond Round 2 and had not taken the scalp of any Football League club in their 108 year history. After beating fellow Conference clubs in Rounds 1 and 2, they visited Midlands neighbours Birmingham City and came away with a 2-1 victory in front of just under 20,000 spectators. Preston North End were then defeated at home as Harriers became only the 5th non-League team to reach the fifth round of the F.A.Cup, when West Ham Utd proved too strong, winning by a single Lee Chapman goal.

With all the associated hype and publicity, league form usually suffers, but while Kidderminster did exit the F.A.Trophy at the first hurdle, points were still regularly collected. A fixture backlog meant that 10 matches were played in the final 18 days of the league season and by the end the cracks were starting to show. Four of the last five fixtures were lost, and Kettering could have snatched the title on the final day, needing at least a six goal win at home to Bromsgrove, while Kiddy had to lose at home to Altrincham. In the final event both lost 1-0, giving the Harriers the title while near neighbours Bromsgrove maintained their Conference status.

However, the Football League was not about to have its first club from Worcestershire. In October 1993, the old stand at Aggborough had been condemned by the authorities and the finances were not in place to replace it. Money was raised from the council, a public appeal, the Cup run and the Football Trust, but the 31st December deadline had passed, and the ground was deemed unacceptable. The club's desire to play the Preston and West Ham Cup-ties at home delayed the start of the building works and even the offer of a groundsharing arrangement with West Bromwich Albion could not redeem the situation. The new stand was eventually built in 14 weeks and opened for the first home game of the 1994-5 season.

Runcorn were also to suffer problems with their ground. During the F.A.Cup-tie with Hull City, a section of wall collapsed, causing the game to be abandoned with Hull leading 1-0. A section of roof was subsequently blown off an area of terracing, before a fire completely gutted the main stand. Even with these traumas, the club finished fifth in the league and reached the F.A.Trophy final where they lost to Woking.

1993/94 Season Results Grid

	Altrincham	Bath City	Bromsgrove Rovers	Dagenham & Redbridge	Dover Athletic	Gateshead	Halifax Town	Kettering Town	Kidderminster Harriers	Macclesfield Town	Merthyr Tydfil	Northwich Victoria	Runcorn	Slough Town	Southport	Stafford Rangers	Stalybridge Celtic	Telford United	Welling United	Witton Albion	Woking	Yeovil Town
Altrincham	X	0-2	2-3	1-2	2-0	0-3	0-0	1-1	1-0	0-1	3-0	2-2	2-1	2-0	1-2	0-0	0-0	2-0	2-0	1-3	0-2	1-0
Bath City	0-1	X	0-1	0-0	0-0	2-3	2-2	0-3	4-0	5-1	0-3	0-0	0-0	3-0	2-1	2-3	1-1	3-0	0-0	1-1	0-1	3-0
Bromsgrove Rovers	1-2	0-1	X	2-0	1-2	3-0	1-0	0-4	0-3	3-0	3-3	0-0	0-0	0-1	2-2	3-3	2-0	0-5	1-1	3-3	0-0	1-2
Dagenham & Redbridge	3-0	3-0	4-2	X	2-1	1-1	3-0	2-3	1-1	1-1	0-1	1-1	2-1	1-0	3-3	1-0	0-1	4-1	2-0	2-1	3-4	2-1
Dover Athletic	1-0	0-3	4-3	1-1	X	3-1	1-2	0-1	3-1	1-2	1-0	2-0	2-3	0-0	0-2	2-0	1-1	0-1	0-1	1-0	5-0	0-2
Gateshead	2-1	1-0	0-1	3-1	1-2	X	2-1	0-0	0-2	1-0	0-0	1-0	2-2	0-0	1-3	0-0	2-1	0-2	1-0	3-0	1-1	2-1
Halifax Town	0-0	0-0	3-0	0-1	0-1	3-1	X	0-0	1-0	1-2	2-1	1-2	1-1	1-0	2-2	1-1	2-1	6-0	1-1	0-0	2-3	1-1
Kettering Town	1-0	0-1	0-1	1-1	1-0	0-0	0-1	X	1-1	0-1	0-0	0-0	2-2	2-0	2-0	2-0	3-2	1-2	2-2	1-0	3-0	1-0
Kidderminster Harriers	0-1	0-0	1-1	3-0	1-1	2-1	0-2	0-2	X	2-1	2-0	2-0	3-0	1-0	2-0	1-0	2-0	1-0	0-0	3-1	2-3	2-0
Macclesfield Town	1-0	0-0	4-3	3-0	0-2	6-1	0-1	0-0	0-0	X	1-2	0-0	0-0	2-2	0-1	0-0	1-3	1-0	1-0	2-0	1-1	1-2
Merthyr Tydfil	0-0	1-1	2-1	0-0	0-0	3-0	2-1	0-1	1-4	2-1	X	5-0	1-1	5-1	2-2	1-2	0-3	0-1	4-3	2-3	1-1	1-1
Northwich Victoria	2-0	3-1	1-1	2-2	0-1	1-2	0-2	1-1	3-0	1-1	1-2	X	1-1	1-1	2-1	0-0	2-0	1-0	3-1	0-1	0-0	1-1
Runcorn	2-1	0-0	4-1	2-1	2-1	1-1	5-0	0-0	0-5	2-1	1-1	1-2	X	3-2	3-0	2-2	1-1	3-2	2-4	1-0	2-1	4-0
Slough Town	0-2	0-0	1-1	3-1	1-0	2-1	2-0	0-2	1-5	1-1	3-2	2-2	3-0	X	0-0	3-0	2-3	0-0	1-1	1-0	0-0	5-2
Southport	3-1	1-1	1-2	0-0	3-2	1-1	2-2	0-1	1-1	1-0	3-2	0-0	1-0	1-0	X	0-2	0-2	1-0	2-1	2-1	2-1	1-1
Stafford Rangers	0-1	2-0	0-0	2-0	2-2	3-1	1-1	1-0	2-3	2-3	5-1	3-1	2-2	0-0	0-2	X	2-2	1-1	3-0	1-0	3-0	4-2
Stalybridge Celtic	1-3	1-3	0-2	5-0	0-0	2-1	1-1	1-1	0-2	0-2	2-2	1-1	1-2	0-0	3-1	1-2	X	1-0	2-1	2-1	1-2	1-2
Telford United	0-2	0-0	0-0	0-0	0-1	0-0	3-2	1-1	1-0	1-3	1-0	2-1	1-1	4-1	1-3	2-1	0-2	X	2-0	2-2	2-0	1-1
Welling United	2-1	0-0	1-1	0-0	2-0	1-2	0-2	2-0	0-3	0-1	1-1	0-1	1-1	6-2	0-2	2-1	1-2	0-0	X	2-1	2-2	2-0
Witton Albion	0-1	0-3	4-1	1-1	1-2	1-0	2-2	0-1	2-0	0-2	2-2	1-1	1-1	1-0	0-2	1-1	0-3	0-0	0-5	X	0-0	1-2
Woking	1-1	4-1	0-0	1-8	3-0	1-0	2-6	0-0	1-0	3-0	2-1	2-1	1-1	2-1	1-0	4-0	3-0	0-0	0-2	3-1	X	1-2
Yeovil Town	0-0	1-2	2-3	2-1	1-3	0-2	0-0	1-0	0-1	4-0	2-2	0-3	4-2	0-2	3-2	0-1	0-1	0-1	0-1	2-0	0-1	X

FINAL TABLE

	P	Home					Away					Total					
		W	D	L	F	A	W	D	L	F	A	W	D	L	F	A	Pts
Kidderminster Harriers	42	13	5	3	31	12	9	4	8	32	23	22	9	11	63	35	75
Kettering Town	42	9	7	5	23	14	10	8	3	23	10	19	15	8	46	24	72
Woking	42	12	5	4	35	25	6	8	7	23	33	18	13	11	58	58	67
Southport	42	10	7	4	26	21	8	5	8	31	30	18	12	12	57	51	66
Runcorn	42	12	6	3	41	26	2	13	6	22	31	14	19	9	63	57	61
Dagenham & Redbridge	42	12	5	4	41	23	3	9	9	21	31	15	14	13	62	54	59
Macclesfield Town	42	7	8	6	24	18	9	3	9	24	31	16	11	15	48	49	59
Dover Athletic	42	9	3	9	28	24	8	4	9	20	25	17	7	18	48	49	58
Stafford Rangers	42	10	7	4	39	22	4	8	9	17	30	14	15	13	56	52	57
Altrincham	42	8	5	8	23	22	8	4	9	18	20	16	9	17	41	42	57
Gateshead	42	10	6	5	23	18	5	6	10	22	35	15	12	15	45	53	57
Bath City	42	6	8	7	28	21	7	9	5	19	17	13	17	12	47	38	56
Halifax Town	42	7	9	5	28	18	6	7	8	27	31	13	16	13	55	49	55
Stalybridge Celtic	42	6	6	9	27	30	8	6	7	27	25	14	12	16	54	55	54
Northwich Victoria	42	7	9	5	26	19	4	10	7	18	26	11	19	12	44	45	52
Welling United	42	7	7	7	25	23	6	5	10	22	26	13	12	17	47	49	51
Telford United	42	8	7	6	24	22	5	5	11	17	27	13	12	17	41	49	51
Bromsgrove Rovers	42	5	8	8	26	32	7	7	7	28	34	12	15	15	54	66	51
Yeovil Town	42	7	4	10	23	26	7	5	9	26	36	14	9	19	49	62	51
Merthyr Tydfil *	42	8	7	6	34	26	4	8	9	26	35	12	15	15	60	61	49
Slough Town	42	8	8	5	30	24	3	6	12	14	34	11	14	17	44	58	47 R
Witton Albion	42	4	8	9	18	30	3	5	13	19	33	7	13	22	37	63	34 R

* Merthyr Tydfill two points deducted

Farnborough Town promoted from Southern League, Stevenage Borough from Isthmian League.

CUP COMPETITIONS

F.A.Cup

First Qualifying Round		
Gateshead	Blyth Spartans	4-0
Northwich Victoria	Emley	2-2
Stalybridge Celtic	Fleetwood Town	6-0
Bromsgrove Rovers	Gresley Rovers	1-1
Telford United	Halesowen Town	4-0
Dagenham & Redbridge	Hitchin Town	1-0
Enfield	Welling United	4-1
Sittingbourne	Dover Athletic	1-1
replay		
Emley	Northwich Victoria	2-0
Gresley Rovers	Bromsgrove Rovers	0-1
Dover Athletic	Sittingbourne	1-2
Second Qualifying Round		
Gateshead	Consett	3-1
Bromsgrove Rovers	Bedworth Utd	2-0
Telford United	Grantham Town	2-2
Stalybridge Celtic	Bootle	2-2
Dagenham & Redbridge	Baldock Town	2-1
Bootle	Stalybridge Celtic	1-3
replay		
Grantham Town	Telford United	1-3
Bootle	Stalybridge Celtic	1-3
Third Qualifying Round		
Billingham Synthonia	Gateshead	1-1
Warrington Town	Stalybridge Celtic	0-1
Solihull Borough	Bromsgrove Rovers	1-2
Raunds Town	Telford United	0-4
Halstead Town	Dagenham & Redbridge	1-3
replay		
Gateshead	Billingham Synthonia	0-1
Fourth Qualifying Round		
Altrincham	Accrington Stanley	0-2
Cambridge City	Dagenham & Redbridge	2-2
Cheltenham Town	Bath City	1-1
Chesham Utd	Kidderminster Harriers	1-4
Crawley Town	Merthyr Tydfil	2-1
Hayes	Slough Town	0-2
Kettering Town	Canvey Island	3-1
Macclesfield Town	Southport	5-3
Rushden & Diamonds	Bromsgrove Rovers	1-3
Stafford Rangers	Knowsley Utd	1-1
Stalybridge Celtic	Whitby Town	0-0
Telford United	Morecambe	2-0
Witton Albion	Northallerton Town	2-1
replay		
Bath City	Cheltenham Town	4-2
Dagenham & Redbridge	Cambridge City	0-2
Knowsley Utd	Stafford Rangers	2-2
Whitby Town	Stalybridge Celtic	0-1
second replay		
Knowsley Utd	Stafford Rangers	1-0
First Round		
Halifax Town	West Bromwich Albion	2-1
Kidderminster Harriers	Kettering Town	3-0
Macclesfield Town	Hartlepool Utd	2-0
Molesey	Bath City	0-4
Northampton Town	Bromsgrove Rovers	1-2
Runcorn	Hull City	0-1
(game abandoned 29 mins, wall collapsed)		
Runcorn	Hull City	0-2
(played at Witton Albion)		
Slough Town	Torquay Utd	1-2
Stalybridge Celtic	Marine	1-1
Telford United	Huddersfield Town	1-1
Witton Albion	Lincoln City	0-2
Woking	Weston-Super-Mare	2-2
Yeovil Town	Fulham	1-0

F.A.Cup

First Round - replay		
Huddersfield Town	Telford United	1-0
Marine	Stalybridge Celtic	4-4
(Stalybridge Celtic won 4-2 on pens)		
Weston-Super-Mare	Woking	0-1
Second Round		
Bath City	Hereford Utd	2-1
Carlisle Utd	Stalybridge Celtic	3-1
Crewe Alexandra	Macclesfield Town	2-1
Kidderminster Harriers	Woking	1-0
Stockport County	Halifax Town	5-1
Yeovil Town	Bromsgrove Rovers	0-2
Third Round		
Birmingham City	Kidderminster Harriers	1-2
Bromsgrove Rovers	Barnsley	1-2
Stoke City	Bath City	0-0
replay		
Bath City	Stoke City	1-4
Fourth Round		
Kidderminster Harriers	Preston North End	1-0
Fifth Round		
Kidderminster Harriers	West Ham Utd	0-1

League Cup

First Round *(two legs)*		
Altrincham	Gateshead	1-3
Gateshead	Altrincham	3-1
Kettering Town	Welling Utd	0-0
Welling Utd	Kettering Town	2-1
Merthyr Tydfil	Dover Athletic	0-2
Dover Athletic	Merthyr Tydfil	2-0
Southport	Runcorn	1-4
Runcorn	Southport	2-1
Stalybridge Celtic	Telford Utd	2-0
Telford Utd	Stalybridge Celtic	2-1
Witton Albion	Macclesfield Town	1-2
Macclesfield Town	Witton Albion	4-1
Second Round		
Bath City	Yeovil Town	0-1
Bromsgrove Rovers	Slough Town	2-1
Dover Athletic	Dagenham & Redbridge	1-2
Halifax Town	Gateshead	3-0
Kidderminster Harriers	Stafford Rangers	3-0
Northwich Victoria	Stalybridge Celtic	1-0
Runcorn	Macclesfield Town	0-4
Welling Utd	Woking	1-0
Third Round		
Dagenham & Redbridge	Yeovil Town	1-2
Halifax Town	Macclesfield Town	1-2
Northwich Victoria	Kidderminster Harriers	3-2
Welling Utd	Bromsgrove Rovers	1-2
Semi Final *(two legs)*		
Bromsgrove Rovers	Yeovil Town	1-2
Yeovil Town	Bromsgrove Rovers	0-1
(Yeovil Town won on away goals)		
Macclesfield Town	Northwich Victoria	2-1
Northwich Victoria	Macclesfield Town	0-1
Final *(two legs)*		
Macclesfield Town	Yeovil Town	4-1
Yeovil Town	Macclesfield Town	0-0

Challenge Shield

Northwich Victoria	Wycombe Wanderers	0-1

First Round

Alfreton Town	Runcorn	0-5
Halifax Town	Emley	2-1
Halesowen Town	Gateshead	0-2
Stalybridge Celtic	Colwyn Bay	1-1
Grantham Town	Witton Albion	3-2
Boston United	Macclesfield Town	1-1
Morecambe	Northwich Victoria	2-1
Telford United	Northallerton	2-1
Marine	Southport	0-0
Altrincham	Stafford Rangers	0-2
Welling United	Chelmsford City	6-1
Kettering Town	Stevenage Borough	2-1
St Albans City	Merthyr Tydfil	4-5
Billericay Town	Slough Town	0-2
Kidderminster Harriers	Dagenham & Redbridge	0-2
Waterlooville	Bromsgrove Rovers	1-1
Bashley	Woking	2-4
Weston super Mare	Dover Athletic	0-2
Yeovil Town	Bath City	3-3
replay		
Colwyn Bay	Stalybridge Celtic	2-2
Macclesfield Town	Boston United	1-0
Southport	Marine	3-1
Bromsgrove Rovers	Waterlooville	2-1
Bath City	Yeovil Town	4-0
second replay		
Colwyn Bay	Stalybridge Celtic	2-1

Second Round

Runcorn	Telford United	2-1
Colwyn Bay	Southport	0-3
Kettering Town	Billingham Synthonia	2-2
Dagenham & Redbridge	Woking	1-2
Worcester City	Macclesfield Town	0-0
Sutton United	Bath City	6-1
Morecambe	Slough Town	1-0
Welling United	Dover Athletic	1-3
Guiseley	Stafford Rangers	3-2
Gateshead	Gretna	0-0
Spennymoor Utd	Halifax Town	1-2
Kingstonian	Merthyr Tydfil	0-2
Grays Ath	Bromsgrove Rovers	1-2
replay		
Billingham Synthonia	Kettering Town	3-1
Macclesfield Town	Worcester City	3-2
Gretna	Gateshead	0-1

Third Round

Macclesfield Town	Billingham Synthonia	0-1
Gateshead	Merthyr Tydfil	3-2
Sutton United	Dover Athletic	0-0
Runcorn	Halifax Town	1-1
Woking	Bromsgrove Rovers	3-2
Morecambe	Southport	2-1

Third Round - replay

Dover Athletic	Sutton United	2-3
Halifax Town	Runcorn	0-2

Fourth Round

Gateshead	Runcorn	0-3
Woking	Billingham Synthonia	1-1
replay		
Billingham Synthonia	Woking	1-2

Semi Final (*two legs*)

Woking	Enfield	1-1
Enfield	Woking	0-0
Runcorn	Guiseley	1-1
(played at Chester City)		
Guiseley	Runcorn	0-1
replay		
Woking	Enfield	3-0
(@ Wycombe Wanderers)		

Final (*@ Wembley*)

Woking	Runcorn	2-1

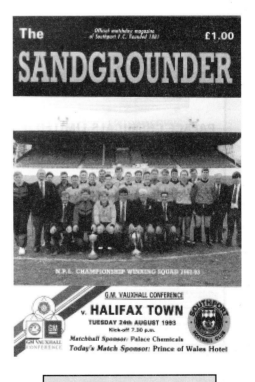

SOUTHPORT 2
HALIFAX TOWN 2
Southport's home Conference bow against fellow newcomers.

65

1994/95

Only once before had the Conference title been retained when Altrincham won the title in 1981, although by now a club would not get the opportunity to achieve this due to their elevation to Division 3 of the Football League. Having become the first club to be denied 'automatic promotion', Kidderminster was the popular choice for the title and the bookmakers had them and Kettering installed as pre-season favourites. Yet the Harriers could only finish mid-table, and after only one defeat in their first eleven games Kettering's form proved too inconsistent to mount a real challenge.

Once the initial skirmishes were over, Macclesfield were the first team to make a positive move. After a home defeat by Kidderminster on 13th September, Macclesfield embarked on a thirteen match unbeaten run. Ten successive victories were recorded, beating the previous league best, held jointly by Altrincham and Wycombe, with eight wins. By the time that the run was brought to an end in mid-December, the Silkmen had already been top of the table for six weeks and it was a position they were to hold for the rest of the season.

Woking were to prove the main, if somewhat distant, challengers for the top spot. After briefly holding the lead in both September and October, the Surrey side settled into second place and went into the New Year eight points behind the leaders from an equal number of games. However, in an eight-week period from 14th January to 11th March, only one league match was played due to a combination of F.A.Trophy matches and postponements, and this was a 4-0 defeat at Halifax. By the time the League campaign was resumed, the gap had grown to 22 points with three games in hand. Continued progress in the F.A.Trophy resulting in their successful retention of the cup, lead to nine matches being played by the Surrey side in the last two weeks of the season. While Woking were never remotely likely to pip Macclesfield, the Cheshire club had taken their foot off the gas, winning only two of the last eleven games and when the season finished, the margin between the teams was down to a mere five points.

Any celebrations of the championship were tempered by the knowledge that Macclesfield would not be progressing to the Football League. Work on an area of covered seating, which should have been finished in October 1994 experienced delays due to problems with the foundations and as a result the ground was not up to standard at the December 31st deadline. A temporary groundshare with Chester City was rejected as this was not within Macclesfield's conurbation. The fact that Macclesfield had provided a temporary home for Chester between 1990-1992, while they were waiting to move into the Deva Stadium, only rubbed salt into the wounds.

1994/95 Season Results Grid

	Altrincham	Bath City	Bromsgrove Rovers	Dagenham & Redbridge	Dover Athletic	Farnborough Town	Gateshead	Halifax Town	Kettering Town	Kidderminster Harriers	Macclesfield Town	Merthyr Tydfil	Northwich Victoria	Runcorn	Southport	Stafford Rangers	Stalybridge Celtic	Stevenage Borough	Telford United	Welling United	Woking	Yeovil Town
Altrincham	X	1-0	1-1	0-1	3-0	2-0	1-3	3-1	2-4	2-0	1-2	1-0	1-3	3-2	0-0	5-1	1-0	1-2	3-1	1-1	1-2	1-3
Bath City	0-3	X	1-1	3-0	0-0	2-0	0-2	0-0	2-0	3-5	1-0	1-0	2-2	4-3	1-2	3-3	2-3	2-1	1-1	2-0	2-0	3-0
Bromsgrove Rovers	0-3	1-1	X	2-2	2-0	2-2	2-2	0-1	2-4	4-3	2-2	2-0	1-4	1-0	1-1	2-1	2-1	2-1	0-1	4-1	5-5	5-0
Dagenham & Redbridge	0-4	1-0	2-0	X	2-0	0-1	0-0	1-4	2-1	1-2	0-4	2-1	1-2	3-2	5-1	3-3	2-2	0-1	3-2	0-0	0-2	0-0
Dover Athletic	1-3	3-0	0-2	1-1	X	1-1	2-2	1-1	0-2	1-0	0-0	2-2	3-1	1-1	3-2	0-0	2-0	2-0	1-1	2-0	1-1	1-1
Farnborough Town	2-3	0-0	0-3	1-3	1-0	X	3-1	2-0	0-0	1-0	1-0	2-1	2-1	0-4	1-4	0-0	0-0	1-1	5-3	1-2	0-2	0-3
Gateshead	1-0	0-1	2-1	2-1	1-0	2-0	X	1-2	0-0	2-1	2-0	4-0	4-0	0-1	1-1	0-0	1-2	0-0	2-1	2-0	2-0	0-3
Halifax Town	1-1	4-2	4-2	1-1	4-0	0-1	3-2	X	2-1	1-2	0-1	2-2	0-0	4-0	2-0	6-0	1-1	0-2	1-1	4-0	4-0	2-1
Kettering Town	2-2	0-0	0-1	2-2	1-0	4-1	2-4	5-1	X	0-0	1-0	4-1	3-3	1-0	1-0	1-0	0-2	3-2	4-3	0-1	3-2	2-1
Kidderminster Harriers	2-2	2-1	0-1	1-1	0-0	0-1	2-3	3-0	1-3	X	1-2	2-0	1-2	1-1	0-1	1-2	3-2	0-3	1-1	3-0	1-3	3-0
Macclesfield Town	4-2	1-0	2-2	2-0	2-0	4-1	2-1	1-1	1-0	1-3	X	0-0	3-1	0-1	1-2	3-0	0-3	2-0	3-1	2-0	1-0	1-0
Merthyr Tydfil	2-5	2-0	2-1	2-0	2-3	1-1	1-2	2-0	2-1	0-1	1-2	X	2-0	3-0	1-2	4-1	4-2	2-2	3-1	1-0	1-1	0-0
Northwich Victoria	1-1	1-1	3-1	5-0	1-3	1-2	1-1	3-0	3-2	3-4	1-3	2-0	X	4-1	2-1	0-1	2-2	0-1	1-1	1-1	2-2	2-2
Runcorn	3-0	1-1	3-1	0-0	3-3	1-0	3-2	0-3	1-2	2-2	2-2	0-0	2-2	X	2-1	3-1	0-3	3-1	4-1	3-2	1-0	2-1
Southport	1-4	3-1	2-1	1-1	2-2	0-1	5-0	4-0	1-1	4-1	2-3	3-1	0-2	5-0	X	3-0	3-1	2-1	1-0	2-0	0-0	2-0
Stafford Rangers	0-1	0-2	1-1	1-2	1-0	1-1	3-1	0-1	2-3	1-2	0-3	2-1	1-3	1-2	1-1	X	5-0	0-3	2-2	1-1	2-3	4-1
Stalybridge Celtic	2-1	0-1	1-1	1-0	2-1	4-1	0-1	1-1	1-4	1-3	2-2	1-1	2-1	0-0	1-1	2-3	X	1-0	1-0	1-3	2-1	3-1
Stevenage Borough	4-2	3-0	1-0	3-1	0-3	3-1	2-3	1-0	2-2	2-3	1-1	0-0	1-1	0-1	1-2	1-0	5-1	X	4-3	1-2	0-1	5-0
Telford United	2-3	3-0	2-2	0-4	1-1	1-1	3-1	1-1	1-0	3-1	2-0	1-1	2-0	0-0	0-0	1-1	1-2	1-1	X	4-2	0-0	1-0
Welling United	0-0	1-5	1-2	4-1	0-1	1-3	3-0	1-1	2-1	0-2	0-1	2-1	1-5	2-1	3-1	3-1	3-3	1-0	1-0	X	1-2	2-1
Woking	4-0	2-2	4-0	3-5	0-0	3-2	1-1	1-3	3-1	0-0	1-0	4-1	1-1	2-0	3-0	2-2	4-1	3-0	2-1	1-1	X	2-2
Yeovil Town	1-3	1-2	2-0	2-2	1-3	0-1	1-1	3-1	1-1	1-1	1-2	1-3	4-4	1-0	0-1	1-0	3-0	0-0	1-1	3-1	1-2	X

Final Table

	P	Home					Away					Total					Pts
		W	D	L	F	A	W	D	L	F	A	W	D	L	F	A	
Macclesfield Town	42	14	3	4	39	18	10	5	6	31	22	24	8	10	70	40	80
Woking	42	11	8	2	46	23	10	4	7	30	31	21	12	9	76	54	75
Southport	42	13	4	4	46	21	8	5	8	22	29	21	9	12	68	50	72
Altrincham	42	10	3	8	34	27	10	5	6	43	33	20	8	14	77	60	68
Stevenage Borough	42	10	4	7	40	27	10	3	8	28	22	20	7	15	68	49	67
Kettering Town	42	12	5	4	40	25	7	5	9	33	31	19	10	13	73	56	67
Gateshead	42	12	4	5	28	13	7	6	8	33	40	19	10	13	61	53	67
Halifax Town	42	11	6	4	46	20	6	6	9	22	34	17	12	13	68	54	63
Runcorn	42	11	7	3	39	28	5	3	13	20	43	16	10	16	59	71	58
Northwich Victoria	42	7	8	6	39	30	7	7	7	38	36	14	15	13	77	66	57
Kidderminster Harriers	42	6	5	10	28	29	10	4	7	35	32	16	9	17	63	61	57
Bath City	42	10	6	5	35	26	5	6	10	20	30	15	12	15	55	56	57
Bromsgrove Rovers	42	9	7	5	42	35	5	6	10	24	34	14	13	15	66	69	55
Farnborough Town	42	8	5	8	23	31	7	5	9	22	33	15	10	17	45	64	55
Dagenham & Redbridge	42	8	5	8	28	32	5	8	8	28	37	13	13	16	56	69	52
Dover Athletic	42	6	10	5	28	25	5	6	10	20	30	11	16	15	48	55	49
Welling United	42	9	3	9	31	33	4	7	10	26	41	13	10	19	57	74	49
Stalybridge Celtic	42	9	6	6	29	27	2	8	11	23	45	11	14	17	52	72	47
Telford United	42	9	9	3	30	20	1	7	13	23	42	10	16	16	53	62	46
Merthyr Tydfil	42	10	4	7	37	27	1	7	13	16	36	11	11	20	53	63	44 R
Stafford Rangers	42	5	5	11	29	34	4	6	11	24	45	9	11	22	53	79	38 R
Yeovil Town *	42	5	8	8	29	31	3	6	12	21	40	8	14	20	50	71	37 R

Yeovil Town 1 point deducted.

Morecambe promoted from N.P.L., Hednesford Town from Southern League, Slough Town from Isthmian League.

F.A.Cup

First Qualifying Round		
RTM Newcastle	Gateshead	0-3
Mossley	Northwich Victoria	2-4
Tamworth	Telford United	1-1
Saffron Walden Town	Stevenage Borough	1-4
Feltham & Hounslow Borough	Dagenham & Redbridge	1-3
(Played at Dagenham)		
Whyteleafe	Dover Athletic	0-0
Windsor & Eton	Welling United	0-1
Yate Town	Merthyr Tydfil	0-3
replay		
Telford United	Tamworth	4-1
Dover Athletic	Whyteleafe	3-0
Second Qualifying Round		
Bishop Auckland	Gateshead	3-1
Northwich Victoria	Nantwich Town	10-0
Halesowen Town	Telford United	1-1
Stevenage Borough	Cambridge City	0-2
Chesham Utd	Dagenham & Redbridge	2-0
Molesey	Dover Athletic	1-4
Welling United	Wembley	1-4
Gloucester City	Merthyr Tydfil	7-1
replay		
Telford United	Halesowen Town	3-1
Third Qualifying Round		
Northwich Victoria	Emley	2-1
Gainsborough Trinity	Telford United	0-3
Chertsey Town	Dover Athletic	0-0
replay		
Dover Athletic	Chertsey Town	1-0
Fourth Qualifying Round		
Altrincham	Marine	2-1
Bishop Auckland	Macclesfield Town	2-2
Chesham Utd	Bromsgrove Rovers	1-1
Dover Athletic	Kingstonian	1-2
Halifax Town	Lancaster City	3-1
Northwich Victoria	Blyth Spartans	2-0
Solihull Borough	Kettering Town	2-4
Southport	Stalybridge Celtic	2-1
Stafford Rangers	Slough Town	0-4
Tiverton Town	Farnborough Town	4-4
Walton & Hersham	Yeovil Town	3-2
Yeading	Telford United	1-0
replay		
Bromsgrove Rovers	Chesham Utd	0-1
Farnborough Town	Tiverton Town	1-5
Macclesfield Town	Bishop Auckland	0-1
First Round		
Altrincham	Southport	3-2
Barnet	Woking	4-4
Bath City	Bristol Rovers	0-5
Halifax Town	Runcorn	1-1
Kettering Town	Plymouth Argyle	0-1
Kidderminster Harriers	Torquay Utd	1-1
Mansfield Town	Northwich Victoria	3-1
replay		
Runcorn	Halifax Town	1-3
Torquay Utd	Kidderminster Harriers	1-0
Woking	Barnet	1-0

F.A.Cup

Second Round		
Altrincham	Wigan Ath	1-0
Halifax Town	Mansfield Town	0-0
Marlow	Woking	2-1
replay		
Mansfield Town	Halifax Town	2-1
Third Round		
Tottenham Hotspur	Altrincham	3-0

League Cup

First Round *(two legs)*		
Altrincham	Telford Utd	1-1
Telford Utd	Altrincham	0-3
Bath City	Welling Utd	3-1
Welling Utd	Bath City	2-6
Gateshead	Stalybridge Celtic	2-3
Stalybridge Celtic	Gateshead	3-2
Halifax Town	Northwich Victoria	0-1
Northwich Victoria	Halifax Town	1-1
Merthyr Tydfil	Bromsgrove Rovers	2-1
Bromsgrove Rovers	Merthyr Tydfil	4-1
Stevenage Borough	Farnborough Town	1-2
Farnborough Town	Stevenage Borough	3-1
Second Round		
Altrincham	Northwich Victoria	3-2
Bath City	Dover Athletic	0-1
Kidderminster Harriers	Kettering Town	1-5
Macclesfield Town	Runcorn	4-2
Stalybridge Celtic	Southport	3-1
Stafford Rangers	Bromsgrove Rovers	1-4
Woking	Farnborough Town	0-0
Yeovil Town	Dagenham & Redbridge	2-4
replay		
Farnborough Town	Woking	0-1
Third Round		
Dagenham & Redbridge	Dover Athletic	4-3
Kettering Town	Woking	2-1
Macclesfield Town	Altrincham	2-1
Stalybridge Celtic	Bromsgrove Rovers	3-3
replay		
Bromsgrove Rovers	Stalybridge Celtic	2-0
Semi Final *(two legs)*		
Kettering Town	Dagenham & Redbridge	0-2
Dagenham & Redbridge	Kettering Town	2-4
Kettering Town won on away goals		
Macclesfield Town	Bromsgrove Rovers	2-1
Bromsgrove Rovers	Macclesfield Town	4-1
Final *(two legs)*		
Bromsgrove Rovers	Kettering Town	4-1
Kettering Town	Bromsgrove Rovers	1-6

Challenge Shield

Kidderminster Harriers	Woking	1-2

First Round

Chelmsford City	Yeovil Town	2-4
Bromsgrove Rovers	Enfield	1-3
Stalybridge Celtic	Hyde United	3-3
Runcorn	Northwich Victoria	2-1
Telford United	Southport	2-0
Gresley Rovers	Stafford Rangers	2-0
Bamber Bridge	Halifax Town	1-0
West Auckland Town	Macclesfield Town	1-2
(played at Macclesfield Town)		
Woking	Chesham Utd	3-0
Merthyr Tydfil	Slough Town	3-2
Stevenage Borough	Dagenham & Redbridge	2-1
St Albans City	Kidderminster Harriers	2-3
Welling United	Marlow	2-2
Farnborough Town	Dover Athletic	1-0
Sutton United	Bath City	1-1
Walton & Hersham	Kettering Town	2-2
Bishop Auckland	Gateshead	0-1
Hednesford Town	Altrincham	1-2

replay

Hyde Utd	Stalybridge Celtic	3-1
Marlow	Welling United	1-5
Bath City	Sutton United	1-0
Kettering Town	Walton & Hersham	1-0

Second Round

Runcorn	Leek Town	4-2
Altrincham	VS Rugby	1-1
Gateshead	Rothwell Town	6-1
Hyde Utd	Telford United	2-0
Welling United	Ilkeston Town	1-1
Kingstonian	Kidderminster Harriers	0-0
Boreham Wood	Kettering Town	2-1
Bath City	Marine	1-2
Ashton Utd	Macclesfield Town	0-5
Merthyr Tydfil	Bamber Bridge	2-1
Woking	Cheltenham Town	3-1
Farnborough Town	Rushden & Diamonds	0-1
Yeovil Town	Stevenage Borough	1-1

replay

VS Rugby	Altrincham	1-2
Ilkeston Town	Welling United	3-0
Kidderminster Harriers	Kingstonian	1-0
Stevenage Borough	Yeovil Town	2-0

Third Round

Runcorn	Hyde United	0-0
Gateshead	Macclesfield Town	0-1
Ilkeston Town	Kidderminster Harriers	2-2
Stevenage Borough	Woking	0-3
Morecambe	Altrincham	2-3
Enfield	Merthyr Tydfil	1-1

replay

Hyde Utd	Runcorn	4-0
Kidderminster Harriers	Ilkeston Town	2-1
Merthyr Tydfil	Enfield	1-1
(abandoned 70 mins, snow)		
Merthyr Tydfil	Enfield	0-1

Fourth Round

Kidderminster Harriers	Altrincham	5-0
Macclesfield Town	Woking	0-1

Semi Final *(two legs)*

Rushden & Diamonds	Woking	1-0
Woking	Rushden & Diamonds	2-0
Kidderminster Harriers	Hyde United	2-0
Hyde Utd	Kidderminster Harriers	1-0

Final *(@ Wembley)*

Woking	Kidderminster Harriers	2-1

BATH CITY   0
BRISTOL ROVERS   5
The F.A. Cup brings together
Landlords and Tenants.

Stevenage Borough, in only their second season in the Conference were crowned champions. This was a remarkable achievement in view of the fact that as recently as the 1990-1 season they were playing in Division Two North of the Isthmian League. Possibly due to their rapid advancement, they were unable to match their progress off the field of play and they were ultimately frustrated in their attempts to gain Football League membership.

Kidderminster, champions two years earlier, were the first team to lead the league for any period of time, holding pole position for most of September and October. The baton was then taken up by Macclesfield who had started their title defence with four defeats in the first eleven games, including a 6-1 defeat at Farnborough. The next ten matches yielded an impressive 26 points until Stevenage inflicted a 4-0 reversal.

The lead was maintained until mid-February, when Stevenage, in the midst of a seventeen match unbeaten run, went to the top and were never replaced. The title was clinched with two games to spare with a 1-1 home draw against Morecambe, and the winning margin was eight points. For Macclesfield, their disappointment at not retaining their crown was tempered with success in the F.A.Trophy, beating Cheshire neighbours Northwich in the final.

The battle now transferred to the High Court, with Stevenage attempting to overturn the League ruling. The deadline of December 31st for ground improvements was a compromise that had been reached in discussions between the Football League and the Conference. The League felt facilities should be up to the required standard before the season started, whereas the Conference were happy to inspect the grounds during the season and rely on guaranties that works would be completed by July 31st. Stevenage, as with Kidderminster and Macclesfield before them, had failed to carry out the necessary improvements in time, and their Chairman Victor Green challenged the League rules on the grounds of restraint of trade.

The case went to court in July and although Stevenage lost, there was sympathy for their position. It was ruled that as the criteria were in place at the start of the season, all clubs were aware of the situation, and if they had been unhappy with the rules this would have been the time to protest. There was also no restraint of trade, as football would still be played, albeit in the Conference. However, two elements were questioned. The New Year deadline for ground improvements was set well before the promotion place was decided and the financial criteria on League entry was harsh when there was no similar criteria for the existing League members. The matter was referred to the Court of Appeal, who dismissed an expedited appeal, but in view of the findings the deadline for ground improvements was moved back to April 1st.

1995/96 Season Results Grid

	Altrincham	Bath City	Bromsgrove Rovers	Dagenham & Redbridge	Dover Athletic	Farnborough Town	Gateshead	Halifax Town	Hednesford Town	Kettering Town	Kidderminster Harriers	Macclesfield Town	Morecambe	Northwich Victoria	Runcorn	Slough Town	Southport	Stalybridge Celtic	Stevenage Borough	Telford United	Welling United	Woking
Altrincham	X	1-2	3-0	3-1	2-2	2-2	1-1	3-2	2-1	1-3	1-1	0-4	3-0	3-4	2-2	0-1	1-1	1-0	0-2	1-0	1-0	2-0
Bath City	2-2	X	0-1	0-2	2-1	2-1	0-1	2-1	1-0	3-1	1-1	1-1	3-2	0-3	3-0	3-1	4-0	0-4	1-2	0-3	1-1	0-3
Bromsgrove Rovers	0-0	4-1	X	2-0	3-0	1-2	3-1	0-1	1-4	3-2	2-1	1-0	1-0	1-1	2-0	0-0	4-1	1-1	1-1	0-2	1-1	2-1
Dagenham & Redbridge	1-0	0-1	2-2	X	3-0	2-2	0-4	1-1	1-2	1-2	4-2	3-0	2-2	0-3	2-3	1-3	1-2	4-1	1-2	1-1	1-1	0-0
Dover Athletic	1-4	1-0	0-2	0-1	X	1-3	1-1	3-2	1-3	2-1	2-1	2-3	2-3	0-1	4-2	0-1	0-1	1-3	1-2	1-0	2-1	4-3
Farnborough Town	1-1	0-0	1-0	2-0	3-2	X	2-3	0-0	1-3	1-1	3-1	6-1	3-1	0-1	0-1	0-1	1-0	1-1	2-2	2-1	0-1	0-2
Gateshead	2-3	3-1	1-0	2-0	1-1	1-1	X	3-2	0-3	1-1	4-1	0-1	3-0	1-1	1-0	2-1	2-2	1-0	2-2	1-2	1-1	0-1
Halifax Town	1-1	3-1	1-1	3-0	1-0	0-0	2-0	X	1-3	2-0	0-2	1-0	1-1	2-0	1-3	1-2	2-2	2-3	2-3	0-0	2-1	2-2
Hednesford Town	2-1	2-1	4-2	0-0	2-2	4-1	0-1	3-0	X	1-0	1-3	0-1	1-2	2-1	2-0	3-1	2-1	2-1	2-1	4-0	1-1	2-1
Kettering Town	4-2	3-0	2-2	2-0	2-2	0-2	1-0	1-2	2-0	X	2-0	2-2	2-3	2-2	4-0	2-0	1-1	1-6	1-2	0-3	1-3	3-0
Kidderminster Harriers	1-1	1-2	1-0	5-1	1-1	3-3	1-1	6-1	3-1	1-0	X	0-4	4-2	2-1	4-1	4-3	2-3	3-0	0-1	2-0	3-0	2-0
Macclesfield Town	2-3	0-1	2-1	3-1	0-1	1-0	1-0	7-0	1-1	1-1	0-2	X	2-0	0-0	1-0	1-1	3-1	1-0	0-0	1-0	2-1	3-2
Morecambe	7-0	1-0	4-1	2-2	3-1	2-3	2-3	0-1	0-1	5-3	3-1	2-4	X	2-2	3-1	1-2	4-3	2-0	1-0	2-0	1-0	4-5
Northwich Victoria	2-1	2-2	2-2	1-0	1-2	1-3	1-2	1-1	0-2	6-2	5-2	2-1	4-0	X	4-3	0-3	1-2	1-0	1-3	2-0	1-2	3-0
Runcorn	0-1	1-0	0-0	2-0	1-3	0-3	1-1	0-1	2-2	4-2	0-1	0-0	1-3	3-4	X	4-3	1-1	0-1	0-8	2-3	1-3	2-3
Slough Town	1-2	1-1	2-3	5-0	3-2	1-1	1-2	2-3	0-2	1-2	5-4	2-2	1-1	1-1	0-1	X	2-5	2-1	2-6	1-2	0-0	2-3
Southport	1-2	2-1	1-2	2-1	0-0	7-1	1-0	0-0	2-2	6-1	0-2	2-1	1-1	2-2	1-1	2-0	X	5-3	0-1	3-2	2-0	2-2
Stalybridge Celtic	1-0	1-0	2-1	2-1	2-0	2-2	0-2	1-0	0-1	3-2	2-2	1-2	0-2	1-5	2-0	0-1	1-4	X	2-5	2-2	2-1	2-4
Stevenage Borough	1-1	2-0	3-3	1-0	3-2	0-0	1-1	1-0	1-0	5-1	4-1	4-0	1-1	5-1	4-1	3-1	1-3	2-2	X	0-1	4-1	4-0
Telford United	2-0	3-1	0-0	0-0	1-0	3-2	0-0	1-1	2-1	3-4	1-1	1-2	2-2	1-0	2-0	2-1	0-1	1-3	0-1	X	0-0	1-2
Welling United	1-1	2-1	5-2	0-0	1-0	0-1	1-2	0-0	1-1	1-0	0-0	1-2	1-0	1-1	1-1	0-3	0-1	1-1	0-3	3-1	X	1-2
Woking	2-0	2-0	1-1	2-2	1-0	2-1	2-0	2-0	3-0	1-1	0-0	3-2	3-0	0-0	2-1	3-0	4-0	2-1	4-1	5-1	3-2	X

FINAL TABLE

	P	Home					Away					Total					
		W	D	L	F	A	W	D	L	F	A	W	D	L	F	A	Pts
Stevenage Borough	42	13	6	2	51	20	14	4	3	50	24	27	10	5	101	44	91
Woking	42	16	5	0	47	13	9	3	9	36	41	25	8	9	83	54	83
Hednesford Town	42	13	3	5	38	21	10	4	7	33	25	23	7	12	71	46	76
Macclesfield Town	42	12	5	4	32	16	10	4	7	34	33	22	9	11	66	49	75
Gateshead	42	9	7	5	32	24	9	6	6	26	22	18	13	11	58	46	67
Southport	42	10	7	4	42	25	8	5	8	35	39	18	12	12	77	64	66
Kidderminster Harriers	42	13	4	4	49	26	5	6	10	29	40	18	10	14	78	66	64
Northwich Victoria	42	9	3	9	38	35	7	9	5	34	29	16	12	14	72	64	60
Morecambe	42	12	2	7	51	33	5	6	10	27	39	17	8	17	78	72	59
Farnborough Town	42	8	6	7	29	23	7	8	6	34	35	15	14	13	63	58	59
Bromsgrove Rovers	42	11	6	4	33	20	4	8	9	26	37	15	14	13	59	57	59
Altrincham	42	9	6	6	33	29	6	7	8	26	35	15	13	14	59	64	58
Telford United	42	8	7	6	27	23	7	3	11	24	33	15	10	17	51	56	55
Stalybridge Celtic	42	9	3	9	29	37	7	4	10	30	31	16	7	19	59	68	55
Halifax Town	42	8	7	6	30	25	5	6	10	19	38	13	13	16	49	63	52
Kettering Town	42	9	5	7	38	32	4	4	13	30	52	13	9	20	68	84	48
Slough Town	42	4	6	11	35	44	9	2	10	28	32	13	8	21	63	76	47
Bath City	42	9	4	8	29	31	4	3	14	16	35	13	7	22	45	66	46
Welling United	42	6	8	7	21	23	4	7	10	21	30	10	15	17	42	53	45
Dover Athletic	42	8	1	12	29	38	3	6	12	22	36	11	7	24	51	74	40
Runcorn	42	4	5	12	25	43	5	3	13	23	44	9	8	25	48	87	35 R
Dagenham & Redbridge	42	5	7	9	31	34	2	5	14	12	39	7	12	23	43	73	33 R

Rushden & Diamonds promoted from Southern League, Hayes from Isthmian League.

CUP COMPETITIONS

F.A.Cup

First Qualifying Round		
Gateshead	Dunston FB	3-2
Northwich Victoria	Burscough	5-0
Morecambe	Sheffield	7-0
Telford United	Shifnal Town	4-0
Hednesford Town	Corby Town	3-1
Dagenham & Redbridge	Hornchurch	4-0
Stevenage Borough	Brook House	0-0
Farnborough Town	Dartford	1-0
Dover Athletic	Bognor Regis Town	1-2
Welling United	Wick	2-0
replay		
Brook House	Stevenage Borough	1-5
Second Qualifying Round		
Gateshead	Barrow	2-2
Lincoln Utd	Northwich Victoria	1-4
Raunds Town	Telford United	1-2
Tamworth	Hednesford Town	1-2
Berkhamstead Town	Dagenham & Redbridge	1-2
Uxbridge	Stevenage Borough	0-1
Fisher 93	Farnborough Town	1-4
Worksop Town	Morecambe	2-3
Welling United	Bromley	2-2
replay		
Barrow	Gateshead	1-0
Bromley	Welling United	3-3
second replay		
Welling United	Bromley	1-2
Third Qualifying Round		
Northwich Victoria	Eastwood Town	0-0
Telford United	Halesowen Town	4-1
Hednesford Town	Solihull Borough	2-2
Morecambe	Gainsborough Trinity	6-2
Dagenham & Redbridge	Purfleet	1-1
Stevenage Borough	Staines Town	2-0
Farnborough Town	Walton & Hersham	3-2
replay		
Eastwood Town	Northwich Victoria	1-2
Purfleet	Dagenham & Redbridge	2-1
Solihull Borough	Hednesford Town	1-2
Fourth Qualifying Round		
Aylesbury Utd	Stevenage Borough	1-3
Canvey Island	Hednesford Town	2-0
Cinderford Town	Bath City	3-2
Farnborough Town	Yeovil Town	2-1
Kettering Town	Bromsgrove Rovers	0-0
Macclesfield Town	Northwich Victoria	0-1
Runcorn	Halifax Town	2-1
Stalybridge Celtic	Colwyn Bay	2-2
Telford United	Southport	3-0
Witton Albion	Morecambe	3-2
Yeading	Slough Town	0-2
replay		
Bromsgrove Rovers	Kettering Town	2-2
Colwyn Bay	Stalybridge Celtic	3-0
second replay		
Kettering Town	Bromsgrove Rovers	1-2
First Round		
Altrincham	Crewe Alexandra	0-2
Barnet	Woking	2-2
Brentford	Farnborough Town	1-1
Cinderford Town	Bromsgrove Rovers	2-1
Hereford United	Stevenage Borough	2-1
Kidderminster Harriers	Sutton Utd	2-2
Northwich Victoria	Scunthorpe Utd	1-3
Runcorn	Wigan Ath	1-1
Slough Town	Plymouth Argyle	0-2
Telford United	Witton Albion	2-1

F.A.Cup

First Round - replay		
Farnborough Town	Brentford	0-4
Sutton Utd	Kidderminster Harriers	1-1
(Sutton Utd won 3-2 on pens)		
Wigan Ath	Runcorn	4-2
Woking	Barnet	2-1
Second Round		
Enfield	Woking	1-1
Telford United	Notts County	0-2
replay		
Woking	Enfield	2-1
(Played at Wycombe Wanderers)		
Third Round		
Swindon Town	Woking	2-0

League Cup

First Round (two legs)		
Dagenham & Redbridge	Slough Town	0-3
Slough Town	Dagenham & Redbridge	3-0
Kidderminster Harriers	Hednesford Town	4-1
Hednesford Town	Kidderminster Harriers	2-0
Bath City	Farnborough Town	0-3
Farnborough Town	Bath City	3-2
Morecambe	Stalybridge Celtic	4-1
Stalybridge Celtic	Morecambe	5-2
(Morecambe won on away goals)		
Telford Utd	Northwich Victoria	1-2
Northwich Victoria	Telford Utd	0-3
Welling Utd	Dover Athletic	1-2
Dover Athletic	Welling Utd	3-0
Second Round		
Farnborough Town	Dover Athletic	1-3
Kettering Town	Stevenage Borough	2-1
Macclesfield Town	Kidderminster Harriers	4-1
Runcorn	Southport	1-5
Bromsgrove Rovers	Telford Utd	3-1
Morecambe	Altrincham	6-4
Slough Town	Woking	3-0
Gateshead	Halifax Town	4-0
Third Round		
Kettering Town	Slough Town	2-0
Dover Athletic	Bromsgrove Rovers	0-1
Morecambe	Macclesfield Town	1-4
Southport	Gateshead	2-1
Semi Final (two legs)		
Bromsgrove Rovers	Kettering Town	2-0
Kettering Town	Bromsgrove Rovers	2-1
Southport	Macclesfield Town	4-4
Macclesfield Town	Southport	2-1
Final (two legs)		
Macclesfield Town	Bromsgrove Rovers	1-1
Bromsgrove Rovers	Macclesfield Town	3-1

Challenge Shield

Macclesfield Town	Woking	3-2

First Round		
Colwyn Bay	Altrincham	3-3
Bath City	Yeovil Town	1-1
Halifax Town	Southport	2-1
Macclesfield Town	Runcorn	1-0
Carshalton Ath	Woking	3-1
Farnborough Town	Slough Town	1-1
Burton Albion	Telford United	3-1
Stalybridge Celtic	Gresley Rovers	1-1
Morecambe	Emley	2-2
Stevenage Borough	Dagenham & Redbridge	3-2
Hednesford Town	Northwich Victoria	1-1
Kidderminster Harriers	Gateshead	0-0
Kettering Town	St Albans City	1-1
Bromsgrove Rovers	Bishop Auckland	1-0
Rothwell Town	Welling United	2-2
Dover Athletic	Cheltenham Town	2-2
replay		
Cheltenham Town	Dover Athletic	1-1
Emley	Morecambe	3-1
Altrincham	Colwyn Bay	2-0
Northwich Victoria	Hednesford Town	2-0
Gateshead	Kidderminster Harriers	2-0
Gresley Rovers	Stalybridge Celtic	1-0
Welling United	Rothwell Town	3-0
Yeovil Town	Bath City	2-3
Slough Town	Farnborough Town	4-3
St Albans City	Kettering Town	2-3
second replay		
Dover Athletic	Cheltenham Town	1-0
Second Round		
Hyde Utd	Welling United	4-1
Guiseley	Altrincham	4-0
Emley	Gateshead	1-2
Boreham Wood	Dover Athletic	2-1
Macclesfield Town	Purfleet	2-1
Slough Town	Kettering Town	1-2
Bath City	Hayes	2-0
Stevenage Borough	Burton Albion	2-1
Wembley	Northwich Victoria	0-2
Halifax Town	Bromsgrove Rovers	0-1
Third Round		
Merthyr Tydfil	Northwich Victoria	1-1
Macclesfield Town	Sudbury Town	1-0
Radcliffe Borough	Gateshead	1-2
Stevenage Borough	Kettering Town	3-0
Bath City	Bromsgrove Rovers	1-1
replay		
Bromsgrove Rovers	Bath City	2-1
Northwich Victoria	Merthyr Tydfil	2-2
second round		
Northwich Victoria	Merthyr Tydfil	3-0

Fourth Round		
Hyde Utd	Stevenage Borough	3-2
Gresley Rovers	Macclesfield Town	0-2
Bromsgrove Rovers	Northwich Victoria	0-1
Chorley	Gateshead	3-1
Semi Final *(two legs)*		
Hyde Utd	Northwich Victoria	1-2
Northwich Victoria	Hyde Utd	1-0
Macclesfield Town	Chorley	3-1
Chorley	Macclesfield Town	1-1
Final *(@ Wembley)*		
Macclesfield Town	Northwich Victoria	3-1

MORECAMBE 2
TELFORD UNITED 0
Opening day victory for Conference newcomers Morecambe.

1996/97

The credibility of the fifth division had been failure of three successive champions to satisfy the Football League that their credentials were worthy of promotion. It was imperative that on this occasion that there should be no problems.

As it turned out, the three major contenders for the title would prove to be the three unsuccessful champions. It was Stevenage who set the early pace, winning their first 12 matches, but as their form dropped away and they became embroiled in a series of cup-ties, it was Kidderminster who assumed the lead. From the beginning of September until Boxing Day, 20 matches produced 15 victories and only one defeat. Come the turn of the year, their lead was 12 points over Macclesfield. The New Year brought a change in fortune, for between 5th January and 7th March, six of their matches were cup-ties and the three league matches yielded only two points, resulting in their fall from the summit.

It was Macclesfield's turn at the top. Their season had been a case of triumph in the face of adversity. The biggest blow had been on 19th September, when their much-loved Chairman, Arthur Jones, had been found dead at his business premises. The Club's subsequent Championship would be dedicated to his memory. On the field their semi-professional international goalkeeper Ryan Price received severe facial injuries during the home match with Southport. His nose was broken, jaw fractured and both cheekbones broken, requiring 42 pins and 7 plates to be inserted into his face. Remarkably he was back in goal ten weeks later for the FA Trophy tie with Kidderminster. The 3-0 defeat allowed the team to concentrate on the league campaign and a run of eight consecutive victories in February and March, gave them a marginal advantage over the Harriers. The lead changed hands on several occasions until a victory at Kettering on the final day secured the title.

Much was expected of Rushden and Diamonds. With their magnificent stadium, big-named playing staff and the financial backing of Max Griggs, there seemed no end to what could be achieved. However, money could not necessarily buy success. No wins in the first six games was the prelude to much disappointment. Still bottom going into March, Brian Talbot took up the reins as head coach. Just two defeats in the last fourteen matches saw the Northamptonshire side rise to a final twelfth place. Having spent over £500,000 on players, and using a dozen semi-professional internationals over the season, a greater return on the investment could have been expected. Surely they would be successful the following season.

1996/97 Season Results Grid

	Altrincham	Bath City	Bromsgrove Rovers	Dover Athletic	Farnborough Town	Gateshead	Halifax Town	Hayes	Hednesford Town	Kettering Town	Kidderminster Harriers	Macclesfield Town	Morecambe	Northwich Victoria	Rushden & Diamonds	Slough Town	Southport	Stalybridge Celtic	Stevenage Borough	Telford United	Welling United	Woking
Altrincham	X	1-3	3-1	1-2	0-3	0-1	2-1	0-2	1-1	4-3	0-1	0-1	0-1	2-3	4-3	0-1	1-0	1-0	1-2	2-3	1-1	1-1
Bath City	1-2	X	1-0	2-1	1-1	3-0	0-0	3-1	2-1	0-2	0-3	0-3	2-1	3-2	3-2	0-0	0-2	0-2	0-0	2-3	3-1	1-1
Bromsgrove Rovers	4-0	2-1	X	3-1	1-1	2-2	3-0	2-2	1-0	1-2	0-1	0-3	2-3	0-5	0-1	4-1	0-1	0-1	1-1	2-1	1-0	0-3
Dover Athletic	2-2	2-2	2-0	X	0-0	0-1	2-2	1-0	2-2	0-1	0-5	2-1	3-0	2-2	1-1	0-0	0-1	2-1	3-3	1-4	2-1	5-1
Farnborough Town	1-1	4-1	2-1	2-3	X	1-2	3-0	1-1	1-0	0-2	2-1	0-1	2-2	2-2	2-2	2-1	3-3	1-3	3-1	0-2	2-1	1-2
Gateshead	1-1	5-0	1-0	1-3	1-0	X	0-1	1-1	0-1	1-1	3-1	0-0	0-3	5-1		2-1	2-2	0-2	2-2	2-3	1-2	3-2
Halifax Town	1-1	4-5	1-0	1-3	3-0	2-0	X	2-2	1-0	2-1	2-3	3-3	1-1	0-3	1-3	4-1	2-0	4-1	4-2	0-3	1-1	0-4
Hayes	3-1	0-1	1-0	2-0	0-0	0-0	0-0	X	4-0	2-1	0-1	0-2	2-3	1-1	1-1	5-0	1-1	0-2	1-3	0-1	1-1	3-2
Hednesford Town	2-2	2-0	3-0	1-1	0-1	0-0	1-1	2-0	X	0-0	1-4	4-1	2-1	3-0	1-0	2-1	0-1	2-1	0-0	0-3	2-0	
Kettering Town	3-1	1-0	2-0	1-1	3-1	4-1	4-1	2-2	0-2	X	3-1	1-4	0-2	1-0	1-5	0-0	0-1	1-0	1-0	2-1	2-3	0-0
Kidderminster Harriers	1-1	6-0	1-2	4-1	2-3	3-2	3-0	5-1	2-1	4-0	X	0-0	2-1	1-0	1-0	1-2	3-0	1-1	3-0	1-0	3-2	1-0
Macclesfield Town	1-1	2-2	4-0	1-0	3-0	3-0	1-0	1-0	4-0	0-1	0-1	X	0-0	0-1	2-1	2-0	3-2	2-0	2-1	2-1	1-1	5-0
Morecambe	2-1	1-1	1-0	3-1	1-1	4-0	1-0	2-4	2-2	5-2	2-3	1-0	X	2-0	2-0	0-0	2-1	0-0	1-2	0-1	1-2	1-2
Northwich Victoria	2-2	1-0	1-0	2-0	1-1	4-2	2-2	2-1	2-1	2-1	1-1	2-1	1-0	X	1-2	0-1	5-1	0-1	0-1	1-1	0-0	1-2
Rushden & Diamonds	3-2	4-1	1-2	1-1	0-2	0-4	2-2	2-2	0-2	1-0	1-1	1-1	2-1	1-1	X	2-2	3-0	1-1	0-1	3-0	3-0	1-1
Slough Town	0-1	5-2	2-2	2-2	1-1	0-1	1-0	1-3	2-2	1-1	0-2	0-0	0-0	3-4	5-0	X	1-1	4-1	1-6	6-0	3-3	3-0
Southport	1-3	3-1	0-0	0-1	0-3	1-1	2-1	0-2	1-2	2-2	1-0	1-5	3-1	0-0	2-1	0-1	X	3-0	0-0	1-0	3-2	4-1
Stalybridge Celtic	1-0	2-2	3-0	4-2	2-0	2-5	2-3	3-1	1-2	3-1	4-1	0-1	2-1	0-1	2-2	2-2	2-2	X	0-3	0-0	0-0	0-2
Stevenage Borough	2-1	2-1	3-0	4-1	3-1	4-1	6-0	2-0	3-2	0-0	2-2	2-3	4-2	2-0	4-1	2-2	2-1	1-1	X	3-0	2-1	0-3
Telford United	0-0	1-1	3-1	1-0	2-0	0-3	1-1	0-0	1-1	1-0	0-0	2-3	2-2	0-5	0-2	1-0	1-1	2-3		X	2-0	1-2
Welling United	1-0	2-0	1-2	1-0	0-2	2-0	0-1	1-0	1-2	0-1	0-3	1-4	1-1	0-1	1-1	3-2	2-3	2-0	2-0	2-1	X	1-1
Woking	7-1	2-2	1-3	1-1	0-2	1-1	2-2	1-2	2-0	2-1	2-1	2-3	1-2	3-1	4-2	2-0	0-1	3-2	3-1	0-0	2-1	X

Final Table

	P	Home					Away					Total						
		W	D	L	F	A	W	D	L	F	A	W	D	L	F	A	Pts	
Macclesfield Town	42	15	4	2	41	11	12	5	4	39	19	27	9	6	80	30	90	P
Kidderminster Harriers	42	14	4	3	48	18	12	3	6	36	24	26	7	9	84	42	85	
Stevenage Borough	42	15	4	2	53	23	9	6	6	34	30	24	10	8	87	53	82	
Morecambe	42	10	5	6	34	23	9	4	8	35	33	19	9	14	69	56	66	
Woking	42	10	5	6	41	29	8	5	8	30	34	18	10	14	71	63	64	
Northwich Victoria	42	11	5	5	31	20	6	7	8	30	34	17	12	13	61	54	63	
Farnborough Town	42	9	6	6	35	29	7	7	7	23	24	16	13	13	58	53	61	
Hednesford Town	42	10	7	4	28	17	6	5	10	24	33	16	12	14	52	50	60	
Telford United	42	6	7	8	21	30	10	3	8	25	26	16	10	16	46	56	58	
Gateshead	42	8	6	7	32	27	7	5	9	27	36	15	11	16	59	63	56	
Southport	42	8	5	8	27	28	7	5	9	24	33	15	10	17	51	61	55	
Rushden & Diamonds	42	8	8	5	30	25	6	3	12	31	38	14	11	17	61	63	53	
Stalybridge Celtic	42	9	5	7	35	29	5	5	11	18	29	14	10	18	53	58	52	
Kettering Town	42	9	4	8	30	28	5	5	11	23	34	14	9	19	53	62	51	
Hayes	42	7	7	7	27	21	5	7	9	27	34	12	14	16	54	55	50	
Slough Town	42	7	7	7	42	32	5	7	9	20	33	12	14	16	62	65	50	
Dover Athletic	42	7	9	5	32	30	5	5	11	25	38	12	14	16	57	68	50	
Welling United	42	9	2	10	24	26	4	7	10	26	34	13	9	20	50	60	48	
Halifax Town	42	9	5	7	39	37	3	7	11	16	37	12	12	18	55	74	48	
Bath City	42	9	5	7	27	28	3	6	12	26	52	12	11	19	53	80	47	R
Bromsgrove Rovers	42	8	4	9	29	30	4	1	16	12	37	12	5	25	41	67	41	R
Altrincham	42	6	3	12	25	34	3	9	9	24	39	9	12	21	49	73	39	R

F I N A L   T A B L E

Leek Town promoted from N.P.L., Cheltenham Town from Southern League, Yeovil Town from Isthmian League.

CUP COMPETITIONS

F.A.Cup

First Qualifying Round		
Oldham Town	Halifax Town	2-3
Brandon Utd	Morecambe	0-6
Yorkshire Amateurs	Stalybridge Celtic	0-1
Rossendale Utd	Southport	0-5
Rocester	Kettering Town	0-3
Westfields	Rushden & Diamonds	0-4
Wednesfield	Hednesford Town	0-0
Arlesey Town	Stevenage Borough	0-3
Three Bridges	Farnborough Town	1-6
Southwick	Welling United	1-2
Mile Oak	Dover Athletic	0-3
Devizes Town	Bath City	2-2
St Helens Town	Gateshead	0-0
Stotfold	Hayes	0-2
replay		
Gateshead	St Helens Town	5-1
Hednesford Town	Wednesfield	6-0
Bath City	Devizes Town	3-1
Second Qualifying Round		
Gateshead	Ossett Town	5-1
Halifax Town	Bishop Auckland	1-4
Morecambe	Guiseley	4-1
Stalybridge Celtic	Ossett Albion	4-1
Southport	Emley	1-1
Kettering Town	Atherstone Utd	0-0
Rushden & Diamonds	Gresley Rovers	4-0
Hednesford Town	Evesham Utd	6-1
Stevenage Borough	Baldock Town	1-1
Hayes	Grays Ath	1-1
Farnborough Town	Carshalton Ath	3-2
Welling United	Dulwich Hamlet	2-1
Dover Athletic	Aldershot Town	2-0
Bath City	Newport AFC	5-2
replay		
Emley	Southport	2-3
Atherstone Utd	Kettering Town	1-6
Baldock Town	Stevenage Borough	1-2
Grays Ath	Hayes	0-0
second replay		
Hayes	Grays Ath	2-0
Third Qualifying Round		
Gateshead	Workington	4-0
Morecambe	Flixton	6-2
Stalybridge Celtic	Ashton Utd	2-1
Southport	Burton Albion	4-1
Kettering Town	Bedworth Utd	0-1
Rushden & Diamonds	Bilston Town	1-0
Hednesford Town	Tamworth	4-2
Stevenage Borough	Braintree Town	3-1
Hayes	Chesham Utd	1-0
Farnborough Town	Bracknell Town	3-2
Welling United	Herne Bay	2-0
Dover Athletic	Hendon	0-1
Bath City	Cirencester Town	2-0
Fourth Qualifying Round		
Barrow	Altrincham	1-1
Bath City	Cheltenham Town	0-0
Cinderford Town	Farnborough Town	0-4
Gateshead	Consett	0-1
Gravesend & Northfleet	Stevenage Borough	1-5
Hayes	Slough Town	1-0
Hednesford Town	Telford Utd	2-0
Lancaster City	Morecambe	1-1
Rushden & Diamonds	Bognor Regis Town	2-0
Shepshed Dynamo	Bromsgrove Rovers	2-0
Spennymoor Utd	Southport	2-2
Staines Town	Welling United	0-1
Stalybridge Celtic	Leek Town	1-0
Witton Albion	Kidderminster Harriers	1-4
replay		
Altrincham	Barrow	4-0
Cheltenham Town	Bath City	4-1
Morecambe	Lancaster City	2-2
Southport	Spennymoor Utd	2-1
second replay		
Morecambe	Lancaster City	4-2

F.A.Cup

First Round		
Boreham Wood	Rushden & Diamonds	1-1
Boston Utd	Morecambe	3-0
Cambridge Utd	Welling United	3-0
Chester City	Stalybridge Celtic	3-0
Crewe Alexandra	Kidderminster Harriers	4-1
Farnborough Town	Barnet	2-2
Hednesford Town	Southport	2-1
Macclesfield Town	Rochdale	0-2
Northwich Victoria	Walsall	2-2
Preston North End	Altrincham	4-1
Stevenage Borough	Hayes	2-2
Woking	Millwall	2-2
replay		
Barnet	Farnborough Town	1-0
Hayes	Stevenage Borough	0-2
Millwall	Woking	0-1
Rushden & Diamonds	Boreham Wood	2-3
Walsall	Northwich Victoria	3-1
Second Round		
Blackpool	Hednesford Town	0-1
Cambridge Utd	Woking	0-2
Leyton Orient	Stevenage Borough	1-2
Third Round		
Stevenage Borough	Birmingham City	0-2
(Played at Birmingham)		
Coventry City	Woking	1-1
Hednesford Town	York City	1-0
replay		
Woking	Coventry City	1-2
Fourth Round		
Hednesford Town	Middlesbrough	2-3
(Played at Middlesbrough)		

League Cup

First Round			
Bath City	Welling Utd		0-2
Dover Athletic	Rushden & Diamonds		2-3
Farnborough Town	Hayes		0-1
Halifax Town	Altrincham	aet	0-1
Kettering Town	Slough Town		1-0
Stalybridge Celtic	Telford Utd	aet	3-1
Second Round			
Altrincham	Macclesfield Town		0-1
Bromsgrove Rovers	Northwich Victoria		3-1
Gateshead	Morecambe		1-3
Hednesford Town	Kidderminster Harriers		1-6
Kettering Town	Farnborough Town		0-2
Rushden & Diamonds	Stevenage Borough		1-0
Stalybridge Celtic	Southport		2-1
Woking	Welling Utd		0-2
Third Round			
Kidderminster Harriers	Rushden & Diamonds		1-0
Macclesfield Town	Bromsgrove Rovers		1-0
Morecambe	Stalybridge Celtic	aet	3-3
Welling Utd	Farnborough Town	aet	1-2
replay			
Stalybridge Celtic	Morecambe		0-1
Semi Final (two legs)			
Farnborough Town	Kidderminster Harriers		2-2
Kidderminster Harriers	Farnborough Town		1-1
(Kidderminster Harriers won on away goals)			
Morecambe	Macclesfield Town		0-2
Macclesfield Town	Morecambe		4-1
Final (two legs)			
Macclesfield Town	Kidderminster Harriers		1-1
Kidderminster Harriers	Macclesfield Town		0-0
(Kidderminster Harriers won on away goals)			

Challenge Shield

Stevenage Borough	Macclesfield Town	aet	1-2

First Round		
Bath City	Stevenage Borough	1-1
Bromsgrove Rovers	Merthyr Tydfil	2-1
Dover Athletic	Dagenham & Redbridge	0-2
Gateshead	Runcorn	1-2
Gresley Rovers	Altrincham	3-3
Guiseley	Telford United	2-1
Kettering Town	Chelmsford City	0-1
Kidderminster Harriers	Macclesfield Town	3-0
Morecambe	Chorley	3-1
Northwich Victoria	Hednesford Town	3-1
Raunds Town	Welling United	0-1
Rushden & Diamonds	Farnborough Town	1-2
Slough Town	Dorchester Town	2-2
Southport	Halesowen Town	0-0
Stalybridge Celtic	Halifax Town	0-1
Wokingham Town	Woking	0-1
Yeovil Town	Hayes	2-2
replay		
Stevenage Borough	Bath City	6-1
Altrincham	Gresley Rovers	1-0
Dorchester Town	Slough Town	1-1
Halesowen Town	Southport	0-2
Hayes	Yeovil Town	2-2
second replay		
Slough Town	Dorchester Town	1-2
Yeovil Town	Hayes	1-2
Second Round		
Bishop Auckland	Northwich Victoria	3-2
Boreham Wood	Stevenage Borough	0-1
Bradford PA	Morecambe	0-1
Bromsgrove Rovers	Hyde United	1-1
Colwyn Bay	Southport	2-0
Farnborough Town	Altrincham	0-2
Gloucester City	Halifax Town	3-0
Hayes	Runcorn	1-2
Kidderminster Harriers	Emley	0-0
St Albans City	Woking	1-1
Welling United	Guiseley	1-1
replay		
Hyde Utd	Bromsgrove Rovers	2-2
Emley	Kidderminster Harriers	1-5
Woking	St Albans City	3-1
Guiseley	Welling United	1-0
second replay		
Bromsgrove Rovers	Hyde United	0-2

Third Round		
Altrincham	Bishop Auckland	0-1
Dorchester Town	Woking	2-3
Heybridge Swifts	Kidderminster Harriers	3-0
Morecambe	Dagenham & Redbridge	0-0
Stevenage Borough	Guiseley	1-0
replay		
Dagenham & Redbridge	Morecambe	2-1
Fourth Round		
Heybridge Swifts	Woking	0-1
Stevenage Borough	Colwyn Bay	2-0
Semi final *(two legs)*		
Woking	Stevenage Borough	1-0
Stevenage Borough	Woking	2-1
replay		
Woking	Stevenage Borough	2-1
(Played at Watford)		
Final *(@ Wembley)*		
Dagenham & Redbridge	Woking	0-1

KETTERING TOWN 1
MACCLESFIELD TOWN 4
Macclesfield secure the Championship
on the final day of the season.

1997/98

One of football's most unpredictability. In terms ons, this has never been better triumph in 97-8. Before the season endearing qualities is its of the Conference champi- illustrated than in Halifax's started, the bookmakers were quoting odds of 66-1 on the Shaymen resuming Football League membership in May, and with good reason.

Since relegation from Division 3 in 1993, Halifax had never finished higher than eighth place. In the 1996-7 season, Conference status had only been preserved on the final day. Bath won their final match, meaning that only a win would be good enough for the Yorkshiremen. Trailing twice, they eventually secured a 4-2 victory over Stevenage, with the danger finally dispelled by a last minute Geoff Horsfield goal. Suitably inspired, Horsfield proceeded to score 30 goals in 1997-8 to make him the league's top goalscorer, and ably supported by Jamie Paterson, their progress to the title was relatively trouble free. The Shaymen were unbeaten until November 1st and were top of the table, save for two weeks, from early September. Victory over Rushden & Diamonds on 21st March opened up a 13 point lead over their opponents and when Kidderminster were beaten on 18th April, the Championship was secured, the earliest a title race had been resolved since 1992-3. They were defeated on only five occasions, twice after they had already been crowned Champions.

Cheltenham Town had their best season thus far in the Conference. They were promoted from the Dr Martens (Southern) League when Gresley Rovers were unable to step up as Champions. They capitalised on their good fortune by finishing as runners-up for the second successive season, winning the F.A.Trophy and enjoying their best ever F.A.Cup run, by progressing from the first qualifying round to a third round replay with Reading. They had a seventeen game unbeaten run, from 25th August to New Years Day, but from then on their challenge faded as cup-ties caused a fixture backlog, which resulted in 11 games being played in the final 26 days of the season. However, during the last week they picked up 10 points to overtake both Rushden & Diamonds and Woking, to claim second place.

Stevenage gained F.A.Cup headlines, not only for their on-field performances, but also for a war of words with 4th round opponents, Newcastle United. Stevenage decided to play the tie at their own ground and installed 1,400 temporary seats to increase the capacity to 8,000. Newcastle claimed they were worried about crowd safety and appealed to the F.A. for a change of venue. Stevenage countered that in reality, the Magpies did not want a repeat of their infamous defeat at Hereford United, 26 years earlier. The F.A sided with 'the Boro' and after a 1-1 draw the Premiership club won the replay with the aid of a goal which subsequent television analysis suggested may not have crossed the line.

1997/98 Season Results Grid

	Cheltenham Town	Dover Athletic	Farnborough Town	Gateshead	Halifax Town	Hayes	Hednesford Town	Hereford Utd	Kettering Town	Kidderminster Harriers	Leek Town	Morecambe	Northwich Victoria	Rushden & Diamonds	Slough Town	Southport	Stalybridge Celtic	Stevenage Borough	Telford United	Welling United	Woking	Yeovil Town
Cheltenham Town	X	3-1	1-0	2-0	4-0	2-1	1-0	1-2	2-0	0-1	1-1	2-1	3-2	2-0	1-1	2-0	2-0	1-1	3-1	1-1	3-2	2-0
Dover Athletic	3-0	X	2-2	0-1	0-1	1-0	1-3	1-1	0-0	0-4	2-1	2-3	4-0	0-3	2-1	3-1	3-1	1-1	6-3	2-1	0-2	1-0
Farnborough Town	1-2	1-0	X	4-0	1-2	0-2	1-3	0-2	3-2	3-3	2-0	0-2	2-3	2-0	1-0	3-2	6-0	1-2	1-0	0-0	3-0	2-2
Gateshead	0-0	1-2	3-0	X	2-2	1-1	2-5	1-1	2-0	2-0	0-2	1-4	2-2	2-1	5-1	0-2	3-3	2-1	0-2	1-1	1-2	0-3
Halifax Town	1-1	1-1	1-0	2-0	X	1-1	1-1	3-0	3-0	2-1	2-1	5-1	4-2	2-0	1-0	4-3	3-1	4-0	6-1	1-0	1-0	3-1
Hayes	1-1	0-0	3-1	1-0	1-2	X	4-0	2-0	0-1	1-1	3-1	0-3	1-1	1-2	0-1	2-0	1-2	1-3	2-1	3-1	3-0	6-4
Hednesford Town	0-1	1-0	1-0	3-0	0-0	2-1	X	1-1	1-1	3-0	1-0	0-1	2-0	0-1	2-1	2-1	1-0	2-1	1-0	3-2	1-1	1-0
Hereford Utd	3-2	0-1	2-1	1-0	0-0	3-0	2-1	X	3-2	1-0	1-0	2-2	1-1	1-1	3-0	0-2	1-1	1-2	2-1	1-1	1-2	2-1
Kettering Town	0-1	2-1	2-1	3-0	1-1	1-1	1-2	1-2	X	2-2	1-1	1-3	0-4	3-3	2-1	3-1	2-0	1-3	0-1	1-1	0-1	1-1
Kidderminster Harriers	1-2	3-3	2-0	1-1	0-2	1-0	1-1	1-4	4-1	X	1-1	1-4	1-1	2-2	0-1	1-5	5-0	1-3	1-1	2-1	1-1	3-1
Leek Town	0-0	5-1	3-1	2-2	2-0	1-2	3-3	2-2	0-4	0-0	X	1-1	1-1	2-0	0-2	0-1	2-2	2-1	3-1	1-2	2-0	2-0
Morecambe	1-0	3-3	1-1	2-0	1-1	0-2	1-3	1-5	1-3	3-1	1-1	X	3-1	3-1	2-1	2-0	3-1	0-2	1-0	4-2	1-2	1-0
Northwich Victoria	2-1	2-1	3-3	1-1	2-0	1-1	1-1	0-2	0-0	1-1	3-1	5-0	X	2-4	0-1	1-1	2-2	5-1	0-2	2-1	0-2	2-1
Rushden & Diamonds	4-1	4-1	5-5	3-2	4-0	1-3	1-1	1-0	4-1	0-1	3-3	0-1	3-3	X	0-1	3-0	2-0	3-2	0-1	2-1	2-2	2-2
Slough Town	1-2	2-4	1-0	1-0	1-1	0-0	2-0	3-0	1-1	2-0	1-1	3-3	3-0	1-2	X	1-0	4-0	3-1	1-0	1-2	1-3	1-0
Southport	1-2	0-1	3-1	3-1	0-0	0-2	4-1	0-0	2-1	1-2	2-2	1-1	0-2	3-2	1-2	X	4-2	1-0	1-2	3-1	0-0	2-1
Stalybridge Celtic	1-4	1-0	1-1	2-2	0-1	1-1	1-1	2-3	3-4	2-1	6-1	3-1	0-1	2-4	0-1	1-3	X	1-1	1-2	2-1	0-3	3-2
Stevenage Borough	1-2	2-2	5-0	6-1	1-2	1-5	1-1	2-0	0-0	3-1	1-1	0-3	1-3	2-1	4-2	1-0	1-1	X	1-1	0-0	0-0	2-1
Telford United	0-0	0-1	0-1	4-4	0-3	1-0	1-1	0-0	1-1	1-1	3-0	1-3	2-1	4-2	1-0	2-2	1-0	3-0	X	0-3	0-3	1-4
Welling United	2-1	2-2	1-0	2-0	6-2	2-0	3-2	3-0	2-2	0-3	2-0	2-2	0-1	0-1	1-1	3-5	1-0	1-0	4-1	X	1-1	1-3
Woking	2-0	4-0	3-0	3-1	2-2	3-0	4-2	3-1	0-1	0-1	5-2	0-2	1-0	0-2	2-1	1-1	3-1	5-3	1-1	3-1	X	2-0
Yeovil Town	3-1	4-1	0-1	6-3	0-1	4-3	1-0	2-0	2-0	1-0	3-1	2-3	2-2	1-2	2-1	0-0	2-0	2-1	5-3	1-1	2-0	X

Final Table

	P	Home					Away					Total						
		W	D	L	F	A	W	D	L	F	A	W	D	L	F	A	Pts	
Halifax Town	42	17	4	0	51	15	8	8	5	23	28	25	12	5	74	43	87	P
Cheltenham Town	42	15	4	2	39	15	8	5	8	24	28	23	9	10	63	43	78	
Woking	42	14	3	4	47	22	8	5	8	25	24	22	8	12	72	46	74	
Rushden & Diamonds	42	12	4	5	44	26	11	1	9	35	31	23	5	14	79	57	74	
Morecambe	42	11	4	6	35	30	10	6	5	42	34	21	10	11	77	64	73	
Hereford Utd	42	11	7	3	30	19	7	6	8	26	30	18	13	11	56	49	67	
Hednesford Town	42	14	4	3	28	12	4	8	9	31	38	18	12	12	59	50	66	
Slough Town	42	10	6	5	34	21	8	4	9	24	28	18	10	14	58	49	64	R
Northwich Victoria	42	8	9	4	34	24	7	6	8	29	35	15	15	12	63	59	60	
Welling United	42	11	5	5	39	27	6	4	11	25	35	17	9	16	64	62	60	
Yeovil Town	42	14	3	4	45	24	3	5	13	28	39	17	8	17	73	63	59	
Hayes	42	10	4	7	36	25	6	6	9	26	27	16	10	16	62	52	58	
Dover Athletic	42	10	4	7	34	29	5	6	10	26	41	15	10	17	60	70	55	
Kettering Town	42	8	6	7	29	29	5	7	9	24	31	13	13	16	53	60	52	
Stevenage Borough	42	8	8	5	35	27	5	4	12	24	36	13	12	17	59	63	51	
Southport	42	9	5	7	32	26	4	6	11	24	32	13	11	18	56	58	50	
Kidderminster Harriers	42	6	8	7	32	31	5	6	10	24	32	11	14	17	56	63	47	
Farnborough Town	42	10	3	8	37	27	2	5	14	19	43	12	8	22	56	70	44	
Leek Town	42	8	8	5	34	26	2	6	13	18	41	10	14	18	52	67	44	
Telford United	42	6	7	8	25	31	4	5	12	28	45	10	12	20	53	76	42	
Gateshead	42	7	6	8	32	35	1	5	15	19	52	8	11	23	51	87	35	R
Stalybridge Celtic	42	6	5	10	33	38	1	3	17	15	55	7	8	27	48	93	29	R

Barrow promoted from N.P.L., Forest Green Rovers from Southern League, Kingstonian from Isthmian League.

F I N A L   T A B L E

F.A.Cup

First Qualifying Round		
Gateshead	Matlock Town	2-0
Halifax Town	Droylsden	4-1
Winsford Utd	Leek Town	1-0
Telford United	Bedworth Utd	1-2
Kettering Town	Mirrlees Blackstone	1-0
Welling United	Leyton Pennant	3-0
Baldock Town	Slough Town	0-0
Uxbridge	Dover Athletic	0-2
Thatcham Town	Cheltenham Town	0-1
Yeovil Town	Witney Town	1-1
replay		
Slough Town	Baldock Town	5-0
Witney Town	Yeovil Town	1-2
Second Qualifying Round		
Gateshead	Gainsborough Trinity	1-4
Halifax Town	Leigh RMI	4-0
Kettering Town	Cambridge City	1-1
Welling United	Sutton Utd	2-2
Walton & Hersham	Slough Town	0-0
Dover Athletic	Kingstonian	0-4
Merthyr Tydfil	Cheltenham Town	0-2
Worcester City	Yeovil Town	1-2
replay		
Cambridge City	Kettering Town	2-4
Sutton Utd	Welling United	2-1
Slough Town	Walton & Hersham	0-0
(Slough Town won 3-2 on pens)		
Third Qualifying Round		
Halifax Town	Ossett Town	5-0
Kettering Town	Hinckley Utd	0-1
Slough Town	Tilbury	6-1
Cheltenham Town	Paulton Rovers	5-0
Yeovil Town	Chippenham Town	4-0
Fourth Qualifying Round		
Altrincham	Morecambe	0-2
Blyth Spartans	Kidderminster Harriers	2-1
Bognor Regis Town	Farnborough Town	0-0
Cheltenham Town	Sutton Utd	1-0
Gainsborough Trinity	Halifax Town	2-1
Halesowen Town	Northwich Victoria	0-2
Rushden & Diamonds	Boreham Wood	1-1
Sittingbourne	Hereford United	2-2
Slough Town	Kingstonian	2-1
Southport	North Ferriby Utd	2-0
Stalybridge Celtic	Solihull Borough	3-3
Yeovil Town	Hayes	1-1
replay		
Boreham Wood	Rushden & Diamonds	1-0
Farnborough Town	Bognor Regis Town	2-1
Hayes	Yeovil Town	1-0
Hereford United	Sittingbourne	3-0
Solihull Borough	Stalybridge Celtic	4-3
First Round		
Carshalton Ath	Stevenage Borough	0-0
Cheltenham Town	Tiverton Town	2-1
Chesterfield	Northwich Victoria	1-0
Farnborough Town	Dagenham & Redbridge	0-1
Hayes	Boreham Wood	0-1
Hereford United	Brighton & Hove Albion	2-1
Hull City	Hednesford Town	0-2
Morecambe	Emley	1-1
Slough Town	Cardiff City	1-1
Southport	York City	0-4
Woking	Southend Utd	0-2
replay		
Cardiff City	Slough Town	3-2
Emley	Morecambe	3-3
(Emley won 3-1 on pens)		
Stevenage Borough	Carshalton Ath	5-0

F.A.Cup

Second Round		
Cambridge Utd	Stevenage Borough	1-1
Cheltenham Town	Boreham Wood	1-1
Colchester Utd	Hereford United	1-1
Hednesford Town	Darlington	0-1
replay		
Boreham Wood	Cheltenham Town	0-2
Hereford United	Colchester Utd	1-1
(Hereford United won 5-4 on pens)		
Stevenage Borough	Cambridge Utd	2-1
Third Round		
Cheltenham Town	Reading	1-1
Hereford United	Tranmere Rovers	0-3
Swindon Town	Stevenage Borough	1-2
replay		
Reading	Cheltenham Town	2-1
Fouth Round		
Stevenage Borough	Newcastle Utd	1-1
replay		
Newcastle Utd	Stevenage Borough	2-1

League Cup

First Round		
Dover Athletic	Kettering Town	1-3
Hayes	Rushden & Diamonds	2-0
Leek Town	Southport	3-1
Slough Town	Welling Utd	1-0
Stalybridge Celtic	Halifax Town	3-1
Yeovil Town	Cheltenham Town	3-1
Second Round		
Kidderminster Harriers	Hednesford Town	0-2
Hayes	Slough Town	2-0
Morecambe	Leek Town	3-2
Woking	Kettering Town	4-0
Stalybridge Celtic	Gateshead	3-4
Telford Utd	Northwich Victoria	1-2
Farnborough Town	Hereford United	2-1
Stevenage Borough	Yeovil Town	0-3
Third Round		
Hayes	Yeovil Town	3-0
Northwich Victoria	Hednesford Town	3-2
Gateshead	Morecambe	1-1
Woking	Farnborough Town	3-1
replay		
Morecambe	Gateshead	3-1
Semi Final *(two legs)*		
Hayes	Woking	0-2
Woking	Hayes	3-1
Morecambe	Northwich Victoria	3-0
Northwich Victoria	Morecambe	3-1
Final *(two legs)*		
Morecambe	Woking	1-1
Woking	Morecambe	1-1
(Morecambe won 4-3 on pens)		

Challenge Shield

Macclesfield Town	Woking	3-1

First Round

Enfield	Cheltenham Town	1-1
Gresley Rovers	Leek Town	4-4
Guiseley	Telford United	0-0
Halifax Town	Blyth Spartans	2-1
Hayes	Cambridge City	3-2
Hednesford Town	Gainsborough Town	2-1
Hereford United	Dulwich Hamlet	3-0
Kettering Town	Dorchester Town	1-0
Kidderminster Harriers	Berkhamsted Town	4-1
Lancaster City	Northwich Victoria	0-3
Morecambe	Solihull Borough	3-2
Purfleet	Dover Athletic	0-1
Rushden & Diamonds	Farnborough Town	3-2
Southport	Winsford Utd	3-0
Stalybridge Celtic	Gateshead	2-4
Stevenage Borough	Chesham Utd	2-2
Welling United	Slough Town	1-1
Woking	Margate	0-1
Yeovil Town	Yeading	0-0

replay

Cheltenham Town	Enfield	5-1
Leek Town	Gresley Rovers	3-1
Telford United	Guiseley	3-2
Chesham Utd	Stevenage Borough	0-3
Slough Town	Welling United	2-1
Yeading	Yeovil Town	1-0

Second Round

Altrincham	Morecambe	2-0
Cheltenham Town	Rushden & Diamonds	3-1
Gateshead	Stevenage Borough	1-2
Halifax Town	Slough Town	1-1
Hayes	Kidderminster Harriers	5-0
Hednesford Town	Leek Town	5-0
Hereford United	Dover Athletic	0-2
Northwich Victoria	Kettering Town	4-0
Telford United	Ashton Utd	0-1
Yeading	Southport	0-6

replay

Slough Town	Halifax Town	2-0

Third Round

Altrincham	Southport	0-2
Ashton Utd	Cheltenham Town	0-1
Barrow	Northwich Victoria	1-0
Grantham Town	Hednesford Town	2-1
Hayes	Bashley	2-0
Hyde Utd	Dover Athletic	0-2
Slough Town	Boreham Wood	1-1
Stevenage Borough	Gloucester City	1-1

replay

Boreham Wood	Slough Town	1-2
Gloucester City	Stevenage Borough	1-2

Fourth Round

Cheltenham Town	Hayes	1-0
Dover Athletic	Barrow	1-1
Grantham Town	Southport	1-1
Stevenage Borough	Slough Town	0-1

replay

Southport	Grantham Town	3-1
Barrow	Dover Athletic	0-0
(Dover Ath won 5-4 pens)		

Semi final *(two legs)*

Slough Town	Southport	0-1
Southport	Slough Town	1-1
Cheltenham Town	Dover Athletic	2-1
Dover Athletic	Cheltenham Town	2-2

Final *(@ Wembley)*

Cheltenham Town	Southport	1-0

Halifax Town

Saturday 18th April 1998, Kick-Off: 3.00pm
Match Sponsors: Wyvern F.M.
The Harrier Issue No. 25   Price: £1.50

KIDDERMINSTER HARRIERS 0
HALIFAX TOWN 2
*Halifax wrap up the title
with time to spare*

81

1998/99

The season started with pre-season favourites, Rushden & Diamonds, doing their best to prove the bookies right. They won their first six matches, with a goal tally of 20-2, but were only successful once in the next half dozen. In comparison, Cheltenham won only two points from their first three matches, but then entered a 12 match unbeaten run and by September 22nd they were league leaders and were never out of the top two for the rest of the season.

When the Gloucestershire side were dislodged from the top, it was Kettering Town who replaced them. Having only survived the previous season due to vastly improved post-Christmas results, Peter Morris had rebuilt his team to good effect. However, they had always played three or four games more than their rivals, and Cheltenham's consistency meant they were able to take the title with three games to spare. A crowd of 6,150 gathered at Whaddon Road on April 22nd to witness the celebration, when a goal by Michael Duff seven minutes into injury time secured a 3-2 victory over Yeovil Town and the Championship.

Despite their relegation from Division 3, things were looking a lot brighter for Doncaster Rovers. Under the previous stewardship of Messrs. Richardson and Weaver the trials and tribulations of the club had looked likely to spell the end for the Rovers. However, with their new owner and the return of the prodigal sons, Ian and Glynn Snodin, as a managerial team, hopes were high. Initially the signings of Neville Southall, Steve Nicol and John Sheridan together with other experienced Football League players, while raising the clubs profile, proved unsuccessful, with only one win in the first nine matches. Over the months, the blend was adjusted and while the side were never out of the bottom eight, the Endsleigh Challenge Trophy was won by beating Farnborough Town over two legs in the final. The supporters responded magnificently with home league gates averaging 3,380, nearly 98% up on the previous season.

For the second season running a club was expelled from the Conference. In 1998 Slough Town were relegated as they were unable to comply with the requirements on seating capacity. They were required to have 499 seats by the 31st May 1998 deadline, but due to problems with the local council, they could not guarantee fulfilling the requirements. This season also saw the demise of Barrow after one season. Their financial plight led to the club going into receivership in January 1999. The chairman and manager left and in the face of adversity they struggled to maintain their status on the pitch, a fight they won on the last day of the season. A new club Barrow (AFC) 1999 was formed, but the Conference felt they did not meet the financial criteria and after much argument they were handed a berth in the Unibond League.

1998/99 Season Results Grid

	Barrow	Cheltenham Town	Doncaster Rovers	Dover Athletic	Farnborough Town	Forest Green Rovers	Hayes	Hednesford Town	Hereford Utd	Kettering Town	Kidderminster Harriers	Kingstonian	Leek Town	Morecambe	Northwich Victoria	Rushden & Diamonds	Southport	Stevenage Borough	Telford United	Welling United	Woking	Yeovil Town
Barrow	X	1-1	2-2	1-0	1-0	2-1	0-1	0-2	0-1	0-0	0-4	0-1	2-1	2-1	0-1	0-2	0-0	0-1	1-1	2-1	1-2	2-0
Cheltenham Town	4-1	X	2-1	1-1	0-0	1-1	3-3	0-0	2-2	3-0	1-0	1-0	0-0	4-1	0-1	1-0	3-0	3-0	2-0	0-0	1-1	3-2
Doncaster Rovers	2-1	2-2	X	5-4	1-2	0-1	0-1	0-1	3-1	1-1	1-0	0-1	0-1	2-1	2-2	1-1	0-1	0-0	2-1	4-1	0-1	0-2
Dover Athletic	1-1	0-0	1-0	X	2-1	1-1	0-0	0-0	3-1	0-1	0-1	5-1	2-1	2-3	0-0	1-1	2-1	1-1	1-1	1-2	3-2	1-2
Farnborough Town	2-2	2-4	1-0	1-2	X	2-2	1-5	0-1	0-4	1-3	2-4	4-2	2-1	1-6	1-6	1-2	1-1	1-0	3-1	1-1	2-1	0-0
Forest Green Rovers	1-1	1-2	0-0	0-1	0-0	X	1-2	1-0	2-1	1-0	5-0	1-0	3-1	2-2	3-1	1-0	1-2	1-1	3-2	0-2	1-2	1-1
Hayes	1-0	3-2	1-2	1-0	0-3	1-0	X	1-0	1-2	0-2	2-1	3-0	2-0	1-2	1-0	2-1	3-0	2-2	4-3	1-2	2-2	1-1
Hednesford Town	1-0	3-2	1-1	1-2	0-0	1-1	0-0	X	3-1	0-2	2-1	1-2	1-1	1-0	1-1	3-1	2-2	1-1	3-2	2-1	2-1	2-3
Hereford Utd	3-0	0-2	1-0	2-0	2-0	4-0	0-1	0-0	X	0-2	1-3	2-0	1-0	2-2	3-2	2-2	0-1	0-0	0-0	0-1	0-1	0-1
Kettering Town	2-0	0-2	0-1	0-2	4-1	2-1	1-0	1-0	1-1	X	1-0	2-0	2-1	6-0	0-0	0-0	1-0	1-2	2-1	1-1	3-0	1-2
Kidderminster Harriers	1-2	0-1	3-3	1-0	2-0	2-2	0-1	1-2	1-0	1-1	X	0-1	1-2	5-2	4-0	0-0	2-1	2-0	3-0	0-1	3-2	0-1
Kingstonian	5-1	1-2	2-1	1-0	1-1	0-1	1-1	1-1	2-0	1-2	1-0	X	3-0	0-0	1-1	1-5	0-2	1-0	1-0	2-1	0-0	0-0
Leek Town	3-1	0-2	1-1	2-0	4-0	0-2	1-4	1-3	3-2	1-2	1-4	2-2	X	7-0	0-3	2-3	0-0	1-1	1-1	2-4	0-3	2-4
Morecambe	3-2	0-2	1-2	0-4	1-0	3-1	2-3	3-1	1-0	3-1	2-1	0-0	2-2	X	3-1	2-3	1-1	1-1	0-1	2-1	0-1	1-1
Northwich Victoria	1-0	1-0	1-3	2-0	3-0	1-0	2-1	1-1	1-0	4-0	1-0	2-3	0-2	1-1	X	2-1	1-2	0-1	1-1	3-0	0-3	1-2
Rushden & Diamonds	4-0	1-2	1-3	2-2	1-0	4-0	5-0	1-1	1-2	1-1	0-0	2-0	3-1	1-2	1-2	X	3-1	2-1	2-3	3-1	2-0	1-2
Southport	0-4	0-2	3-2	3-0	2-2	1-1	1-2	1-1	0-0	0-1	1-1	1-1	3-1	1-0	2-2	0-1	X	1-1	2-1	5-2	0-0	2-3
Stevenage Borough	1-2	2-2	2-0	1-0	3-1	1-1	2-1	3-1	0-3	2-2	3-0	3-3	2-0	1-3	0-0	0-0	2-0	X	2-2	1-1	5-0	1-1
Telford United	1-1	0-3	0-2	1-1	3-1	1-2	2-0	1-1	0-2	0-0	1-1	2-0	2-3	3-0	2-2	0-3	2-1	0-3	X	0-0	1-1	2-2
Welling United	1-1	2-1	1-1	0-3	0-0	0-2	0-2	1-1	2-2	0-2	0-1	1-3	1-0	3-2	2-3	0-1	2-1	1-1	0-1	X	0-1	1-2
Woking	2-3	1-0	2-0	1-2	4-0	1-1	2-0	2-1	0-1	0-0	2-1	0-1	1-0	0-3	2-1	1-1	2-3	1-2	3-0	0-0	X	0-0
Yeovil Town	1-0	2-2	2-2	1-1	6-3	0-4	1-1	1-2	3-0	2-1	3-1	1-3	2-0	0-1	1-2	0-1	3-1	1-3	4-0	1-3	0-1	X

Final Table

	P	Home					Away					Total					
		W	D	L	F	A	W	D	L	F	A	W	D	L	F	A	Pts
Cheltenham Town	42	11	9	1	35	14	11	5	5	36	22	22	14	6	71	36	80	P
Kettering Town	42	11	5	5	31	16	11	5	5	27	21	22	10	10	58	37	76
Hayes	42	12	3	6	34	25	10	5	6	29	25	22	8	12	63	50	74
Rushden & Diamonds	42	11	4	6	41	22	9	8	4	30	20	20	12	10	71	42	72
Yeovil Town	42	8	4	9	35	32	12	7	2	33	22	20	11	11	68	54	71
Stevenage Borough	42	9	9	3	37	23	8	8	5	25	22	17	17	8	62	45	68
Northwich Victoria	42	11	3	7	29	21	8	6	7	31	30	19	9	14	60	51	66
Kingstonian	42	9	7	5	25	19	8	6	7	25	30	17	13	12	50	49	64
Woking	42	9	5	7	27	20	9	4	8	24	25	18	9	15	51	45	63
Hednesford Town	42	9	8	4	30	24	6	8	7	19	20	15	16	11	49	44	61
Dover Athletic	42	7	9	5	27	21	8	4	9	27	27	15	13	14	54	48	58
Forest Green Rovers	42	9	5	7	28	22	6	8	7	27	28	15	13	14	55	50	58
Hereford Utd	42	9	5	7	25	17	6	5	10	24	29	15	10	17	49	46	55
Morecambe	42	9	5	7	31	29	6	3	12	29	47	15	8	19	60	76	53
Kidderminster Harriers	42	9	4	8	32	22	5	5	11	24	30	14	9	19	56	52	51
Doncaster Rovers	42	7	5	9	26	26	5	7	9	25	29	12	12	18	51	55	48
Telford United	42	7	8	6	24	24	3	8	10	20	36	10	16	16	44	60	46
Southport	42	6	9	6	29	28	4	6	11	18	31	10	15	17	47	59	45
Barrow	42	7	5	9	17	23	4	5	12	23	40	11	10	21	40	63	43	R
Welling United	42	4	7	10	18	30	5	7	9	26	35	9	14	19	44	65	41
Leek Town	42	5	5	11	34	42	3	3	15	14	34	8	8	26	48	76	32	R
Farnborough Town	42	6	5	10	29	48	1	6	14	12	41	7	11	24	41	89	32	R

FINAL TABLE

Altrincham promoted from N.P.L., Nuneaton Borough from Southern League, Sutton United from Isthmian League.

F.A.Cup

Third Qualifying Round		
Doncaster Rovers	Flixton	2-0
Gateshead	Barrow	2-1
Morecambe	Farsley Celtic	4-2
Droylsden	Northwich Victoria	2-0
Ramsbottom Utd	Southport	0-5
Kidderminster Harriers	Blakenall	3-1
Sutton Coldfield Town	Telford United	1-1
Congleton Town	Hednesford Town	1-1
Buxton	Leek Town	0-0
Hastings Town	Yeovil Town	0-3
Hereford United	Newport (IOW)	2-3
Gravesend & Northfleet	Dover Athletic	0-0
Farnborough Town	Heybridge Swifts	2-0
Taunton Town	Kettering Town	4-3
Welling United	Weymouth	3-2
Barnstaple Town	Cheltenham Town	0-1
Rushden & Diamonds	Forest Green Rovers	2-0
Hayes	Bromley	1-0
Maidenhead Utd	Kingstonian	2-4
Minehead	Woking	1-5
Witney Town	Stevenage Borough	1-2
replay		
Telford United	Sutton Coldfield Town	1-0
Hednesford Town	Congleton Town	1-0
Leek Town	Buxton	3-0
Dover Athletic	Gravesend & Northfleet	3-2
Fourth Qualifying Round		
Southport	Stourbridge	4-0
Leek Town	Lancaster City	0-3
Telford United	Burscough	2-1
Doncaster Rovers	Guiseley	3-1
Morecambe	Hednesford Town	1-2
Aldershot Town	Woking	0-0
St Albans City	Kingstonian	1-1
Havant & Waterlooville	Hayes	2-2
Dagenham & Redbridge	Stevenage Borough	0-3
Basingstoke Town	Dover Athletic	2-2
Welling United	Whyteleafe	3-1
Leatherhead	Rushden & Diamonds	1-1
Kidderminster Harriers	Gloucester City	2-1
Farnborough Town	Yeovil Town	1-3
Cheltenham Town	Taunton Town	3-2
replay		
Woking	Aldershot Town	2-1
Kingstonian	St Albans City	1-1
(Kingstonian won 5-4 on pens)		
Hayes	Havant & Waterlooville	1-1
(Hayes won 4-3 on pens)		
Dover Athletic	Basingstoke Town	1-2
Rushden & Diamonds	Leatherhead	4-0
First Round		
Bristol Rovers	Welling United	3-0
Cheltenham Town	Lincoln City	0-1
Dulwich Hamlet	Southport	0-1
Hednesford Town	Barnet	3-1
Kingstonian	Burton Albion	1-0
Mansfield Town	Hayes	2-1
Plymouth Argyle	Kidderminster Harriers	0-0
Runcorn	Stevenage Borough	1-1
Rushden & Diamonds	Shrewsbury Town	1-0
Southend Utd	Doncaster Rovers	0-1
Telford United	Cambridge Utd	0-2
Woking	Scunthorpe Utd	0-1
Yeovil Town	West Auckland Town	2-2

F.A.Cup

First Round - replay		
Kidderminster Harriers	Plymouth Argyle	0-0
(abandoned half time, fog)		
Kidderminster Harriers	Plymouth Argyle	0-0
(Plymoutn Argyle won 5-4 on pens)		
Stevenage Borough	Runcorn	2-0
West Auckland Town	Yeovil Town	1-1
(Yeovil Town won 5-3 on pens)		
Second Round		
Cardiff City	Hednesford Town	3-1
Doncaster Rovers	Rushden & Diamonds	0-0
Kingstonian	Leyton Orient	0-0
Lincoln City	Stevenage Borough	4-1
Mansfield Town	Southport	1-2
Yeovil Town	Northampton Town	2-0
replay		
Leyton Orient	Kingstonian	2-1
Rushden & Diamonds	Doncaster Rovers	4-2
Third Round		
Cardiff City	Yeovil Town	1-1
Rushden & Diamonds	Leeds Utd	0-0
Southport	Leyton Orient	0-2
replay		
Leeds Utd	Rushden & Diamonds	3-1
Yeovil Town	Cardiff City	1-2

League Cup

First Round		
Kettering Town	Hayes	0-3
Barrow	Leek Town	2-1
Dover Athletic	Stevenage Borough	2-3
Farnborough Town	Kingstonian	4-2
Forest Green Rovers	Kidderminster Harriers	2-4
Southport	Telford United	2-1
Second Round		
Hayes	Welling United	3-2
Morecambe	Barrow	2-0
Stevenage Borough	Cheltenham Town	0-1
Doncaster Rovers	Southport	2-0
Hednesford Town	Northwich Victoria	1-3
Farnborough Town	Rushden & Diamonds	3-1
Kidderminster Harriers	Hereford United	1-2
Woking	Yeovil Town	3-0
Third Round		
Cheltenham Town	Hayes	2-1
Doncaster Rovers	Northwich Victoria	3-2
Farnborough Town	Woking	4-3
Hereford United	Morecambe	3-2
Semi Final *(two legs)*		
Farnborough Town	Cheltenham Town	2-0
(only one leg played)		
Morecambe	Doncaster Rovers	1-2
Doncaster Rovers	Morecambe	3-0
Final *(two legs)*		
Farnborough Town	Doncaster Rovers	0-1
Doncaster Rovers	Farnborough Town	3-0

Challenge Shield

Cheltenham Town	Halifax Town	0-1

Second Round		
Kidderminster Harriers	Lincoln Utd	2-2
Doncaster Rovers	Frickley Ath	0-2
Bromsgrove Rovers	Hednesford Town	1-2
Atherstone Utd	Southport	0-0
Northwich Victoria	Netherfield Kendal	3-0
Blakenall	Telford United	1-1
Ashton Utd	Leek Town	1-0
Leigh RMI	Morecambe	4-1
Stevenage Borough	Uxbridge	4-0
Rushden & Diamonds	Bath City	2-0
Hayes	Folkestone Invicta	1-1
Hucknall Town	Barrow	2-1
Gloucester City	Kingstonian	1-2
Dover Athletic	Welling United	4-1
Kettering Town	Andover	4-0
Forest Green Rovers	Boreham Wood	4-1
Yeovil Town	Tonbridge Angels	1-0
Woking	Salisbury City	2-1
Farnborough Town	Dartford	1-1
Cheltenham Town	Bashley	2-1
Hereford United	Hitchin Town	1-1
replay		
Lincoln Utd	Kidderminster Harriers	2-1
Southport	Atherstone Utd	2-1
Telford United	Blakenall	2-1
Folkestone Invicta	Hayes	3-2
Dartford	Farnborough Town	1-2
Hitchin Town	Hereford United	2-1
Third Round		
Radcliffe Borough	Northwich Victoria	1-2
Colwyn Bay	Hednesford Town	1-1
Droylsden	Telford United	2-3
Leigh RMI	Southport	0-1
Basingstoke Town	Yeovil Town	0-2
Stevenage Borough	Dover Athletic	3-2
Forest Green Rovers	Witney Town	4-0
Kingstonian	Kettering Town	5-2
Cheltenham Town	Canvey Island	2-1
Slough Town	Rushden & Diamonds	1-2
Dagenham & Redbridge	Farnborough Town	1-1
Woking	Folkestone Invicta	8-4
replay		
Hednesford Town	Colwyn Bay	2-2
(Colwyn Bay won 5-4 on pens)		
Farnborough Town	Dagenham & Redbridge	1-1
(Dagenham & Redbridge won 4-2 pens)		
Fourth Round		
Cheltenham Town	Stevenage Borough	0-0
Dagenham & Redbridge	Telford United	4-0
Northwich Victoria	Worcester City	1-0
Runcorn	Southport	2-3
Weymouth	Forest Green Rovers	1-2
Whyteleafe	Kingstonian	0-3
Woking	Rushden & Diamonds	0-0
Yeovil Town	Hinckley Utd	3-2

replay		
Rushden & Diamonds	Woking	1-2
Stevenage Borough	Cheltenham Town	0-0
(Cheltenham Town won 5-4 on pens)		
Fifth Round		
Cheltenham Town	Hendon	3-0
Hitchin Town	Forest Green Rovers	1-2
Kingstonian	Yeovil Town	1-0
Northwich Victoria	Colwyn Bay	3-1
Woking	Southport	0-0
replay		
Southport	Woking	1-0
Sixth Round		
Emley	Cheltenham Town	0-1
Forest Green Rovers	Southport	4-1
Northwich Victoria	Kingstonian	0-2
Semi Final *(two legs)*		
Kingstonian	Cheltenham Town	2-2
Cheltenham Town	Kingstonian	1-3
St Albans City	Forest Green Rovers	1-1
Forest Green Rovers	St Albans City	3-2
Final *(@ Wembley)*		
Forest Green Rovers	Kingstonian	0-1

RUSHDEN & DIAMONDS 0
LEEDS UNITED 0
Diamonds produce their best
ever F.A. Cup performance.

1999/00

Six years after having been denied a place in the Football League, Kidderminster Harriers were finally rewarded for their endeavours with promotion to Division 3. The portents at the start of the campaign were not good. The previous two seasons had seen the Harriers languish in 17th and 15th position and five defeats in the first eight games did nothing to suggest that the situation was improving. It was Stevenage who set the pace with six straight wins, a run ended by the Harriers in early September.

As 'Boro' subsequently faded, Kingstonian, Nuneaton, Rushden & Diamonds and Yeovil all had spells at the top of the league, but no one team could break clear. This played into Kidderminster's hands and once an early bout of injuries had cleared, Jan Molby's side embarked upon a devastating run, losing only two of their last 27 games, one of which was suffered on the day that promotion was secured. They were spared any fixture congestion by losing at the first attempt in the three main cup competitions.

It was a case of *deja-vu* for Welling United in their quest to maintain Conference status. For the second season running the final day's fixtures would decide their fate. If both Altrincham and Forest Green failed to win their matches, a win at Hednesford would see Welling safe in 19th place. The three points were duly won and with Altrincham drawing, hopes were high, until Forest Green scored in the 84th and 86th minutes of their match with Kettering to secure the win and Conference survival on goal difference. This time there was to be no reprieve and after a 14 year stay at the top of the non-League pyramid, always battling against the odds, Welling were returned to the Dr Martens League.

History was made at the Conference match between Kidderminster and Nuneaton Borough on 13th September. For the first time in 'Senior' football the match was officiated by three women. Referee Wendy Toms and assistants Janie Frampton and Amy Rayner took charge of the Midlands Derby and received considerable pre-match publicity. The game passed off without controversy and their performances were acclaimed in the media.

On a sad note, Blackpool striker Martin Aldridge died from injuries sustained in a head-on car crash. Aldridge was on loan at Rushden & Diamonds and was travelling back from the home match with Northwich Victoria on January 29th, when the accident happened near Wellingborough. A one minute silence was held at all Conference fixtures the following week.

1999/00 Season Results Grid

	Altrincham	Doncaster Rovers	Dover Athletic	Forest Green Rovers	Hayes	Hednesford Town	Hereford Utd	Kettering Town	Kidderminster Harriers	Kingstonian	Morecambe	Northwich Victoria	Nuneaton Borough	Rushden & Diamonds	Scarborough	Southport	Stevenage Borough	Sutton United	Telford United	Welling United	Woking	Yeovil Town
Altrincham	X	1-2	3-0	1-1	1-2	0-1	2-1	1-1	0-0	1-3	2-2	2-0	2-2	1-2	2-1	3-0	0-1	3-0	3-3	0-1	1-1	2-2
Doncaster Rovers	0-1	X	0-1	3-2	0-0	2-1	2-2	2-1	1-2	1-0	0-1	2-0	0-1	0-1	0-1	1-1	1-2	1-0	2-0	1-1	0-0	0-3
Dover Athletic	2-2	1-3	X	4-0	2-2	4-1	2-0	1-1	0-1	0-1	3-1	4-1	3-1	0-4	1-1	1-1	4-2	1-1	3-0	2-1	2-2	3-0
Forest Green Rovers	1-1	1-0	3-1	X	0-1	3-0	0-1	2-0	3-2	0-3	1-2	5-1	1-2	1-0	0-1	1-0	3-2	1-2	5-2	1-2	0-0	3-0
Hayes	1-1	3-4	1-2	3-0	X	2-1	0-0	0-1	2-0	1-2	0-1	2-1	3-0	0-5	0-1	0-2	1-2	1-0	1-2	1-0	0-0	2-3
Hednesford Town	5-0	2-1	1-0	1-0	2-1	X	0-1	1-1	0-2	2-3	1-3	1-0	0-0	1-2	0-3	1-2	2-2	1-0	2-1	0-1	3-0	1-0
Hereford Utd	2-2	5-3	2-0	1-0	0-2	3-0	X	4-2	1-1	0-2	1-1	3-0	1-1	4-0	4-4	2-1	2-1	4-1	2-2	1-2	2-4	0-1
Kettering Town	0-0	2-2	1-2	1-0	1-1	4-2	2-0	X	3-1	2-1	1-1	1-1	1-1	1-1	0-0	0-3	1-0	1-0	0-0	2-1	0-0	1-2
Kidderminster Harriers	1-1	1-0	1-2	3-3	2-1	3-0	1-1	1-0	X	2-0	2-1	3-1	1-2	2-0	2-0	5-0	3-1	1-0	2-0	4-1	3-2	4-0
Kingstonian	2-2	0-1	4-1	0-1	1-3	0-2	0-0	2-0	0-1	X	0-0	3-3	2-0	0-1	2-0	4-2	1-0	4-2	4-2	1-0	0-2	0-1
Morecambe	3-3	2-1	2-0	1-1	1-4	4-0	3-2	2-1	0-1	1-2	X	5-0	1-1	0-0	0-1	3-3	3-3	6-2	5-2	2-1	1-0	1-1
Northwich Victoria	1-1	2-1	1-1	0-0	0-0	3-2	0-2	2-6	1-1	0-3	0-0	X	3-1	2-1	2-0	0-1	3-3	2-0	2-1	3-2	3-1	3-0
Nuneaton Borough	3-1	0-0	0-2	2-3	2-1	3-0	0-1	0-1	2-3	2-0	1-1	3-1	X	1-1	1-1	0-2	0-1	2-0	1-1	4-3	0-1	1-1
Rushden & Diamonds	1-0	0-0	1-1	3-2	1-0	1-1	0-0	2-0	5-3	1-0	0-2	6-0	1-1	X	0-0	4-2	2-1	4-0	1-1	2-0	1-3	1-1
Scarborough	1-0	0-0	1-2	5-0	4-1	1-1	3-0	0-0	0-0	0-1	0-2	3-0	1-1	0-1	X	3-0	1-3	3-0	2-0	0-0	3-2	5-0
Southport	2-0	1-0	1-2	2-1	4-1	2-0	0-1	0-1	0-1	0-0	1-1	0-1	2-0	2-1	2-2	X	2-1	1-1	1-3	3-2	4-1	1-1
Stevenage Borough	1-1	3-0	3-1	1-1	3-0	1-1	0-3	3-0	0-2	0-1	1-2	3-1	2-1	2-2	0-1	1-1	X	1-0	2-0	0-1	0-1	0-0
Sutton United	3-0	1-0	0-1	3-2	2-2	0-0	1-1	1-1	0-3	2-2	0-1	2-2	1-2	0-4	1-2	1-1	0-2	X	2-1	2-3	1-1	0-1
Telford United	0-1	0-2	1-1	2-0	1-2	6-2	1-1	3-1	3-2	1-0	3-2	0-1	1-0	1-1	1-0	0-0	2-1	2-0	X	2-1	1-2	3-1
Welling United	2-2	0-1	1-1	1-1	1-2	1-2	3-1	1-0	1-2	0-1	0-0	1-3	0-0	0-3	2-1	4-1	2-1	2-3	2-0	X	1-2	2-5
Woking	0-1	1-3	2-0	2-1	0-3	0-1	0-2	1-1	1-0	1-1	0-0	1-1	1-1	1-3	0-2	0-0	0-2	1-2	1-0	2-3	X	2-0
Yeovil Town	3-0	1-3	1-1	1-0	2-4	3-0	1-0	2-0	1-0	3-2	2-0	3-2	1-3	5-1	1-2	1-1	2-2	1-2	2-1	1-1	0-3	X

FINAL TABLE

	P	Home W	Home D	Home L	Home F	Home A	Away W	Away D	Away L	Away F	Away A	Total W	Total D	Total L	Total F	Total A	Pts	
Kidderminster Harriers	42	16	3	2	47	16	10	4	7	28	24	26	7	9	75	40	85	P
Rushden & Diamonds	42	11	8	2	37	18	10	5	6	34	24	21	13	8	71	42	76	
Morecambe	42	10	7	4	46	29	8	9	4	24	19	18	16	8	70	48	70	
Scarborough	42	10	6	5	36	14	9	6	6	24	21	19	12	11	60	35	69	
Kingstonian	42	9	4	8	30	24	11	3	7	28	20	20	7	15	58	44	67	
Dover Athletic	42	10	7	4	43	26	8	5	8	22	30	18	12	12	65	56	66	
Yeovil Town	42	11	4	6	37	28	7	6	8	23	35	18	10	14	60	63	64	
Hereford Utd	42	9	6	6	43	31	6	8	7	18	21	15	14	13	61	52	59	
Southport	42	10	5	6	31	21	5	8	8	24	35	15	13	14	55	56	58	
Stevenage Borough	42	8	5	8	26	20	8	4	9	34	34	16	9	17	60	54	57	
Hayes	42	7	3	11	24	28	9	5	7	33	30	16	8	18	57	58	56	
Doncaster Rovers	42	7	5	9	19	21	8	4	9	27	27	15	9	18	46	48	54	
Kettering Town	42	8	10	3	25	19	4	6	11	19	31	12	16	14	44	50	52	
Woking	42	5	6	10	17	27	8	7	6	28	26	13	13	16	45	53	52	
Nuneaton Borough	42	7	6	8	28	25	5	9	7	21	28	12	15	15	49	53	51	
Telford United	42	12	4	5	34	21	2	5	14	22	45	14	9	19	56	66	51	
Hednesford Town	42	10	3	8	27	23	5	3	13	18	45	15	6	21	45	68	51	
Northwich Victoria	42	10	8	3	33	25	3	4	14	20	53	13	12	17	53	78	51	
Forest Green Rovers	42	11	2	8	35	23	2	6	13	19	40	13	8	21	54	63	47	
Welling United	42	6	5	10	27	32	7	3	11	27	34	13	8	21	54	66	47	R
Altrincham	42	6	8	7	31	26	3	11	7	20	34	9	19	14	51	60	46	R
Sutton United	42	4	8	9	23	32	4	2	15	16	43	8	10	24	39	75	34	R

Leigh R.M.I. promoted from N.P.L., Boston United from Southern League, Dagenham & Redbridge from Isthmian League.

CUP COMPETITIONS

F.A.Cup

Fourth Qualifying Round		
Altrincham	Stalybridge Celtic	0-0
Doncaster Rovers	Crook Town	7-0
Dulwich Hamlet	Hayes	0-0
Hereford United	Burgess Hill Town	4-1
Kingstonian	Boston Utd	0-0
Morecambe	Bishop Auckland	1-0
Northwich Victoria	Hednesford Town	2-2
Nuneaton Borough	Guiseley	2-3
Rothwell Town	Kettering Town	1-1
Rushden & Diamonds	Sutton United	4-1
Scarborough	Tamworth	0-1
Southport	Emley	1-1
Stevenage Borough	Bath City	1-1
Telford United	Gateshead	0-0
Welling United	Kidderminster Harriers	2-0
Woking	Burton Albion	1-1
Worcester City	Forest Green Rovers	2-5
Worthing	Dover Athletic	1-1
Yeovil Town	Witney Town	2-1
replay		
Stalybridge Celtic	Altrincham	2-1
(replay ordered ,ineligible player, Stalybridge Celtic)		
Stalybridge Celtic	Altrincham	3-2
Hayes	Dulwich Hamlet	3-0
Boston Utd	Kingstonian	0-3
Hednesford Town	Northwich Victoria	1-0
Kettering Town	Rothwell Town	2-1
Emley	Southport	0-2
Bath City	Stevenage Borough	1-0
Gateshead	Telford United	2-1
Burton Albion	Woking	3-1
Dover Athletic	Worthing	0-1
First Round		
Aldershot Town	Hednesford Town	1-1
Darlington	Southport	2-1
Doncaster Rovers	Halifax Town	0-2
Forest Green Rovers	Guiseley	6-0
Hayes	Runcorn	2-1
Hereford United	York City	1-0
Lincoln City	Welling United	1-0
Luton Town	Kingstonian	4-2
Oxford Utd	Morecambe	3-2
Reading	Yeovil Town	4-2
Rushden & Diamonds	Scunthorpe Utd	2-0
Wrexham	Kettering Town	1-1
replay		
Hednesford Town	Aldershot Town	1-2
Kettering Town	Wrexham	0-2

F.A.Cup

Second Round		
Hayes	Hull City	2-2
Ilkeston Town	Rushden & Diamonds	1-1
Forest Green Rovers	Torquay Utd	0-3
Hereford United	Hartlepool Utd	1-0
replay		
Hull City	Hayes	3-2
Rushden & Diamonds	Ilkeston Town	3-0
Third Round		
Hereford United	Leicester City	0-0
Sheffield Utd	Rushden & Diamonds	1-1
replay		
Leicester City	Hereford United	2-1
Rushden & Diamonds	Sheffield Utd	1-1
(Sheffield Utd won 6-5 on pens)		

League Cup

First Round		
Altrincham	Kidderminster Harriers	1-0
Forest Green Rovers	Telford United	1-2
Hednesford Town	Nuneaton Borough	1-2
Hereford United	Sutton United	2-0
Morecambe	Southport	1-2
Welling United	Dover Athletic	3-0
Second Round		
Doncaster Rovers	Nuneaton Borough	4-0
Kettering Town	Hayes	0-1
Northwich Victoria	Altrincham	1-6
Rushden & Diamonds	Telford United	0-1
Southport	Scarborough	1-2
Welling United	Kingstonian	0-1
Woking	Stevenage Borough	3-1
Yeovil Town	Hereford United	3-0
Third Round		
Altrincham	Telford United	1-3
Hayes	Yeovil Town	2-1
Kingstonian	Woking	2-0
Scarborough	Doncaster Rovers	1-2
Semi Final *(two legs)*		
Hayes	Kingstonian	0-0
Kingstonian	Hayes	1-0
Telford United	Doncaster Rovers	1-2
Doncaster Rovers	Telford United	1-0
Final		
Doncaster Rovers	Kingstonian	2-0

Challenge Shield

Cheltenham Town	Kingstonian	0-1

Second Round		
Barrow	Southport	2-3
Morecambe	Hucknall Town	6-1
Kidderminster Harriers	Telford United	2-4
Ilkeston Town	Scarborough	2-4
Runcorn	Northwich Victoria	2-0
Bedworth Town	Hednesford Town	0-2
Ossett Town	Doncaster Rovers	0-1
Guiseley	Nuneaton Borough	2-0
Altrincham	Gateshead	1-0
Hereford United	Barton Rovers	1-0
Hayes	Worcester City	0-2
Rushden & Diamonds	Havant & Waterlooville	1-0
Harlow Town	Dover Athletic	2-3
Cirencester Town	Forest Green Rovers	0-3
Folkestone Invicta	Kingstonian	0-1
Weymouth	Yeovil Town	0-0
Merthyr Tydfil	Stevenage Borough	0-0
Ashford Town	Woking	0-5
Welling United	Gloucester City	2-1
Salisbury City	Sutton United	2-5
Kettering Town	Thame Utd	2-2
replay		
Yeovil Town	Weymouth	2-1
Stevenage Borough	Merthyr Tydfil	4-0
Thame Utd	Kettering Town	0-1
Third Round		
Blakenall	Morecambe	2-1
Doncaster Rovers	Halesowen Town	1-1
Stocksbridge Park Steel	Scarborough	0-0
Whitby Town	Telford United	1-3
Southport	Altrincham	0-0
Hednesford Town	Hyde Utd	1-1
Sutton United	Canvey Island	1-0
Forest Green Rovers	Hendon	4-1
Gravesend & Northfleet	Dover Athletic	1-1
Billericay Town	Hereford United	3-1
Wealdstone	Kingstonian	0-5
Kettering Town	Welling United	2-0
Bath City	Rushden & Diamonds	1-2
Woking	Whyteleafe	4-2
Yeovil Town	Stevenage Borough	2-1
replay		
Halesowen Town	Doncaster Rovers	2-3
Scarborough	Stocksbridge Park Steel	5-0
Altrincham	Southport	1-1
(Southport won 4-3 on pens)		
Hyde Utd	Hednesford Town	2-0
Dover Athletic	Gravesend & Northfleet	2-1
Fourth Round		
Bedford Town	Yeovil Town	0-4
Billericay Town	Rushden & Diamonds	0-0
Burnham	Scarborough	1-1
Dover Athletic	Doncaster Rovers	1-0
Kettering Town	Walton & Hersham	2-2
Kingstonian	Moor Green	2-1
Southport	Emley	2-0
Sutton United	Forest Green Rovers	3-0
Telford United	Farnborough Town	2-1
Woking	Aldershot Town	0-0

replay		
Rushden & Diamonds	Billericay Town	2-1
Walton & Hersham	Kettering Town	0-2
Scarborough	Burnham	6-0
Aldershot Town	Woking	0-1
Fifth Round		
Bishop Auckland	Scarborough	2-1
Rushden & Diamonds	Marine	1-0
Southport	Woking	3-0
Sutton United	Dover Athletic	2-1
Telford United	Worcester City	4-1
Workington	Kettering Town	0-1
Yeovil Town	Kingstonian	0-1
Sixth Round		
Kingstonian	Southport	0-0
Sutton United	Rushden & Diamonds	1-1
Kettering Town	Bishop Auckland	2-2
Telford United	Runcorn	2-0
replay		
Southport	Kingstonian	0-1
Rushden & Diamonds	Sutton United	1-3
Bishop Auckland	Kettering Town	1-2
Semi Final *(two legs)*		
Sutton United	Kingstonian	1-1
Kingstonian	Sutton United	6-0
Kettering Town	Telford United	1-0
Telford United	Kettering Town	0-0
Final *(@ Wembley)*		
Kingstonian	Kettering Town	3-2

**KINGSTONIAN 6
SUTTON UNITED 0
The 'K's' thump their local
rivals to reach Wembley.**

This was the season that the inevitable happened. With the resources that were available to the manager, it was only a matter of time before Rushden & Diamonds secured a place in the Football League. But it was to Yeovil's great credit that they were able to keep the promotion issue open until the final week of the season.

It was perhaps the year when the Conference showed the football world what it had to offer. Both championship challengers were full-time, both had splendid new stadiums, and both had sound finances. Rushden were early pacesetters and were undefeated in their first dozen matches. Meanwhile Yeovil lost two of their first eight games before enjoying a fourteen game unbeaten run that took them through to mid-January. Even the change of manager from Dave Webb to Colin Addison had no ill-effects. At the turn of the year, Yeovil led by seven points with two games in hand.

It was now that Rushden came good. After losing on December 2nd, they did not suffer another reversal until April 14th when Hereford beat them 3-1 at Edgar Street. The sixteen match unbeaten run realised thirty-eight points and saw them overtake Yeovil. The crunch match was two weeks before the end of the season, when the top two met at Yeovil. The resulting draw kept Rushden in pole position and when Hereford scored an injury time winner at Yeovil in the penultimate match, the title was Rushden's.

The F.A.Cup saw five Conference clubs reach the third round and all performed creditably. Yeovil were beaten at Bolton, Chester succumbed to Blackburn Rovers and Morecambe could not upset Premiership Ipswich Town. Kingstonian won away from home for the third round in succession at Southend United, and only an injury time equaliser prevented Bristol City following suit in round four. The replay in front of the Sky cameras at Kingsmeadow resulted in a disappointing 1-0 defeat for the K's and there was further disappointment with their relegation at the end of the season.

The other F.A.Cup giant-killers were Dagenham & Redbridge. Having won at Lincoln City in Round 2, an away tie at Charlton Athletic appeared to be no more than a money-spinning reward. It was nearly so much more as Charlton were grateful for an equaliser four minutes from time. The replay went to extra-time before the 'Daggers' were beaten, with a prized 4th Round tie with Tottenham in sight. The club was able to build on their cup success and embarked on a run of nine consecutive victories which saw them rise from thirteenth to third in a six week period. Their third place finish was the highest achieved by a club with part-time status.

For some years, the Conference has been pushing for two promotion places to the Football League, a move that has been rejected every time. However, in recognition of the strides that had been made by the "Fifth Division" in improving the quality and facilities of their member clubs, eight Conference clubs were allowed entry into the L.D.V. Vans Trophy for the first time (a competition for members of the Football League Second and Third Divisions). The places were allocated to Chester City, as the team relegated from the Football League, Doncaster Rovers, as holders of the League Cup plus Rushden & Diamonds, Morecambe, Scarborough, Kingstonian, Dover Athletic and Yeovil Town, the teams placed from 2nd to 7th in the Conference in the 1999-2000 season; Kingstonian were replaced by Hereford United who finished 8th, as it was found that the Surrey side's ground was not up to the required standard.

	Boston United	Chester City	Dagenham & Redbridge	Doncaster Rovers	Dover Athletic	Forest Green Rovers	Hayes	Hednesford Town	Hereford Utd	Kettering Town	Kingstonian	Leigh RMI	Morecambe	Northwich Victoria	Nuneaton Borough	Rushden & Diamonds	Scarborough	Southport	Stevenage Borough	Telford United	Woking	Yeovil Town
Boston United	X	0-0	5-1	3-1	1-2	0-0	0-1	3-4	5-3	4-3	2-1	0-1	2-1	1-1	4-1	1-1	2-2	1-0	3-3	2-1	0-0	4-1
Chester City	2-2	X	1-1	3-0	1-0	0-1	0-0	0-1	2-1	2-1	0-0	1-1	1-0	1-1	4-0	1-2	3-2	0-1	1-1	1-0	3-3	2-1
Dagenham & Redbridge	2-1	1-1	X	2-1	1-1	3-1	2-0	6-1	2-1	5-1	1-2	2-1	3-2	1-0	1-1	0-2	1-0	0-1	3-0	0-0	1-2	2-0
Doncaster Rovers	4-2	1-0	1-0	X	1-1	3-0	0-0	3-1	2-1	0-0	0-2	4-0	0-2	1-1	3-2	0-2	1-1	0-0	0-0	1-2	0-1	2-0
Dover Athletic	0-0	1-1	3-1	1-1	X	1-2	4-1	4-0	1-0	1-0	1-3	1-2	2-2	3-0	2-1	4-1	0-2	0-1	1-0	1-3	0-0	1-1
Forest Green Rovers	0-3	1-1	4-4	2-2	2-1	X	1-2	0-2	1-1	3-2	3-1	3-1	0-0	1-0	0-0	0-0	2-3	2-0	2-3	1-1	0-0	0-1
Hayes	1-1	1-3	4-1	0-3	3-2	1-0	X	1-1	0-2	2-1	1-1	1-2	1-1	2-2	0-0	0-3	0-1	1-0	0-1	0-1	1-2	2-3
Hednesford Town	2-4	0-0	0-2	2-4	0-0	1-1	1-3	X	0-3	1-2	3-2	1-2	0-0	7-1	0-3	2-3	0-1	0-1	1-1	1-1	1-2	1-2
Hereford Utd	1-1	2-0	0-1	0-1	4-2	3-1	3-2	1-1	X	0-0	0-0	1-1	2-0	0-1	1-1	3-1	1-1	0-0	1-1	2-0	0-1	2-2
Kettering Town	2-2	4-0	0-0	0-0	0-2	1-3	0-2	2-0	0-2	X	3-1	0-1	1-5	2-3	1-2	0-2	1-1	1-1	1-2	0-1	2-0	2-1
Kingstonian	0-0	1-3	2-3	1-1	0-0	0-1	0-1	1-0	0-3	0-1	X	0-2	1-6	1-0	2-2	2-4	2-2	3-1	0-2	0-1	0-3	3-4
Leigh RMI	2-2	0-1	1-2	0-1	2-1	1-1	4-0	2-2	2-1	1-0	2-1	X	1-0	3-0	6-2	1-0	2-0	2-2	1-4	1-1	2-0	2-3
Morecambe	2-0	0-2	2-3	2-1	1-2	0-2	4-0	0-0	1-1	0-2	3-2	1-2	X	4-0	4-2	2-1	4-4	1-3	1-2	0-0	3-0	0-0
Northwich Victoria	0-3	1-1	3-0	1-1	2-0	3-4	2-0	1-0	1-2	2-1	1-1	1-0	X	2-2	0-0	3-0	0-2	3-2	0-1	4-0	4-0	1-2
Nuneaton Borough	3-1	1-2	2-0	1-0	1-2	2-0	1-1	5-1	1-2	1-1	2-1	2-1	5-1	3-1	X	1-1	1-2	1-2	0-3	1-1	1-1	0-2
Rushden & Diamonds	0-0	2-0	2-1	0-0	2-1	0-0	4-0	5-1	1-0	1-1	2-1	1-1	4-1	2-1	2-1	X	1-0	4-0	2-2	3-0	2-0	1-2
Scarborough	2-2	0-2	0-1	3-1	2-0	1-0	2-0	0-0	2-4	0-1	1-0	1-1	2-2	4-0	0-0	0-3	X	1-1	2-2	1-1	3-2	2-2
Southport	3-1	1-0	0-1	1-0	2-1	1-1	2-0	2-0	1-1	2-3	2-2	1-2	1-2	1-1	1-2	1-3	3-1	X	2-2	3-0	0-1	3-0
Stevenage Borough	3-2	1-2	0-2	0-0	1-1	3-1	3-3	4-1	2-1	2-0	2-5	3-0	1-1	3-1	1-1	0-2	1-1	1-3	X	5-3	0-3	0-0
Telford United	3-2	3-0	0-1	1-0	0-2	1-0	2-0	2-1	1-0	2-1	0-1	2-1	0-0	2-3	2-1	1-2	1-0	2-3	2-2	X	3-1	1-2
Woking	1-1	1-0	4-4	1-1	4-1	2-0	1-2	1-1	0-3	1-1	0-0	1-1	3-1	1-1	0-2	1-4	1-1	1-2	1-1	3-0	X	2-3
Yeovil Town	2-1	2-1	1-3	2-0	4-0	2-0	3-0	4-2	2-3	2-0	3-1	6-1	3-2	1-0	0-0	0-0	0-1	0-1	1-1	2-0	1-0	X

			Home			Away					Total					
	P	W	D	L	F	A	W	D	L	F	A	W	D	L	F	A	Pts
Rushden & Diamonds	42	14	6	1	41	13	11	5	5	37	23	25	11	6	78	36	86	P
Yeovil Town	42	14	3	4	41	17	10	5	6	32	33	24	8	10	73	50	80
Dagenham & Redbridge	42	13	4	4	39	19	10	4	7	32	35	23	8	11	71	54	77
Southport	42	9	5	7	33	24	11	4	6	25	22	20	9	13	58	46	69
Leigh RMI	42	11	5	5	38	24	8	6	7	25	33	19	11	12	63	57	68
Telford United	42	13	1	7	33	23	6	7	8	18	28	19	8	15	51	51	65
Stevenage Borough	42	8	7	6	36	33	7	11	3	35	28	15	18	9	71	61	63
Chester City	42	9	8	4	29	19	7	6	8	20	24	16	14	12	49	43	62
Doncaster Rovers	42	11	5	5	28	17	4	8	9	19	26	15	13	14	47	43	58
Scarborough	42	7	9	5	29	25	7	7	7	27	29	14	16	12	56	54	58
Hereford Utd	42	6	12	3	27	19	8	3	10	33	27	14	15	13	60	46	57
Boston United	42	10	7	4	43	28	3	10	8	31	35	13	17	12	74	63	56
Nuneaton Borough	42	9	5	7	35	26	4	10	7	25	34	13	15	14	60	60	54
Woking	42	5	10	6	30	30	8	5	8	22	27	13	15	14	52	57	54
Dover Athletic	42	9	6	6	32	22	5	5	11	22	34	14	11	17	54	56	53
Forest Green Rovers	42	6	9	6	28	28	5	6	10	15	26	11	15	16	43	54	48
Northwich Victoria	42	8	7	6	31	24	3	6	12	18	43	11	13	18	49	67	46
Hayes	42	5	6	10	22	31	7	4	10	22	40	12	10	20	44	71	46
Morecambe	42	8	5	8	35	29	3	7	11	29	37	11	12	19	64	66	45
Kettering Town	42	5	5	11	23	31	6	5	10	23	31	11	10	21	46	62	43	R
Kingstonian	42	3	5	13	19	40	5	5	11	28	33	8	10	24	47	73	34	R
Hednesford Town	42	2	6	13	24	38	3	7	11	22	48	5	13	24	46	86	28	R

FINAL TABLE

Stalybridge Celtic promoted from N.P.L., Margate from Southern League, Farnborough Town from Isthmian League.

CUP COMPETITIONS

F.A.Cup

Fourth Qualifying Round		
Hendon	Dagenham & Redbridge	1-3
Aldershot Town	Dover Athletic	1-0
Yeovil Town	Horsham	1-1
Bedlington Terriers	Morecambe	1-3
Billericay Town	Hednesford Town	0-0
Boston United	Burton Albion	1-1
Chesham Utd	Kettering Town	0-2
Doncaster Rovers	Southport	2-2
Easington Colliery	Chester City	0-2
Forest Green Rovers	Bath City	3-1
Hayes	Dulwich Hamlet	4-2
Hinckley Utd	Telford United	1-1
Kingstonian	Devizes Town	5-2
Nuneaton Borough	Stevenage Borough	1-1
Rushden & Diamonds	Grantham Town	5-4
Scarborough	Leigh RMI	3-4
Sheffield	Northwich Victoria	1-5
(Played at Sheffield United)		
Woking	Hereford United	1-0
replay		
Telford United	Hinckley Utd	4-1
Horsham	Yeovil Town	0-2
Burton Albion	Boston United	3-2
Southport	Doncaster Rovers	1-0
Stevenage Borough	Nuneaton Borough	1-2
Hednesford Town	Billericay Town	2-1
First Round		
Leigh RMI	Millwall	0-3
(Played at Millwall)		
Blackpool	Telford United	3-1
Brentford	Kingstonian	1-3
Bury	Northwich Victoria	1-1
Carlisle Utd	Woking	5-1
Chester City	Plymouth Argyle	1-1
Dagenham & Redbridge	Hayes	3-1
Forest Green Rovers	Morecambe	0-3
Havant & Waterlooville	Southport	1-2
Hednesford Town	Oldham Ath	2-4
Kettering Town	Hull City	0-0
Stoke City	Nuneaton Borough	0-0
Yeovil Town	Colchester United	5-1
Luton Town	Rushden & Diamonds	1-0
replay		
Hull City	Kettering Town	0-1
Northwich Victoria	Bury	1-0
Plymouth Argyle	Chester City	1-2
Nuneaton Borough	Stoke City	1-0
Second Round		
Blackpool	Yeovil Town	0-1
Bournemouth	Nuneaton Borough	3-0
Bristol City	Kettering Town	3-1
Chester City	Oxford Utd	3-2
Lincoln City	Dagenham & Redbridge	0-1
Morecambe	Cambridge Utd	2-1
Northwich Victoria	Leyton Orient	3-3
Southport	Kingstonian	1-2

F.A.Cup

Second Round - replay		
Leyton Orient	Northwich Victoria	3-2
Third Round		
Southend Utd	Kingstonian	0-1
Morecambe	Ipswich Town	0-3
Charlton Ath	Dagenham & Redbridge	1-1
Bolton Wanderers	Yeovil Town	2-1
Blackburn Rovers	Chester City	2-0
replay		
Dagenham & Redbridge	Charlton Ath	0-1
Fourth Round		
Bristol City	Kingstonian	1-1
replay		
Kingstonian	Bristol City	0-1

League Cup

First Round		
Boston United	Nuneaton Borough	1-5
Dagenham & Redbridge	Stevenage Borough	1-2
Hayes	Woking	3-5
Hednesford Town	Telford United	1-0
Kettering Town	Forest Green Rovers	3-0
Northwich Victoria	Leigh RMI	3-3
replay		
Leigh RMI	Northwich Victoria	1-0
Second Round		
Chester City	Hednesford Town	2-2
Dover Athletic	Kingstonian	0-1
Hereford United	Kettering Town	0-1
Morecambe	Leigh RMI	5-2
Nuneaton Borough	Scarborough	2-0
Rushden & Diamonds	Stevenage Borough	2-1
Southport	Doncaster Rovers	1-0
Woking	Yeovil Town	0-1
replay		
Hednesford Town	Chester City	(aet) 1-3
Third Round		
Kingstonian	Rushden & Diamonds	1-0
Nuneaton Borough	Morecambe	2-0
Southport	Chester City	0-3
Yeovil Town	Kettering Town	2-0
Semi Final		
Yeovil Town	Kingstonian	0-5
Chester City	Nuneaton Borough	2-1
Final		
Kingstonian	Chester City	(aet) 0-0
(Chester City won 4-2 on pens)		

Challenge Shield

Kidderminster Harriers	Kingstonian	2-1

F.A. Trophy

Third Round

Aldershot Town	Stevenage Borough	1-5
Forest Green Rovers	Barton Rovers	6-1
Histon	Kettering Town	3-0
Bilston Town	Nuneaton Borough	3-2
Burscough	Morecambe	3-3
Chester City	Doncaster Rovers	2-0
Dagenham & Redbridge	Weymouth	0-1
Hayes	Rushden & Diamonds	0-1
Hereford United	Dover Athletic	1-0
Leigh RMI	Hucknall Town	1-0
Tamworth	Boston United	0-3
Matlock Town	Northwich Victoria	2-0
Runcorn	Scarborough	0-4
Southport	Hednesford Town	3-0
Staines Town	Kingstonian	2-2
Trafford	Telford United	1-1
Woking	Margate	1-2
Yeovil Town	Bath City	2-1
replay		
Kingstonian	Staines Town	2-0
Morecambe	Burscough	3-0
Telford United	Trafford	7-1

Fourth Round

Scarborough	Burton Albion	0-1
Chester City	St Albans City	3-2
Kingstonian	Southport	0-1
Hereford United	Leigh RMI	0-0
Tiverton Town	Boston United	2-1
Stevenage Borough	Margate	2-1
Kings Lynn	Telford United	1-2
Emley	Yeovil Town	2-4
Matlock Town	Forest Green Rovers	2-2
Evesham Utd	Morecambe	0-0
Marine	Rushden & Diamonds	0-6
replay		
Forest Green Rovers	Matlock Town	3-1
Morecambe	Evesham Utd	4-1
Leigh RMI	Hereford United	1-2

Fifth Round

Burton Albion	Yeovil Town	2-1
Weymouth	Southport	1-2
Morecambe	Hereford United	0-0
Canvey Island	Stevenage Borough	1-1
Billericay	Telford United	2-3
Chester City	Blyth Spartans	4-2
Forest Green Rovers	Rushden & Diamonds	2-0
replay		
Hereford United	Morecambe	1-1
(Hereford Utd won 3-1 pens)		
Stevenage Borough	Canvey Island	0-0
(Canvey Island won 4-2 pens)		

Sixth Round

Hereford United	Burton Albion	1-0
Canvey Island	Telford United	1-0
Forest Green Rovers	Worksop	2-1
Chester City	Southport	1-0

Semi Final *(two legs)*

Forest Green Rovers	Hereford United	2-2
Hereford United	Forest Green Rovers	1-4
Canvey Island	Chester City	2-0
Chester City	Canvey Island	0-2

Final *(@ Villa Park)*

Canvey Island	Forest Green Rovers	1-0

L.D.Van Trophy

Northern Section		
First Round		
Chester City	Hull City	1-0
Doncaster Rovers	Rochdale	3-2
Lincoln City	Morecambe	3-2
Stoke City	Scarborough	3-1
Second Round		
Hartlepool Utd	Doncaster Rovers	3-1
Port Vale	Chester City	2-0

Southern Section		
First Round		
Barnet	Rushden & Diamonds	2-0
Bournemouth	Dover Athletic	1-1
(Bournemouth won 4-2 pens)		
Hereford United	Yeovil Town	4-0
Second Round		
Hereford United	Reading	1-2

DAGENHAM 0
CHARLTON ATHLETIC 1
The Daggers F.A.Cup campaign ends in disappointment.

A.P.Leamington

Founded: 1945   Career 1979-82
Ground: The Windmill, Tachbrook Road, Leamington

	P	W	D	L	F	A	Pts
Home:	59	12	19	28	65	97	44
Away:	59	9	13	37	54	137	34
Total:	118	21	32	65	119	234	78

Records:

Win:	Home:	5-0	Telford United (80-1)
	Away:	2-0	Barrow (80-1)
Defeat:	Home:	1-5	Stafford Rangers (81-2)
	Away:	0-7	Bath City (81-2)

Barnet

Founded: 1888   Career: 1979-91
Ground: Underhill, Barnet

	P	W	D	L	F	A	Pts
Home:	247	123	54	70	430	286	381
Away:	247	86	56	105	329	372	307
Total:	494	209	110	175	759	658	688

Records:

Win:	Home:	8-1	Fisher Ath (90-1)
	Away:	7-0	Wycombe W. (87-8)
Defeat:	Home:	1-5	Bath City (80-1)
	Away:	0-6	Wealdstone (82-3)

Altrincham

Founded 1903   Career: 1979-97, 99-00
Ground: Moss Lane, Altrincham

	P	W	D	L	F	A	Pts
Home:	394	192	95	107	664	443	601
Away:	394	125	117	152	511	580	475
Total:	788	317	212	259	1175	1023	1076

Records:

Win:	Home:	9-2	Merthyr Tyd.(90-1)
	Away:	6-2	Boston Utd (90-1)
Defeat:	Home:	3-7	Slough Town (91-2)
	Away:	0-7	Morecambe (95-6)

Barrow

Founded: 1901   Career: 1979-83, 84-86, 89-92, 98-99
Ground: Holker Street Stadium, Wilkie Road

	P	W	D	L	F	A	Pts
Home:	206	86	58	62	287	239	285
Away:	206	33	55	118	205	399	145
Total:	412	119	113	180	492	638	430

Records:

Win:	Home:	6-0	Frickley Ath.(84-5)
	Away:	6-2	Bangor City (80-1)
Defeat	Home:	0-5	Telford Utd.(82-3)
	Away:	0-6	Bath City (85-6)

Aylesbury United

Founded: 1897   Career: 1988-89
Ground: The Stadium, Buckingham Road, Aylesbury

	P	W	D	L	F	A	Pts
Home:	20	7	4	9	27	30	25
Away:	20	2	5	13	16	41	11
Total:	40	9	9	22	43	71	36

Records:

Win:	Home:	4-1	Weymouth (88-9)
	Away:	2-0	Fisher Ath (88-9)
Defeat:	Home:	1-5	Kidderminster Harriers (88-9)
	Away:	0-5	Runcorn (88-9) Welling U. (88-9)

Bath City

Founded: 1889   Career: 1979-88, 90-97
Ground: Twerton Park, Twerton

	P	W	D	L	F	A	Pts
Home:	332	141	92	99	487	385	469
Away:	332	88	88	156	353	515	342
Total:	664	229	180	255	840	900	811

Records:

Win:	Home:	7-0	AP Leamington (81-2)
	Away:	5-0	Welling Utd (91-2)
Defeat:	Home:	1-6	Kettering T.(84-5)
	Away:	0-6	Maidstone U.(79-0), Kidderminster H.(96-7)

Bangor City

Founded: 1896   Career: 1979-81, 82-84
Ground: The Stadium, Farrar Road, Bangor

	P	W	D	L	F	A	Pts
Home:	80	29	25	26	114	113	91
Away:	80	15	20	45	87	160	59
Total:	160	44	45	71	201	273	150

Records:

Win:	Home:	4-0	Telford U., Trowbridge T.(83-4)
	Away:	5-1	Redditch U.(79-80), Barrow (82-3)
Defeat:	Home:	2-6	Barrow (80-1)
	Away:	1-6	Maidstone Utd (82--3)

Boston United

Founded: 1934   Career: 1979-93, 2000-
Ground: York Street, Boston

	P	W	D	L	F	A	Pts
Home:	310	156	72	82	585	422	488
Away:	310	79	81	150	370	552	307
Total:	620	235	153	232	955	974	795

Records:

Win:	Home:	6-0	Maidstone U.(81-2) Gateshead (86-7)
	Away:	5-1	Nuneaton B. (86-7) Cheltenham T. (87-8)
Defeat:	Home:	0-6	Runcorn (88-9)
	Away:	1-7	Frickley Ath (83-4)

Bromsgrove Rovers

Founded: 1885   Career: 1992-97
Ground: Victoria Ground, Bromsgrove

	P	W	D	L	F	A	Pts
Home:	105	42	32	31	165	139	158
Away:	105	29	29	47	122	169	116
Total:	210	71	61	78	287	308	274

Records:

Win:	Home:	5-0	Yeovil Town (94-5)
	Away:	3-0	Bath C.(92-3) Farnborough T.(94/5)
Defeat:	Home:	0-5	Telford U.(93-4), Northwich V.(96-7),
	Away:	0-4	Woking (94-5), Macclesfield T.(96-7)

Colchester United

Founded: 1937   Career: 1990-92
Ground: Layer Road, Colchester

	P	W	D	L	F	A	Pts
Home:	42	35	5	2	98	24	110
Away:	42	18	15	9	68	51	69
Total:	84	53	20	11	166	75	179

Records:

Win:	Home:	5-0	Barrow Bath C. (91-2)
	Away:	4-0	Boston Utd (91-2)
Defeat:	Home:	2-3	Farnborough Town (91-2)
	Away:	1-4	Welling Utd (91-2)

Cheltenham Town

Founded: 1892   Career: 1985-92, 97-99
Ground: Whaddon Road, Cheltenham

	P	W	D	L	F	A	Pts
Home:	188	88	56	44	319	224	307
Away:	188	50	59	79	235	313	209
Total:	376	138	115	123	554	537	516

Records:

Win:	Home:	6-1	Dagenham (86-7)
	Away:	5-2	Fisher Ath (89-0)
Defeat	Home:	0-7	Redbridge Forest (91-2)
	Away:	0-5	Altrincham (89-0), Runcorn (85-6)

Dagenham

Founded:1948 (See also 'Dagenham & Redbridge' and 'Redbridge Forest')
Ground: Victoria Road, Dagenham   Career: 1981-88

	P	W	D	L	F	A	Pts
Home:	147	53	38	56	199	206	173
Away:	147	34	32	81	175	288	134
Total:	294	87	70	137	374	494	307

Records:

Win:	Home:	6-2	Trowbridge Town (83-4)
	Away:	4-0	AP Leamington (81-2),Wealdstone (85-6)
Defeat	Home:	0-5	Kettering Town (87-8)
	Away:	0-6	Altrincham (87-8)

Chester City

Founded: 1885   Career: 2000-
Ground: Deva Stadium, Bumpers Lane, Chester

	P	W	D	L	F	A	Pts
Home:	21	9	8	4	29	19	35
Away:	21	7	6	8	20	24	27
Total:	42	16	14	12	49	43	62

Records:

Win:	Home:	4-0	Nuneaton Borough (2000-1)
	Away:	3-1	Hayes, Kingstonian (2000-1)
Defeat	Home:	1-2	Rushden & D.(2000-1)
	Away:	0-4	Kettering Town (2000-1)

Dagenham & Redbridge

Founded: 1992 (See also Dagenham' and 'Redbridge Forest')
Ground: Victoria Road, Dagenham   Career: 1992-96, 2000 -

	P	W	D	L	F	A	Pts
Home:	105	48	26	31	187	137	170
Away:	105	29	32	44	120	160	119
Total:	210	77	58	75	307	297	288*

Records: (* 1 point deducted)

Win:	Home:	6-1	Merthyr Tyd. (92-3) Hednesford T. (2000-1)
	Away:	8-1	Woking (93-4)
Defeat	Home:	0-4	Altrincham (94-5) Macclesfield T. (94-5) Gateshead (95-6)
	Away:	0-5	Stalybridge C. (93-4) Northwich V. (94-5) Slough T. (95-6)

Chorley

Founded: 1883   Career: 1988-90
Ground: Victory Park, Duke St, Chorley

	P	W	D	L	F	A	Pts
Home:	41	15	9	17	52	58	54
Away:	41	11	3	27	47	80	36
Total:	82	26	12	44	99	138	90

Records:

Win:	Home:	4-0	Welling Utd (88-9)
	Away:	4-0	Northwich Vic.(88-9), Telford U.(89-0)
Defeat:	Home:	1-4	Cheltenham Town (88-9) Barnet (89-0)
	Away:	0-5	Barnet (89-0)

Darlington

Founded: 1883   Career: 1989-90
Ground: Feethams Ground, Darlington

	P	W	D	L	F	A	Pts
Home:	21	13	6	2	43	12	45
Away:	21	13	3	5	33	13	42
Total:	42	26	9	7	76	25	87

Records:

Win:	Home:	6-1	Boston Utd (89-90)
	Away:	4-0	Stafford Rangers (89-90)
Defeat:	Home:	1-2	Barnet (89-90)
	Away:	2-3	Kidderminster Harriers (89-90)

Dartford

Founded: 1921   Career: 1981-82, 84-86
Ground: Watling Street, Dartford

	P	W	D	L	F	A	Pts
Home:	63	21	18	24	87	83	67
Away:	63	14	13	36	68	116	55
Total:	126	35	31	60	155	199	122

Records:

Win:	Home:	5-0	Yeovil Town (81-2)
	Away:	5-2	Worcester City (84-5)
Defeat:	Home:	0-3	Dagenham (81-2)
	Away:	0-5	Runcorn (85-6)

Farnborough Town

Founded: 1967   Career: 1989-90, 91-93, 94-99
Ground: John Roberts Gound, Cherrywood Road, Farnborough

	P	W	D	L	F	A	Pts
Home:	168	64	42	62	256	251	234
Away:	168	41	49	78	203	296	172
Total:	336	105	91	140	459	547	406

Records:

Win:	Home:	6-0	Stalybridge C. (97-8)
	Away:	5-0	Slough Town (91-2)
Defeat:	Home:	1-6	Morecambe, Northwich V.(98-9)
	Away:	1-7	Southport (95-6)

Doncaster Rovers

Founded: 1879   Career: 1998 -
Ground: Belle Vue Ground, Doncaster

	P	W	D	L	F	A	Pts
Home:	63	25	15	23	73	64	90
Away:	63	17	19	27	71	82	70
Total:	126	42	34	50	144	146	160

Records:

Win:	Home:	4-0	Leigh RMI (2000-1)
	Away:	3-0	Hayes (2000-1)
Defeat:	Home:	0-3	Yeovil Town (99-2000)
	Away:	0-3	Stevenage A.(99-0), Chester C.(2000-1)

Fisher Athletic

Founded: 1908   Career: 1987-91
Ground: The Surrey Docks Stadium, Salter Road, London.SE16

	P	W	D	L	F	A	Pts
Home:	83	26	21	36	115	119	99
Away:	83	14	25	43	91	164	70
Total:	166	40	46	79	206	283	169

Records:

Win:	Home:	5-1	Dagenham (87-8)
	Away:	5-1	Dagenham (87-8)
Defeat:	Home:	2-5	Cheltenham T. (89-90)
	Away:	1-8	Barnet (90-1)

Dover Athletic

Founded: 1983   Career: 1993-
Ground: Crabble Athletic Ground, Lewisham Road, Dover

	P	W	D	L	F	A	Pts
Home:	168	66	49	53	253	215	247
Away:	168	47	41	80	184	261	182
Total:	336	113	90	133	437	476	429

Records:

Win:	Home:	5-0	Woking (93-4)
	Away:	4-0	Morecambe (98-9)
Defeat:	Home:	0-5	Kidderminster H. (96-7)
	Away:	1-5	Leek Town (97-8)

Forest Green Rovers

Founded: 1890   Career: 1998-
Ground: The Lawn, Nympsfield Road, Forest Green, Nailsworth

	P	W	D	L	F	A	Pts
Home:	63	26	16	21	91	73	94
Away:	63	13	20	30	61	94	59
Total:	126	39	36	51	152	167	153

Records:

Win:	Home:	5-0	Kidderminster H. (98-9)
	Away:	4-0	Yeovil Town (98-9)
Defeat:	Home:	0-3	Kingstonian (99-0), Boston U.(2000-1)
	Away:	0-5	Scarborough (99-00)

Enfield

Founded: 1893   Career: 1981-90
Ground: Southbury Road, Enfield

	P	W	D	L	F	A	Pts
Home:	188	97	38	53	371	238	247
Away:	188	72	42	74	301	303	182
Total:	376	169	80	127	672	541	553

Records:

Win:	Home:	6-0	Worcester C.(84-5)
	Away:	5-0	Gateshead (84-5)
Defeat:	Home:	1-4	Scarborough (81-2), Telford U.(87-8)
	Away:	0-9	Runcorn (89-90)

Frickley Athletic

Founded: 1910   Career: 1980-87
Ground: Westfield Lane, South Elmsall, Pontefract

	P	W	D	L	F	A	Pts
Home:	145	78	31	36	273	178	214
Away:	145	30	38	77	159	280	123
Total:	290	108	69	113	432	458	337

Records:

Win:	Home:	7-1	Boston Utd (83-4)
	Away:	3-0	Boston Utd (85-6)
Defeat:	Home:	2-5	Wealdstone (83-4)
	Away:	1-7	Telford Utd (81-2)

Gateshead

Founded: 1976   Career: 1983-85, 86-87, 90-98
Ground: International Stadium, Neilson Road, Gateshead

	P	W	D	L	F	A	Pts
Home:	231	88	65	78	316	313	317
Away:	231	54	58	119	270	434	220
Total:	462	142	123	197	586	747	536*

Records: * 1 point deducted
Win: Home: 5-0   Bath City (96-7)
        Away: 4-0   Four matches.
Defeat: Home: 0-9   Sutton Utd (90-1)
        Away: 0-6   Boston Utd (86-7) Welling Utd. (90-1)

Hednesford Town

Founded: 1880   Career: 1995-01
Ground: Keys Park, Hednesford

	P	W	D	L	F	A	Pts
Home:	126	58	31	37	175	135	205
Away:	126	34	35	57	147	209	137
Total:	252	92	66	94	322	344	342

Records:
Win: Home: 7-1   Northwich Victoria (2000-1)
        Away: 5-2   Gateshead (97-8)
Defeat: Home: 1-4   Kidderminster Harriers (96-7)
        Away: 1-6   Dagenham & R.(2000-1)

Gravesend & Northfleet

Founded: 1946   Career: 1979-82
Ground: Stonebridge Road, Northfleet

	P	W	D	L	F	A	Pts
Home:	59	27	14	18	96	70	75
Away:	59	13	14	32	52	98	43
Total:	118	40	28	50	148	168	118

Records:
Win: Home: 5-1   Barrow (79-80)
        Away: 4-2   Frickley Ath (80-1)
Defeat: Home: 2-4   Runcorn (81-2)
        Away: 0-5   Scarborough (81-2)

Hereford United

Founded: 1924   Career: 1997-
Ground: Edgar Street, Hereford

	P	W	D	L	F	A	Pts
Home:	84	35	30	19	125	86	135
Away:	84	27	22	35	101	107	103
Total:	168	62	52	54	226	193	238

Records:
Win: Home: 4-0   Forest Green R.(98-9), Rushden & D.(99-0)
        Away: 5-1   Morecambe (97-8)
Defeat: Home: 2-4   Woking (1999-00)
        Away: 0-3   Five matches.

Halifax Town

Founded: 1911   Career: 1993-98
Ground: The Shay Stadium, Shaw Hill, Halifax

	P	W	D	L	F	A	Pts
Home:	105	52	31	22	194	115	187
Away:	105	28	34	43	107	168	118
Total:	210	80	65	65	301	283	305

Records:
Win: Home: 6-0   Telford Utd (93-4) Stafford R. (94-5)
        Away: 6-2   Woking (93-4)
Defeat: Home: 0-4   Woking (96-7)
        Away: 0-7   Macclesfield Town (95-6)

Kettering Town

Founded: 1872   Career: 1979-01
Ground: Rockingham Road, Kettering

	P	W	D	L	F	A	Pts
Home:	457	220	116	121	751	526	726
Away:	457	133	130	194	564	714	515
Total:	914	353	246	315	1315	1240	1241

Records:
Win: Home: 6-0   Morecambe (98-9)
        Away: 6-1   Bath C.(84-5)
Defeat: Home: 1-6   Stalybridge Celtic (95-6)
        Away: 0-8   Sutton Utd (86-7)

Hayes

Founded: 1909   Career: 1996 -
Ground: Townfield House, Church Road, Hayes

	P	W	D	L	F	A	Pts
Home:	105	41	23	41	143	130	146
Away:	105	37	27	41	137	156	138
Total:	210	78	50	82	280	286	284

Records:
Win: Home: 5-0   Slough T.(96-7)
        Away: 5-1   Stevenage A.(97-8),Farnborough T.(98-9)
Defeat: Home: 0-5   Rushden & Diamonds (99-2000)
        Away: 0-5   Rushden & Diamonds (98-9)

Kidderminster Harriers

Founded:1886   Career: 1983-00
Ground: Aggborough Stadium, Hoo Road, Kidderminster

	P	W	D	L	F	A	Pts
Home:	356	167	88	101	641	469	562
Away:	356	132	75	149	522	565	471
Total:	712	299	163	250	1163	1034	1033

Records:
Win: Home: 8-2   Wycombe Wandrers (85-6)
        Away: 5-0   Runcorn (93-4), Dover A.(96-7)
Defeat: Home: 1-5   Farnborough T.(92-3)
        Away: 0-5   Maidstone U.(86-7),Redbridge F.(91-2),
                      Forest Green R.(98-9)

Kingstonian

Founded: 1885   Career: 1998-01
Ground: Kingsmeadow Stadium, Kingston Road, Kingston-upon-Thames

	P	W	D	L	F	A	Pts
Home:	63	21	16	26	74	83	79
Away:	63	24	14	25	81	83	86
Total:	126	45	30	51	155	166	165

Records:

Win:	Home:	5-1	Barrow (98-9)
	Away:	5-2	Stevenage B.(2000-1)
Defeat:	Home:	1-6	Morecambe (2000-1)
	Away:	1-5	Dover Ath (98-9)

Leek Town

Founded: 1946   Career: 1997-99
Ground: Harrison Park, Macclesfield Road, Leek

	P	W	D	L	F	A	Pts
Home:	42	13	13	16	68	68	52
Away:	42	5	9	28	32	75	24
Total:	84	18	22	44	100	143	76

Records:

Win:	Home:	7-0	Morecambe (98-9)
	Away:	2-0	Gateshead (97-8) Northwich V.(98-9)
Defeat:	Home:	0-4	Kettering Town (97-8)
	Away:	1-6	Stalybridge Celtic (97-8)

Leigh R.M.I.

Founded: 1896   Career: 2000-
Ground: Hilton Park, Kirkhall Lane, Leigh

	P	W	D	L	F	A	Pts
Home:	21	11	5	5	38	24	38
Away:	21	8	6	7	25	33	30
Total:	42	19	11	12	63	57	68

Records:

Win:	Home:	6-2	Nuneaton B. (2000-1)
	Away:	2-0	Kingstonian (2000-1)
Defeat:	Home:	1-4	Stevenage B. (2000-1)
	Away:	1-6	Yeovil Town (2000-1)

Lincoln City

Founded: 1883   Career: 1987-88
Ground: Sincil Bank, Lincoln

	P	W	D	L	F	A	Pts
Home:	21	16	4	1	53	13	52
Away:	21	8	6	7	33	35	30
Total:	42	24	10	8	86	48	82

Records:

Win:	Home:	5-0	Altrincham (87-8)
	Away:	4-1	Welling Utd, Stafford R.(87-8)
Defeat:	Home:	0-1	Kettering Town (87-8)
	Away:	1-4	Runcorn Sutton Utd. (87-8)

Macclesfield Town

Founded: 1874   Career: 1987-97
Ground: The Moss Rose Ground, London Road, Macclesfield

	P	W	D	L	F	A	Pts
Home:	209	103	56	50	324	195	365
Away:	209	80	53	76	276	285	293
Total:	418	183	109	126	600	480	658

Records:

Win:	Home:	7-0	Halifax Town (95-6)
	Away:	5-1	Boston Utd (91-2)
Defeat:	Home:	0-3	Enfield (87-8), Stevenage B.94-5)
	Away:	1-6	Farnborough T.(95-6)

Maidstone United

Founded: 1891   Career: 1979-89
Ground: Athletic Ground, London Road, Maidstone *

	P	W	D	L	F	A	Pts
Home:	205	111	53	41	410	207	334
Away:	205	68	60	77	274	285	255
Total:	410	179	113	118	684	492	589

Records:

Win:	Home:	6-0	Four matches.
	Away:	5-1	Wycombe Wanderers (87-8)
Defeat:	Home:	1-4	Enfield (81-2) Kidderminster H. Weymouth (84-5)
	Away:	0-6	Boston Utd (81-2)

(* From 1988-9: Watling Street, Dartford)

Merthyr Tydfil

Founded: 1945   Career: 1989-95
Ground: Penydarren Park, Merthyr Tydfil

	P	W	D	L	F	A	Pts
Home:	126	54	38	34	215	168	200
Away:	126	33	35	58	137	215	134
Total:	252	87	73	92	352	383	332*

* 2 points deducted

Records:

Win:	Home:	7-0	Fisher Ath (90-1)
	Away:	5-1	Barrow (89-90)
Defeat:	Home:	1-5	Woking (92-3)
	Away:	2-9	Altrincham (90-1)

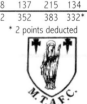

Morecambe

Founded: 1920   Career: 1995-
Ground: Christie Park, Lancaster Road, Morecambe

	P	W	D	L	F	A	Pts
Home:	126	60	28	38	232	173	208
Away:	126	41	35	50	186	209	158
Total:	252	101	63	88	418	382	366

Records:

Win:	Home:	7-0	Altrincham (95-6)
	Away:	6-1	Farnborough T. (98-9) Kingstonian (2000-1)
Defeat:	Home:	1-5	Hereford Utd (97-8)
	Away:	0-7	Leek Town (98-9)

Newport County

Founded 1912: Career: 1988-89 (Resigned from league, record expunged)
Ground: Somerton Park, Newport, Monmouthshire

	P	W	D	L	F	A	Pts
Home:	13	3	3	7	18	26	12
Away:	16	1	4	11	13	36	2
Total:	29	4	7	18	31	62	19

Records:

Win:	Home:	4-0	Weymouth (88-9)
	Away:	2-0	Chorley (88-9)
Defeat:	Home:	1-7	Barnet (88-9)
	Away:	0-5	Wycombe W. (88-9)

Redditch United

Founded: 1948   Career: 1979-80
Ground: Valley Stadium, Bromsgrove Road, Redditch

	P	W	D	L	F	A	Pts
Home:	19	4	5	10	18	29	13
Away:	19	1	3	15	8	40	5
Total:	38	5	8	25	26	69	18

Records:

Win:	Home:	4-1	Wealdstone (79-80)
	Away:	2-0	AP Leamington (79-80)
Defeat:	Home:	1-5	Bangor City (79-80)
	Away:	0-6	Weymouth (79-80)

Northwich Victoria

Founded: 1874   Career: 1979-
Ground: The Drill Field, Drill Field Road, Northwich

	P	W	D	L	F	A	Pts
Home:	457	200	128	129	700	518	680
Away:	457	123	130	204	562	746	489
Total:	914	323	258	333	1262	1264	1169

Records:

Win:	Home:	6-0	Boston Utd (87-8)
	Away:	6-0	Stalybridge Celtic (92-3)
Defeat:	Home:	2-6	Kettering Town (99-2000)
	Away:	1-7	Hednesford Town (2000-1)

Runcorn

Founded: 1918   Career: 1981-96
Ground: Canal Street, Wivern Place, Runcorn

	P	W	D	L	F	A	Pts
Home:	314	165	83	66	584	368	550
Away:	314	93	91	130	385	499	370
Total:	628	258	174	196	969	867	920

Records:

Win:	Home:	9-0	Enfield (89-90)
	Away:	6-0	Boston Utd (88-9)
Defeat:	Home:	0-8	Stevenage B. (95-6)
	Away:	1-6	Bath City (90-1)

Nuneaton Borough

Founded: 1937   Career: 1979-81, 82-87, 99-
Ground: Manor Park, Beaumont Road, Nuneaton

	P	W	D	L	F	A	Pts
Home:	185	86	52	47	316	213	257
Away:	185	43	57	85	218	308	181
Total:	370	129	109	132	534	521	438

Records:

Win:	Home:	5-0	Bath City (82-3) Yeovil T.(84-5)
	Away:	5-2	Bangor C.(80-1)
Defeat:	Home:	1-5	Kettering T.(80-1) Enfield (85-6) Boston U.(86-7)
	Away:	0-6	Wealdstone (86-7)

Rushden & Diamonds

Founded 1992 (Merger of 'Rushden Town' and 'Irthlingborough Diamonds')
Ground: Nene Park, Diamond Way, Irthlingborough   Career 1996-01

	P	W	D	L	F	A	Pts
Home:	105	56	30	19	193	104	198
Away:	105	47	22	36	167	136	163
Total:	210	103	52	55	360	240	361

Records:

Win:	Home:	6-0	Northwich Victoria (99-2000)
	Away:	5-0	Telford U.(96-7) Hayes (99-2000)
Defeat:	Home:	0-4	Gateshead (96-7)
	Away:	0-5	Slough Town (96-7)

Redbridge Forest

Founded: 1989 (See also 'Dagenham' and 'Dagenham & Redbridge)
Ground: Victoria Road, Dagenham   Career: 1991-92

	P	W	D	L	F	A	Pts
Home:	21	12	4	5	42	27	40
Away:	21	6	5	10	27	29	23
Total:	42	18	9	15	69	56	63

Records:

Win:	Home:	5-0	Kidderminster Harriers (91-2)
	Away:	7-0	Cheltenham Town (91-2)
Defeat:	Home:	0-5	Wycombe Wanderers (91-2)
	Away:	1-5	Kidderminster Harriers (91-2)

Scarborough

Founded: 1873   Career: 1979-87, 1999-
Ground: McCain Stadium, Seamer Road, Scarborough

	P	W	D	L	F	A	Pts
Home:	206	98	70	38	328	193	316
Away:	206	71	59	76	259	289	316
Total:	412	169	129	114	587	482	577

Records:

Win:	Home:	6-1	Bath C. (79-80) AP Leamington (81-2)
	Away:	4-0	Nuneaton Borough (80-1)
Defeat:	Home:	0-4	Northwich V.(81-2) Enfield (83/4)
	Away:	0-6	Maidstone Utd (82-3)

Slough Town

Founded: 1890   Career: 1990-94, 95-98
Ground: Wexham Park Stadium, Wexham Road, Slough

	P	W	D	L	F	A	Pts
Home:	147	57	37	53	237	217	208
Away:	147	41	32	74	157	248	155
Total:	294	98	69	127	394	465	363

Records:

Win:	Home:	6-0	Telford U.(96-7)
	Away:	7-3	Altrincham (91-2)
Defeat:	Home:	0-5	Farnborough Town (91-2)
	Away:	2-7	Yeovil Town (90-1)

Stevenage Borough

Founded: 1976   Career: 1994-
Ground: Stevenage Stadium, Broadhall Way, Stevenage

	P	W	D	L	F	A	Pts
Home:	147	71	43	33	278	173	256
Away:	147	61	40	46	230	196	223
Total:	294	132	83	79	508	369	479

Records:

Win:	Home:	6-0	Halifax Town (96-7)
	Away:	8-0	Runcorn (95-6)
Defeat:	Home:	1-5	Hayes (97-8)
	Away:	0-4	Halifax T.(97-8)

Southport

Founded: 1881   Career: 1993-
Ground: Haig Avenue, Southport

	P	W	D	L	F	A	Pts
Home:	168	75	47	46	266	194	272
Away:	168	55	44	69	203	251	209
Total:	336	130	91	115	469	445	481

Records:

Win:	Home:	7-1	Farnborough Town (95-6)
	Away:	5-2	Slough Town (95-6)
Defeat:	Home:	1-5	Macclesfield Town (96-7)
	Away:	0-5	Kidderminster H. (99-00)

Sutton United

Founded: 1898   Career: 1986-91, 99-00
Ground: Borough Sports Ground, Gander Green Lane, Sutton

	P	W	D	L	F	A	Pts
Home:	125	55	33	37	230	164	198
Away:	125	29	36	60	161	216	123
Total:	250	84	69	97	391	380	321

Records:

Win:	Home:	8-0	Kettering Town (86-7)
	Away:	9-0	Gateshead (90-1)
Defeat:	Home:	0-4	Rushden & Diamonds (99-2000)
	Away:	2-6	Barnet (87-8) Morecambe (99-00)

Stafford Rangers

Founded: 1876   Career: 1979-83, 85-95
Ground: Marston Road, Stafford

	P	W	D	L	F	A	Pts
Home:	289	108	88	93	400	349	388
Away:	289	65	85	139	335	482	277
Total:	578	173	173	232	735	831	665

Records:

Win:	Home:	5-1	Dartford (85-6) Merthyr T.(93-4)
	Away:	5-0	Welling U.(87-8)
Defeat:	Home:	2-6	Yeovil Town (88-9)
	Away:	0-6	Witton Alb.(91-2) Halifax T.(94-5)

Telford United

Founded: 1876   Career: 1979-
Ground: Bucks Head Ground, Watling Street, Wellington, Telford

	P	W	D	L	F	A	Pts
Home:	457	216	115	126	683	523	711
Away:	457	129	115	213	533	742	492
Total:	914	345	230	339	1216	1265	1203

Records:

Win:	Home:	7-1	Frickley Ath (81-2)
	Away:	5-0	Barrow (82-3) Bromsgrove R.(93-4)
Defeat:	Home:	0-5	Rushden & Diamonds (96-7)
	Away:	0-6	Maidstone U. (83-4) Halifax T.(93-4)
			Slough T.((96-7)

Stalybridge Celtic

Founded: 1909   Career: 1992-98
Ground: Bower Fold, Mottram Road, Stalybridge

	P	W	D	L	F	A	Pts
Home:	126	46	35	45	178	187	173
Away:	126	29	33	64	136	214	120
Total:	252	75	68	109	314	401	293

Records:

Win:	Home:	6-1	Leek T.(97-8)
	Away:	6-1	Kettering T.(95-6)
Defeat:	Home:	0-6	Northwich Victoria (92-3)
	Away:	0-6	Farnborough Town (97-8)

Trowbridge Town

Founded: 1880   Career: 1981-84
Ground: Frome Road, Trowbridge

	P	W	D	L	F	A	Pts
Home:	63	20	16	27	72	87	73
Away:	63	9	9	45	55	142	36
Total:	126	29	25	72	127	229	109

Records:

Win:	Home:	3-0	Maidstone U.(81-2)
	Away:	3-1	Barnet (82-3)
Defeat:	Home:	0-4	Barnet (83-4)
	Away:	0-6	Maidstone U.(82-3) Wealdstone (83-4)

Wealdstone

Founded: 1899 Career: 1979-81, 82-88
Ground: Lower Mead Stadium, Station Road, Harrow, Middlesex

	P	W	D	L	F	A	Pts
Home:	164	67	55	42	258	196	212
Away:	164	46	44	74	186	247	175
Total:	328	113	99	116	444	443	387

Records:
Win:	Home:	6-0	Barnet (82-3) Trowbridge T.(83-4), Nuneaton B.(86-7)
	Away:	5-1	Yeovil T.(82-3)
Defeat:	Home:	0-6	Barnet (87-8)
	Away:	0-7	Barnet (84-5)

Woking

Founded: 1889 Career: 1992-
Ground: Kingsfield Stadium, Kingsfield, Woking

	P	W	D	L	F	A	Pts
Home:	189	91	49	49	320	222	322
Away:	189	74	47	68	246	270	269
Total:	378	165	96	117	566	492	591

Records:
Win:	Home:	7-1	Altrincham (96-7)
	Away:	5-1	Merthyr T.(92-3)
Defeat:	Home:	1-8	Dagenham & Redbridge (93-4)
	Away:	0-5	Dover A.(93-4) Macclesfield T.(96-7)
			Stevenage B.(98-9)

Welling United

Founded: 1963 Career: 1986-00
Ground: Park View Road, Welling

	P	W	D	L	F	A	Pts
Home:	293	110	79	104	427	398	409
Away:	293	70	77	146	330	491	287
Total:	586	180	156	250	757	889	696

Records:
Win:	Home:	6-0	Boston U.(89-90) Gateshead (90-1)
	Away:	5-0	Witton Albion (93-4)
Defeat:	Home:	0-5	Stafford R.(87-8) Bath C.(91-2)
	Away:	1-6	Barrow (91-2)

Worcester City

Founded: 1902 Career: 1979-85
Ground: St George's Lane, Barbourne, Worcester

	P	W	D	L	F	A	Pts
Home:	122	60	32	30	208	154	174
Away:	122	33	26	63	139	222	114
Total:	244	93	58	93	347	376	288

Records:
Win:	Home:	6-2	Kettering T.(82-3)
	Away:	4-0	Bath City (79-80)
Defeat:	Home:	0-4	Wealdstone (84-5)
	Away:	0-6	Enfield (84-5)

Weymouth

Founded: 1890 Career: 1979-89
Ground: Wessex Stadium, Radipole Lane, Weymouth (Formerly Rec. Ground)

	P	W	D	L	F	A	Pts
Home:	205	106	49	50	355	232	314
Away:	205	58	53	94	248	321	210
Total:	410	164	102	144	603	553	524

Records:
Win:	Home:	6-0	Redditch Utd (79-80)
	Away:	5-0	Yeovil Town (80-1)
Defeat:	Home:	0-4	Wealdstone (83-4)
	Away:	0-5	Boston U.(85-6) Welling U.(86-7)

Wycombe Wanderers

Founded: 1887 Career: 1985-86, 87-93
Ground: Adam's Park, Hillbottom Rd., Sands, High Wycombe (Formerly Loakes Park)

	P	W	D	L	F	A	Pts
Home:	146	81	33	32	279	173	269
Away:	146	52	40	54	201	213	196
Total:	292	133	73	86	480	386	465

Records:
Win:	Home:	6-1	Stafford R.(88-9) Fisher A.(89-90) Telford U.(91-2)
	Away:	5-0	Redbridge Forest (91-2)
Defeat:	Home:	0-7	Barnet (87-8)
	Away:	2-8	Kidderminster Harriers (85-6)

Witton Albion

Founded: 1887 Career: 1991-94
Ground: Wincham Park, Chapel Street, Wincham, Northwich

	P	W	D	L	F	A	Pts
Home:	63	20	23	20	89	90	83
Away:	63	14	17	32	73	98	59
Total:	126	34	40	52	162	188	142

Records:
Win:	Home:	6-0	Stafford Rangers (91-2)
	Away:	3-0	Telford Utd (92-3)
Defeat:	Home:	0-5	Welling U.(93-4)
	Away:	0-4	Wycombe Wanderers (91-2)

Yeovil Town

Founded: 1897 Career: 1979-85, 88-95, 97-
Ground: Huish Park, Lufton Way, Yeovil (Formerly Huish)

	P	W	D	L	F	A	Pts
Home:	352	156	83	113	571	458	521
Away:	352	89	90	173	413	626	347
Total:	704	245	173	286	984	1084	867*

* 1 point deducted.

Records:
Win:	Home:	7-2	Slough Town (90-1)
	Away:	6-2	Stafford Rangers (88-9)
Defeat:	Home:	0-5	Weymouth (80-1)
	Away:	1-7	Altrincham (81-2)

25 Of The Best
Players who 'Made It' in the Football League

Tony Agana
Born: Bromley
2/10/63
Weymouth

For a small club with humble beginnings, Welling United have a tremendous record for developing young players through their youth team, into the first eleven and then sending them on their way to join the ranks of the full-time professionals. Tony Agana was one of the first to follow this path.

Tony was only twenty years old when he left Welling for Weymouth, but he had already been at the Kent club for five years. It was his blistering pace as a winger that attracted the scouts' attention, but he scored his fair share of goals and was Welling's leading scorer in 1983-84, despite leaving the club in March that season. The fee involved was nominal, but as Tony had to transfer his employment to Poole a move was necessary. Over the next three seasons Tony missed less than twenty league and cup games and scored at least a dozen goals each campaign. This tremendous consistency for a winger earned him two England semi-professional caps in 1986.

In the summer of 1987, Watford paid £35,000 for Tony, who was in the unenviable position of being looked upon as a replacement for the recently departed John Barnes. It was a near impossible task for a non-League player and after six months Agana was on the move to Sheffield United, who were soon to be relegated to Division 3. The climb back to the top was spearheaded by Agana and Brian Deane, who scored seventy-seven League goals between them in two successive promotion campaigns.

The goals dried up once back in the top flight, and there was a lengthy spell on the sidelines for Tony to endure. However, Notts County, themselves desperate to stay in Division One, were prepared to spend £750,000 for his goalscoring potential. Unfortunately, the potential was never realised and in the next five and a half years, Tony could only find the net fifteen times in nearly 150 matches. There were two relegations during his stay, but the highlights were provided by two Anglo Italian Cup Finals at Wembley, with Tony scoring in the victorious 1995 showdown against Ascoli.

In March 1997, Tony left Notts County on a free transfer for Hereford United, but two goals in five games could not stop Hereford slipping into the Conference on the final day of the season. After one year in the Conference with the Bulls, he moved on to Leek Town, but another season of struggle ended with their relegation to the Unibond League in 1999 and Tony left to continue his career at Guiseley.

Steve Claridge
Born: Portsmouth
10/4/66
Weymouth

Steve joined his hometown club as an associate schoolboy but was released by them during his spell as an apprentice professional. He started playing for nearby Fareham Town until he was recommended to A.F.C. Bournemouth manager Harry Redknapp, by a mutual friend who had faith in Steve's abilities.

He made his League debut on New Year's Day, 1985, at home to Gillingham, and scored his only first team goal in his seven appearances on the final day of the season, in a 3-0 home win against Newport County. It was while playing in the reserves, that Weymouth manager Stuart Morgan spotted him and after an initial loan period he was signed for £10,000 in October 1985. He scored twenty goals in his first season, but the following was less successful. In 1987-88, Steve was back to his best finishing the season as top goalscorer and was voted Player of the Year. Things turned sour before the last game of the season, the G.M.A.C. Cup Final against Horwich R.M.I., when Steve found himself dropped to the bench, and he decided it was time to leave. Due to an oversight, he was not sent a contract renewal, so he was free to go.

There was interest from several non-League clubs, but after playing some pre-season games for Basingstoke, he was recommended to Steve Coppell at Crystal Palace, who signed him. By October he was back in Hampshire, at Aldershot, and so started an odyssey through the lower echelons of the Football League. There were two spells at Cambridge United and one at both Luton Town and Birmingham City. Successes came with successive promotions at Cambridge and another, plus an Auto Windscreens Shield victory, with Birmingham.

In March 1996 Leicester City paid Birmingham £1.2 million for Steve, hoping he would boost their chances of promotion to the Premiership. It was money well spent as he scored the winning goal in the Play-off final at Wembley. The following season he also scored the only goal in the League Cup final replay against Middlesborough.

With Steve no longer a fixture in the first team, he returned to Portsmouth for two months on loan, before a £350,000 transfer to Wolverhampton Wanderers saw him play in the 1998 F.A.Cup Semi-final against Arsenal. His permanent return to Pompey was completed in August 1998, where he was voted Player of the Year in 1999 and 2000 and was also top goalscorer in the latter season. When Tony Pulis was sacked early in the 2000-01 season, Steve was installed as player/ manager, much to the fans delight. Unfortunately , the results were not to the Chairman's liking, and when Steve was relieved of this position, he moved to Millwall for the remainder of the campaign, helping them to clinch the 2000-01 Division Two championship.

```
┌─────────────────────────┐
│      Andy Clarke        │
│   Born: Islington       │
│        22/7/67          │
│        Barnet           │
└─────────────────────────┘
```

Andy Clarke was playing Sunday league football in Edmonton when he was spotted by Barry Fry, and he signed for Barnet towards the end of the 1988-89 season and made his debut in the final league game of the season at Sutton. A weakened side lost a meaningless fixture 5-1, but Clarke scored the consolation goal. He was in the side for the first game of the next campaign and while the goals did not flow he was making an impact with his pace and power. As the season progressed, Andy began to find the net on a regular basis and the Barry Fry publicity machine went into overdrive. Leicester City, Manchester United and Newcastle United all watched him, Arsenal arranged a special trial match, and six figure bids from Cambridge United and Bournemouth were rejected. Clarke finished the season as Conference Player of the Year and he also won two England semi-professional caps.

Over the 1990 close season, Swindon bid £500,000 for Clarke and his team mate Phil Gridelet, whilst Queens Park Rangers were also said to be interested, but it was not until February 21st 1991 that Clarke was finally sold to Wimbledon. The fee was in instalments, initially £ 150,000, eventually rising to £300,000. During his time at Barnet he had made 111 appearances, and scored 48 goals.

The jump to the First Division proved difficult and while Clarke went straight into the first team squad, most of his appearances were as a substitute, where his explosive pace could be used against tiring opponents. Having never established a regular place in the team, Clarke left The Dons in the 1999 close season to join his old mentor, Barry Fry, at Peterborough United. He was top scorer at the end of his first season and scored the only goal of the play-off final at Wembley to secure promotion to Division Two for the Posh.

```
┌─────────────────────────┐
│     Stan Collymore      │
│     Born: Stone         │
│        22/1/71          │
│    Stafford Rangers     │
└─────────────────────────┘
```

Stan's footballing life began in Birmingham where he played for the county schoolboy's team. After spells at Birmingham City and Walsall, he spent a year with Wolverhampton Wanderers on their Youth Training Scheme, but was released by the club in the summer of 1989. He joined Stafford Rangers and made his debut at home to Merthyr on October 7th. Stan scored his first goal a week later in the F.A.Cup-tie at Lye Town and during the course of the season he made sixteen appearances, plus a dozen as substitute, and notched eight goals. The next year he netted twelve goals in twenty-three games and his displays persuaded Crystal Palace to pay £100,000 for his services.

At Palace, he was in the shadow of Wright and Bright and was not given a regular first team spot when they left the club. His potential was spotted by Colin Murphy at Southend United, who signed him on loan prior to a permanent £150,000 deal being completed in November 1992. Eighteen goals in thirty- three matches helped Southend preserve their First Division status and earned a transfer to Nottingham Forest. Looking to return to the Premiership, Forest paid a club record £2 million fee in July 1993, hoping they had bought someone who could provide a constant supply of goals. It was a story of total success. Over two seasons, Stan scored fifty goals in seventy-eight games, Forest gained promotion in the 1993-94 season, and finished third in the Premiership the following year during which time Stan won two England caps in the 1995 Umbro Cup.

When Stan joined Liverpool that summer, it was for a British record transfer fee of £8.5 million. His return of thirty-five League and cup goals in two seasons did not measure up to expectations and Stan was happy to move back to the Midlands to join the club he supported as a boy, Aston Villa, for £7 million. By now Collymore was creating more headlines off the pitch than on and the move was a major disappointment all round. At the start of the 1999-2000 season he was sent to Fulham on loan, but failed to secure a permanent move. It was Leicester City who gave him the chance to resurrect his career, but he suffered a broken leg after six games. Bradford City, who needed a goalscorer signed him the following season, but after brief spells in Yorkshire and Spain, with Real Oviedo, he announced his retirement at the age of thirty.

> ## Efan Ekoku
> ### Born: Manchester
> ### 8/6/67
> ### Sutton United

Anyone fortunate enough to have been present at the Sutton United v Coventry City F.A.Cup-tie in January 1989 may not have spent long studying the report of the latest reserve match. If they had, they would have read about Efan's first game in a Sutton Utd shirt.

Signed from local side Merton, he made his first team debut on 4th February in an F.A.Trophy tie against Bishop Auckland and remained in the first team squad for the remainder of the campaign. A hat-trick in the final game at home to Barnet set him up for the following season when he was to be the second highest scorer in the Conference with twenty-five goals. His pairing up front with record goalscorer Paul McKinnon produced forty goals and Efan's strength and direct running earned a call up to the England semi-Professional squad as well as attracting the League scouts. It was A.F.C. Bournemouth who secured his signature for a transfer fee of £100,000 in May 1990.

Efan's first two seasons were dogged by injury and of his forty-eight League appearances, nearly half were as a substitute. An injury to his right ankle meant that Efan did not play in the 1992-93 season until January 9th, but two goals on his return heralded a spell of seven goals in fourteen games. The run was concluded by a £765,000 move to Premier League Norwich City where he scored three times in four games before the season's end. His good form continued in the 1993-94 season but in October 1994, Efan was heading back to Surrey to join Wimbledon for just under £1 million. While not a prolific goalscorer he was the club's top League marksman in 1994-95 and 1997-98 and played a significant part in the Don's efforts to stay in the top flight.

In August 1999, Roy Hodgson paid £500,000 to take Efan to Grasshoppers Zurich where he stayed until answering the call from struggling Sheffield Wednesday. Already in a perilous position in Division One, the Yorkshire club signed Efan for the remainder of the season in October 2000 to beef up their attack and his experience and goals were crucial in securing Wednesdays eventual safety.

Steve Finnan
Born: Chelmsford
20/4/76
Welling United

Another product of the Kent club's nursery, Steve joined Welling United as part of the Youth Training Scheme. A member of the club's successful youth team, Steve made his first team debut when he came on as a substitute in the Drinkwise Cup-tie with Kettering on 7th September 1993. Even at the age of seventeen he was not out of his depth, and became a regular first team squad member for the rest of the season. Steve also had the distinction of becoming the 'Wings' first full-time professional when he signed a contract mid-season. Frustration followed in 1994-95, with a five month spell on the sidelines. However, his form on either side of the lay-off was enough to persuade Barry Fry to take the youngster to Birmingham City for an initial £35,000 fee.

Steve made a dozen first team appearances for the Blues in 1995-96 before spending the last two months of the season on loan to Notts County. His form clearly impressed County who went back to Birmingham in November 1996 and paid £300,000 to make the transfer permanent. The following season Steve was an integral part in County's Division Three Championship winning team.

In November 1998, Fulham brought him to London for £600,000 and since then Steve has been a regular performer in the right-wing-back position. Division Two and Division One Championship medals have been secured and Steve has also gained international recognition with the Republic of Ireland, making his full debut against Greece in April 2000.

```
┌─────────────────────────┐
│     Paul Furlong        │
│  Born: Wood Green       │
│       1/10/68           │
│      Enfield            │
└─────────────────────────┘
```

Paul was a product of Enfield's youth and reserve sides who made his first team bow when he appeared as a substitute in a Middlesex Senior Cup-tie against Feltham in December 1986. It was not until the following September that he made his Conference debut, at home to Kidderminster Harriers. He kept his place for the next game at Maidstone where he opened his goals account. The promise that he showed meant that he stayed in the side for the majority of the season as Enfield progressed to the F.A.Trophy final. In the Final replay, Furlong scored twice, including the winning goal eight minutes from time.

Over the next two seasons, as Enfield descended to the foot of the table, Furlong's form was one of the rare highlights. Top goalscorer in each campaign, Paul was called up to the England semi-professional side, a place he held even after Enfield's relegation to the Vauxhall League, a rare feat for a non-Conference player.

At the end of the 1990-91 season, Coventry City paid £130,000 for Paul. He started the season on the City bench, but earned a first eleven spot with four goals in his initial eight appearances. But the step up in class proved too great and after one year he moved to Watford for £250,000. Paul regained his goal-scoring touch with forty-one goals in two seasons, prompting Chelsea to spend £2.5 million on him in May 1994. Once again the Premiership defences proved a tougher nut to crack and after two moderately successful seasons, Birmingham City paid £1.5 million to take him back to Division One. The goals started to flow again, although his latter years have been dogged with injury, which also interrupted a loan spell back in London at Queens Park Rangers.

```
┌─────────────────────────┐
│     Barry Hayles        │
│  Born: London           │
│       17/4/72           │
│  Stevenage Borough      │
└─────────────────────────┘
```

It was while playing for Willesden Hawkeye in the Spartan League, that Barry got his big break. He was selected to play for the Middlesex F.A against the Hertfordshire F.A at Stevenage and his performance that evening caught the attention of the watching Stevenage Borough manager. He was signed during the 1993-4 season, but played only a peripheral role in their Isthmian League Championship campaign. After a disappointing start to 'Boro's debut Conference season, Hayles was given a regular place in the side and finished as top scorer as the club climbed the table to fifth position. He was selected to play in the F.A.X1 versus the Highland League at the end of the 1994-95 season, and followed this up with an exceptional 1995-96 campaign. Named Conference 'Player of the Year' and Mail on Sunday goalscorer of the year with, 29 , Hayles played a major part in Stevenage's championship success and was capped twice at semi-professional level, scoring in each game.

Naturally enough, Hayles was now the subject of attention from several League teams and Bristol Rovers had a bid of £200,000 turned down. His level of performance in 1996-97 dropped from its previous high standard and a broken leg sustained at Welling kept him sidelined for two months. A goalscoring burst at the end of the season rekindled interest and he eventually signed for Bristol Rovers in the close season for £300,000. 32 League goals in sixty-two games attracted a successful bid of £2,000,000 from Kevin Keegan's big spending Fulham. After promotion to Division One, Hayles struggled to adapt to the higher standard, but in his second full season he formed a devastating attacking line up with Saha and Boa Morte as the Championship and Premiership status were secured.

Andy Hessenthaler
Born: Gravesend
17/8/65
Redbridge Forest

The proverbial human dynamo in midfield, Andy's career has seen him return to his roots on the North Kent coast. His formative years were spent at Dartford where he was a product of their youth policy and graduated to the reserves. When Dartford disbanded the reserves, Andy moved to Charlton Athletic where he played thirty-five games in the Football Combination in 1983-84.

Released by the Addicks, Andy joined Kent non-League side Corinthian and during his two year stay the club successfully stepped up to the Southern League. In October 1986, Dartford signed him and under manager Peter Taylor, the club had a successful period, albeit without winning the silverware. In four seasons, the Darts always finished in the top four in the Southern League and twice reached the F.A. Trophy semi-finals. During his last season with Dartford, Andy's exploits gained him his only England semi-professional cap and also earned him the club's 'Player of the Year' award. They also attracted the attention of other clubs and in the summer of 1990, Redbridge Forest signed him in a cash plus player exchange deal valued at £25,000.

In his first season at Redbridge, the Vauxhall-Opel League was won and the club was promoted to the Conference. For Andy it was a brief stay as his old mentor Peter Taylor, newly installed as Watford Manager, decided to pay £65,000 to take him to Vicarage Road. It was a small price to pay for nearly five years service and over two hundred first team appearances. In August 1996, Gillingham brought him back to Kent for £235,000 and Andy was at the forefront in their struggle for promotion from the Second Division. The Gills lost the play-off final in 1999 but twelve months later, guided by Peter Taylor, they won a place in the First Division via the play-offs. When Taylor left for Leicester City Hessenthaler was installed as player-manager and while injury has restricted his appearances, his leadership qualities have seen Gillingham settle comfortably at the higher level.

```
┌─────────────────────────────┐
│         Lee Hughes          │
│      Born: Birmingham       │
│           22/5/76           │
│    Kidderminster Harriers   │
└─────────────────────────────┘
```

Lee joined Kidderminster Harriers as a fifteen year old and progressed through the youth and reserve teams. He signed a full contract with the club in August 1994 and made his Conference debut when appearing as a substitute against Northwich Victoria on September 5th. His full debut came in the next fixture with his first goal being scored against eventual champions Macclesfield Town three days later. A first hat-trick followed against Bath on September 24th and while learning from two of the great non-League strikers, Kim Casey and Paul Davies, Hughes kept his place in the first team squad for the remainder of the season. With Kidderminster reaching the F.A. Trophy Final, Hughes finished the campaign with a place on the Wembley bench as his side lost to Woking 2-1.

Season 1995-96 saw steady progress. Despite a regular place in the side Lee could only score thirteen goals, but his performances were sufficient to earn him two semi-professional international caps. The major breakthrough was made the following season. With thirty-four goals in League, Trophy and F.A.Cup, Lee notched seven goals more than his nearest challenger, and despite Kidderminster narrowly missing out on the major trophies, Lee captured his dream move to the club he had always supported, West Bromwich Albion, for an initial fee of £250,000.

During his four seasons with The Baggies, Hughes has been top League goalscorer each campaign, with the best return of 31 League goals in season 1998-99. He has been linked with moves to several Premiership clubs but remains with West Bromwich where he currently forms a prolific striking partnership with another Conference old boy, Jason Roberts.

```
┌─────────────────────────────┐
│         Andy Hunt           │
│      Born: Thurrock         │
│           9/6/70            │
│       Kettering Town        │
└─────────────────────────────┘
```

Andy was playing village football for Ashill when he was spotted by Kings Lynn who signed him in 1989. He was to spend less than a season with the Beazer Homes League side before his transfer to Kettering Town in exchange for Neil Horwood in August 1990.

Andy made his Kettering debut at home to Gateshead on August 25th, and during his spell at Kettering, he played his part in taking the Poppies to the top of the table. Although he only scored six goals in twenty-seven appearances the watching scouts were obviously impressed with what they saw. A fee of £150,000, the second highest paid for a Conference player, took Andy to St James Park, Newcastle, at the end of January 1991. Manager Ossie Ardiles introduced Andy to the team at the beginning of March and he was a regular until Kevin Keegan replaced the Argentinian the following February.

Hunt never figured in Keegan's plans and in March 1993 he moved to West Bromwich Albion on loan. Ossie Ardiles was now manager at West Brom., and he must have been delighted with the impact his new signing made. Nine goals in ten games, including a hat-trick on his home debut pushed Albion to the play-offs where Andy scored again in the Final at Wembley. A permanent £100,000 transfer was quickly completed.

Over the next five seasons, Andy was top scorer twice, netting at least a dozen goals in each campaign and he formed a striking partnership with Bob Taylor that helped to keep Albion in Division 1.

In the summer of 1998, he was signed by Charlton Athletic to score the goals to help them maintain their newly acquired Premiership status. However, the player was unable to prevent the Londoners returning to Division 1, but in season 1999-2000, Andy was the division's top goalscorer with twenty-four, as Charlton won the Championship. A good start to 2000-01 was brought to a conclusion by illness which was diagnosed as post viral fatigue syndrome, and after several unsuccessful attempts at a comeback Andy was forced to retire at the age of 30.

Paul Jones
Born: Chirk
18/4/67
Kidderminster Harriers

Born on the English/Welsh border, Paul's football career started as a youngster at Wem Town in Shropshire. After a spell at local Football League side Shrewsbury Town, he moved to Bridgnorth Town in the Southern League in 1984. His displays attracted the attention of Kidderminster Harriers manager Graham Allner who signed him in October 1986. Although the Harriers already had two goalkeepers on their books, Paul was quickly drafted into the first team, making his debut on October 7th away to Kettering Town. He played in the first two rounds of Kidderminster's F.A. Trophy campaign, but in January 1987, Jim Arnold was signed and the veteran 'keeper was first choice for the remainder of the season, saving a vital penalty in the Trophy Final replay at the Hawthorns.

Although disappointed to miss out on the Final, Paul benefitted from coaching by Arnold, who had played in the Football League with Everton and Blackburn Rovers. It was in December 1987 that Jones gained a regular first team berth, a position that he was to retain for the next three and a half seasons.

During that time he missed only six matches and earned F.A. recognition as well as being put on standby for the England Semi-professional side. His final game for the Harriers was at Wembley in the 1991 F.A. Trophy final which ended in defeat at the hands of Wycombe Wanderers.

In the Summer, Wolverhampton Wanderers paid £40,000 for Paul, who spent the next five seasons as understudy to Mike Stowell. During this period, Paul could only amass thirty-three League appearances and it was only after a £60,000 transfer to Stockport County that he was able to establish himself as a first team regular. During the 1996-97 season, Paul gained his first Welsh Cap and when Manager Dave Jones moved to Southampton in the close season, he took Paul with him. A model of consistency, he has been first choice at the Dell for four seasons, only missing games due to injury. His form has also seen him secure the Welsh goalkeeper's shirt on a regular basis.

Vinnie Jones
Born: Watford
5/11/65
Wealdstone

As a schoolboy, Vinnie was on the books of his hometown club, but when he was released, he gave up football for a time, apart from a brief spell at Hertford Town. It was his mates who persuaded him to play again, this time with Bedmond Social, in the village where he by now lived.

Vinnie's breakthrough came when he was working as a groundsman at a college in Bushey where Wealdstone trained pre-season. One day Vinnie asked if he could join in and did sufficiently well for Wealdstone to sign him in August 1984. As the season progressed he secured a place in the first team squad which was the most successful in Wealdstone's history. The Gola League title was secured and although he played in the second leg of the Semi-final, Vinnie missed out on a place in the F.A. Trophy Final. The following season, he was a squad member again, and to further his football education he went to Sweden to play for IFK Holmsund in the summer of 1986. The move was arranged by Dave Bassett, who kept an eye on his progress, and on Vinnie's return to England he was offered a trial at Wimbledon which ended in his transfer in November 1986 for a fee of £8,000.

He first hit the headlines in his home debut, scoring the only goal in a victory over Manchester United. His uncompromising approach saw him earn a regular place in the team which he only lost due to a knee injury early in the 1987-88 campaign. Success was on the horizon as Wimbledon reached the F.A.Cup Final in 1988, and Vinnie's midfield battle with Steve McMahon was one of the decisive factors as the Dons caused a massive upset with their 1-0 victory.

Vinnie was subsequently sent-off in the pre-season friendly match at Shanklin on the Isle of Wight and he received a lengthy suspension. However, his poor disciplinary record (13 dismissals in 12 years) did not deter clubs from seeking his services. In 1989, he commenced a two year spell in Yorkshire at Leeds United and Sheffield United before returning to London with Chelsea. In 1992 he returned to Wimbledon where he played nearly two hundred games and earned nine caps for Wales, qualifying by way of his Welsh grandfather. In 1998, Q.P.R. signed Vinnie but a dispute with the club, together with a budding career as an actor saw him hang up his boots in 1999. His big screen debut in *'Lock, Stock and Two Smoking Barrels'* brought forth much praise and it seems likely that Vinnie could achieve even more success as an actor than he did on the football field.

John McGinlay
Born: Inverness
8/4/64
Yeovil Town

Born in the Scottish Highlands, John's football career began further south when he played for Celtic Boys Club. His career continued nearer to home when he joined Highland League Club Nairn County. He had an unsuccessful trial with Sunderland, but impressed one of the coaches, Cecil Irwin. As a former Yeovil manager, Irwin recommended him to the struggling Somerset team who signed him up. He made his first team debut against Telford on 30th March 1985, replacing a certain Ian Botham in the No.9 shirt. He scored twice in a 3-3 draw, but was unable to save Yeovil from certain relegation.

In total, John spent three seasons at the 'Huish' and scored fifty six-goals in over one hundred and twenty games. He left Yeovil towards the end of the 1987-88 season, as a move back up to the Conference was being secured and he returned to his native Highlands with Elgin City. He was leading goalscorer with his new club when Shrewsbury Town brought him back south of the border in exchange for £25,000 in February 1989. He scored on his full debut, but it was in season 1989-90 that he hit the headlines scoring twenty-four goals. Much in demand, John signed for Bury in the summer of 1990 for £175,000, a club record fee. Eight months and nine goals later, Millwall signed him after a loan spell, but when manager Bruce Rioch moved to Bolton Wanderers, John followed him and his career took-off.

During his five full seasons with Bolton, John was instrumental in securing three promotions and a place in the 1995 Coca-Cola Cup Final. He was leading scorer in four consecutive seasons and was selected for the Scottish National Team on fourteen occasions, scoring four goals. In November 1997 Bradford City paid a club record fee of £625,000 to take him to Valley Parade, but an Achilles injury soon sidelined him and forced him to miss the 1998 World Cup. Having been released by Bradford, he attempted a comeback with Oldham before injury problems struck again. John is now using his experience in a managerial capacity at Dr Martens League side Gresley Rovers.

Eddie McGoldrick
Born: Islington
30/4/65
Kettering Town/Nuneaton Borough

Originally with Kettering Town as a schoolboy, Eddie was signed on schoolboy forms by Peterborough United in December 1979. But when not offered an apprenticeship, he returned to his former club. His exploits in the youths and reserves earned him trials for the England U-18 side and it was no surprise when he made his first team debut in a minor competition in December 1981. By the end of the season, Eddie had grabbed his chance and made the number two shirt his own for the 1982-83 season. In the summer of 1984, he joined Nuneaton where he showed his versatility by appearing at full-back and in midfield before establishing himself as a winger.

In 1986, McGoldrick was signed by Northampton Town in a joint deal with young goalkeeper Alan Harris. For a fee of £10,000, the Cobblers obtained a player who used his pace to get at opposing defenders and supplied the crosses for the forwards. He played an important role in the team's successes and it was no surprise when after two and a half years and over one hundred appearances he moved on to Crystal Palace for £200,000.

In his first season with the Eagles, Eddie helped them back to the First Division. Injury meant that he missed the 1990 F.A.Cup Final, but he did appear at Wembley the following season in the ZDS Final. Eddie's parents originated from Co. Dublin, and he made his international debut for the Republic of Ireland in 1992. When Palace were relegated in 1993 he moved across London to Arsenal for £1 million. After a successful first season, including an appearance in the European Cup Winners Cup Final, his luck took a turn for the worse. His confidence was dented by some crowd barracking and injuries which restricted his appearances.

A loan move to Manchester City in September 1996 was made permanent one month later and for the remainder of the season Eddie was a first team regular. The following year, Eddie played only seven League games for City and two on loan to Stockport County. With City in free fall and with a massive first team squad, Eddie was surplus to requirements and he was transfer-listed in February 1998 before being given a free transfer at the end of the season.

The earliest part of Trevor's football career was spent on the books of Derby County as an apprentice professional. Having failed to make the grade he drifted into the non-League scene at Corby Town where he attracted the attention of Nuneaton Borough. He was signed for a club record fee of £7,700 in a joint deal, with Corby team-mate Derek Walker, and immediately started repaying the fee not only with goals but with also his tireless work for the team. Under manager Graham Carr, Nuneaton finished runners-up in the Alliance in consecutive seasons (1983-84 and 1984-85) and Trevor was an integral part of their success, providing chances for goal-scoring machine Paul Culpin. Trevor also earned five England Semi-pro caps.

When Carr left to manage Northampton Town in the summer of 1985, Morley and team-mate Richard Hill followed for a joint fee of £35,000. With a line-up which included many ex non-League players, the Cobblers won the Fourth Division title in 1986-87 and narrowly missed out on a play-off place the following season. Morley, with 45 goals in 130 matches, left the Cobblers in January 1988. He was bound for Watford but when their manager Dave Bassett left the club the day before the move, Manchester City stepped in with a deal worth £260,000. After nearly two years and twenty-one goals with the Maine Road club, West Ham United paid half a million pounds for Morley. Over the next five and a half seasons, the Hammers received an excellent return on their investment. Trevor scored seventy goals in over two hundred games for the club, helping them to return to Division 1 in 1990-91 when he was top goalscorer.

In 1995 he joined Reading and stayed for three seasons before emigrating to Norway where he had played for Brann Bergen during several close seasons.

As a youngster, Stuart trained with his local League club Queens Park Rangers for a short time, but his career was kick-started when his school caretaker recommended some pupils to Wealdstone. He joined the club and after spells in the youth and reserve teams, he made his first team debut as a sixteen year old in a 5-1 defeat at Dorchester in March 1979.

During the next four and a half years, Stuart played two hundred and forty-two games, scoring fifteen goals. He set a club record of ninety-two consecutive league appearances between 1980-1982 and helped the club win the Southern League and Cup Double in 1982. His reputation as a strong tackling wholehearted defender drew the scouts to Lower Mead and Stuart did go to Hull City for a trial. However, with Coventry in need of a left-back, Bobby Gould agreed to pay £25,000 for his services, and within a month Stuart was making his full debut, ironically against Queens Park Rangers.

In the summer of 1985, a joint transfer with Ian Butterworth took Pearce to Nottingham Forest for £200,000. While Butterworth was gone within eighteen months, Stuart was to stay with Forest for twelve seasons and in the process become one of the most popular of players to wear the team's colours. He made a total of 522 first team appearances, scoring 88 goals which included a large percentage of free-kicks and penalties. Seventy-six England Caps were won during his stay at the City ground, making him the club's most capped player.

The most memorable moments of his international career came during the 1990 World Cup and the 1996 European Championship when he surrounded his contrasting fortunes from the penalty spot. Domestically Stuart won the League Cup in 1989 and 1990 and the Full Members Cup in 1989 and 1992, while in the F.A.Cup he was a losing finalist in 1991 despite scoring an early goal to give Forest the lead.

Such was his stature at the club that he was given the job of player/caretaker manager during the 1996-97 season but he was unable to inspire Forest to avoid relegation and left in the summer.

He was signed by Kenny Dalglish to strengthen Newcastle United's defence and finished his first season at the club with another losers medal from the F.A.Cup Final. A change of Manager the following season saw Stuart left on the sidelines and in the Summer of 1999 he moved to West Ham United on a free transfer. His early season form saw him recalled to the England team but two broken legs in quick succession looked to have ended his career.

However, Stuart was back at the start of the 2000-01 campaign and playing as well as ever. His contribution to football was recognised when he was awarded the M.B.E. in 1998.

As a youngster, Graham was on the books of his hometown club on Associate Schoolboy forms. When he was released, he spent a short spell playing in the Hampshire League with Sholling Sports before signing for A.F.C. Bournemouth where he played in the youth team. From there, he had a short spell at Portsmouth before joining Dorchester Town, initially on loan, in March 1977.

The early part of his career was spent as a striker and his goals helped Dorchester gain promotion in 1977-78. In the following season, he was top goalscorer and after 33 goals in 79 League appearances, Weymouth decided to pay £6,000 for his services in August 1979.

Now playing as a midfield ball-winner with an eye for goal, Graham had played twenty-nine League games in the Alliance's inaugural season when fate took a hand in his future. Bill Nicholson was on an unsuccessful scouting trip for Tottenham Hotspur when a chance conversation with a stranger on Swindon station threw up Roberts' name as a promising young non-League player. The next week, Nicholson went to watch him. Graham scored twice, and in May 1980 a deal was completed for a fee of £20,000 plus a visit to the Dorset club by the 'Spurs Team.

By December, Roberts was a fixture in the side. F.A.Cup wins in 1980-81 and 1981-82 were followed by U.E.F.A. Cup success in 1984 when Roberts captained the side. His performances as the holding midfield player alongside Hoddle's creativity earned him six England caps. In December 1986 he joined the English influx at Rangers where he won a Scottish Premier League winners medal in 1987. After twenty months in Scotland it was back to London with Chelsea where he was the defensive kingpin in Chelsea's record breaking Second Division championship success.

In November 1990, Roberts was signed by Second Division West Bromwich for £250,000, but he was unable to prevent their relegation at the end of the season. By the summer of 1992, he was released and joined Diadora League Enfield, eventually becoming player/manager.

After leaving Enfield, Graham has played and managed at several non-League clubs - Slough Town (twice), Stevenage Borough, Yeovil Town, Wealdstone, Chesham United, Hertford Town and Boreham Wood. His most successful period was at Yeovil where he helped them gain promotion to the Conference in 1997.

```
┌─────────────────────────────────────┐
│          Malcolm Shotton            │
│   Born: Newcastle-upon-Tyne         │
│            16/2/57                   │
│        Nuneaton Borough             │
└─────────────────────────────────────┘
```

A native of the North-East, Malcom's football career began at Leicester City where he progressed as far as the reserves without making his first team debut. When he was released, he drifted into the Midlands non-League scene at Atherstone Town. Working as a dyer in a small factory, it was his hope that one day he could return to League football.

It was with Nuneaton Borough that his performances brought him to the attention of the League scouts. A physical and dependable centre-half, he benefitted from the coaching that he received from his Manager, ex-Coventry City defender Roy Barry. At the end of the Alliance's first season, Third Division Oxford United paid £15,000 to secure his services, where he was to form a no-nonsense central defensive partnership with Gary Briggs. As Captain of the side, he led United to the most successful period in their history. Two promotions brought First Division football to the Manor Ground in 1985 and the Milk Cup was won at Wembley with a 3-0 victory over Queens Park Rangers.

He was transferred to Portsmouth in 1987 in an attempt to shore up their defence on their return to Division 1, but ultimately this proved unsuccessful and he moved onto Yorkshire where he had spells at Huddersfield Town, Barnsley, and Hull City, with a brief sojourn to Ayr United in between. Coaching posts at Barnsley and Bradford City followed before a short-lived return to Oxford United as Manager.

```
┌─────────────────────────────────────┐
│           Mark Taylor               │
│   Born: Hildesheim, Germany         │
│            4/9/71                    │
│        Farnborough Town             │
└─────────────────────────────────────┘
```

Mark was born in Germany where his father was in the Armed Forces. As a Schoolboy he played as a sweeper, but successfully converted to a goalkeeper. He joined the Army, posted at Aldershot, and represented both the Army and the Combined Services. Mark started playing for Farnborough's reserve side in the Capital League and after a ten match loan spell at Basingstoke Town, he established himself as the first team 'keeper in their Beazer Homes Premier League championship winning team in 1993-94. After one season in the Conference, he did enough in a trial to convince former England goalkeeper Ray Clemence that he was capable of playing at a higher level, and the Barnet manager paid £700 to buy him out of the Army and take him to Underhill in June 1995.

His Football League career had an inauspicious start when a clearance from Hereford United 'keeper Chris McKenzie ended up in the Barnet net. Thankfully, this was a momentary slip and during the 1995-96 season, Mark missed just one game and was voted 'Player of the Year' by the supporters. In December 1996 Barnet sold him to Southampton, the club he had supported as a lad, for £500,000. He made his debut for the Saints on 11th January 1997 and stayed in the side for the rest of the season, as they pulled away from the foot of the table to maintain their Premiership status.

When Dave Jones was appointed the Saints manager in the summer, he brought Paul Jones with him from Stockport, leaving Mark out in the cold. In November 1997 ambitious Fulham signed Mark for £700,000, where he benefitted from coaching by another former England goalkeeper, Peter Bonetti. In three and a half seasons with the Londoners, Mark has missed just three matches and has played a major role in their promotions from Division 2 to the Premiership. His form has also earned him international recognition with Northern Ireland for whom he made his full debut in March 1999 against the country of his birth, Germany.

Shaun Teale
Born: Southport
10/3/64
Northwich Victoria/Weymouth

The earliest part of Shaun's football career was spent on the books of Everton and Huddersfield Town, but he left both clubs without breaking into their first teams. He returned to his Merseyside roots where he played for Burscough and Ellesmere Port & Neston in the North West Counties League before signing for his hometown club in 1984. In the next two and a half years, Shaun made well over a hundred appearances and started to attract the attention of bigger clubs.

Northwich Victoria were in the relegation zone when they signed Shaun in January 1987 and his influence helped to tighten up the defence. The Vics finished the season in seventeenth position, but after only eight games of the 1987-88 campaign, Weymouth paid a club record fee of £15,000 to take Teale to the South coast. Already boasting an impressive defence, only five goals were conceded in Shaun's first sixteen matches.

Unfortunately Weymouth suffered a loss of form, but Shaun was selected for the England Semi-professional team to play Wales in 1988. He was in the squad again to play Italy in January 1989, where he would have faced Fabrizio Ravanelli, but his transfer to A.F.C. Bournemouth the week before cost him his place, and the Dorset club £50,000. Shaun played over a hundred games for the Cherries but was unable to prevent them from being relegated to the Third Division in 1990.

Shaun's career reached its high point when Aston Villa signed him in the summer of 1991 for £350,000. He regularly played as part of a three man central defence and was in the side that won the Coca-Cola Cup at Wembley in 1994. The arrival of Gareth Southgate in July 1995 saw Shaun's place in jeopardy and he moved on to Tranmere Rovers for £500,000 where he spent the next two seasons. A spell in Hong Kong with Happy Valley followed but in 1998 he returned to British football with Motherwell. In February 2000, he joined Carlisle on a non-contract basis and helped the club to avoid the drop into the Conference. He subsequently returned to Southport where he spent the 2000-01 season.

Son of former Charlton Athletic and Crystal Palace defender Don Townsend, Andy left school at sixteen and worked as a bricklayer. He joined Athenian League Welling United and by the age of seventeen was a first team regular. His performances in midfield attracted the Football League scouts and his name was linked to Tottenham Hotspur and Chelsea. He had a pre-season trial with the latter in 1982, but the club could not match his wages as a computer operator with Greenwich Council together with his playing expenses with Welling, who by now were a top Southern League outfit.

It was while watching team-mate Tony Agana that Weymouth manager Brian Godfrey spotted Townsend and the pair moved to the South Coast in March 1984. Andy, who had played over 100 Southern League games for Welling, initially signed only on loan to the end of the season, when the move was made permanent. Never a prolific goalscorer, Townsend scored thirteen goals in twenty-nine appearances for Weymouth before Southampton paid £35,000 to take him to The Dell in January 1985. His first team debut was three months later as a left-back, but a move back to the midfield had transpired, when in 1986, he broke a leg - ironically in a pre-season friendly with Weymouth. He returned to action in February 1987 and was a first team fixture until his transfer to Norwich in the 1988 close season.

With Andy's Grandmother coming from County Kerry, he was eligible for the Republic of Ireland and made his international debut in 1989. After his performances in the 1990 World Cup, Chelsea paid £1.2 million for his services and after three years and over 100 games he was sold to Aston Villa for £2.1 million. Andy led the Republic to the 1994 World Cup finals in America and won his first major honours with two League Cup victories. Having started the 1997-98 season at Aston Villa, Andy was soon on his way to Middlesbrough who saw him as the man to lead them back to the Premiership. This was accomplished at the first time of asking and after a season back in the top flight, West Bromwich Albion signed him for £50,000 hoping that he could repeat the feat with them. Unfortunately, injuries disrupted his season and he was forced into premature retirement. Having initially indicated a desire to go into coaching, Andy is now seen regularly as a TV pundit.

As with so many professional footballers, Mark's career suffered an early setback, for after one year as an apprentice professional he was released by Everton in the summer of 1981. He was signed up by Northwich Victoria's manger Lammie Robertson after some impressive performances in the pre-season games.

It was not long before he had established himself as a fixture in the first team, making forty-eight appearances in his first season. Mark was converted from an orthodox winger to a midfielder, but could play up front when required. His second season with the Vics culminated in the F.A.Trophy Final against Telford where he was to finish on the losing side. This was to be his last game for the club as during the summer he gave up his job in a bakery to return to the professional ranks with Oldham Athletic.

The £10,000 transfer fee was repaid in full as Mark did not miss a match in his two seasons with the Latics and he scored a dozen goals. First Division West Ham United signed Mark for £250,000 in August 1985 and he was an ever present when West Ham finished in third place in the League in 1985-86, their highest placing ever. After four and a half years and two hundred games, Mark was the subject of two, million pound moves, firstly to Manchester City and then the return to his first club, Everton.

In March 1994, he went on loan to Birmingham City before making the move permanent and taking up the position of player/coach. In 1995 he helped the Midlanders win the Division 2 title and the Auto Windscreens Shield, but after Trevor Francis replaced Barry Fry as manager, Mark was on his way again, this time for a brief spell at Huddersfield Town. Once his Football League career was over, Mark returned to the non-League ranks, helping Leigh RMI reach the Conference in 2000. He subsequently joined Altrincham as Manager but left towards the end of the 2000-01 campaign.

Guy Whittingham
Born: Evesham
10/11/64
Yeovil Town

While serving in the Armed Forces, Guy embarked on his footballing career with Oxford City in the Vauxhall-Opel League, and was spotted by the Waterlooville manager Ernie Bradwell who signed him up at the start of the 1988-89 season. Partnered up front by Paul Moody, who would also progress to the Football League, Guy helped the side reach the first round proper of the F.A.Cup, where he scored in a 4-1 defeat by Aylesbury United.

This was to be his last game for the club as he was signed by Yeovil Town, for whom he made his debut a week later, scoring on his first home outing the following Saturday. By the end of the season he was top scorer with eighteen goals in twenty-three games.

During the course of the 1988-89 season, Guy played for Waterlooville, Yeovil Town, the Combined Services, the Army, and Portsmouth Reserves - and netted ninety goals in one hundred matches. This kind of a scoring record convinced Portsmouth to pay the 450 required to buy him out of the Army. In his four seasons with Pompey, he finished top goalscorer each term, helping the club to the F.A.Cup semi-finals in 1991-92 and setting a club record of 42 League goals the following season. Having missed out on promotion to the Premiership, Guy made the step-up by signing for Aston Villa for £1.2 million. The move was not a success and despite a productive loan spell at Wolverhampton Wanderers he was transferred to Sheffield Wednesday in December 1994.

After three and a half seasons, Guy found himself surplus to requirements and spent a season on loan at Wolverhampton Wanderers, Portsmouth and Watford. At the end of the 1998-99 season, Guy returned to Portsmouth where he combined playing, with a coaching role under Steve Clandge. When Clandge was removed from the 'hot seat', Guy moved to Wycombe Wanderers on loan where played in the F.A.Cup semi final against Liverpool.

> **Ian Woan**
> **Born: Heswall**
> **14/12/67**
> **Runcorn**

Although Ian was born on the Wirral peninsular, his football career started as a trainee at Manchester City. He then had a spell with Heswall in the West Cheshire League before deciding to try his luck over the border in Wales. Initially he played for Caernarfon before moving to Newtown, where his ability with his left foot persuaded Runcorn to sign him during the 1989 close season.

During his seven months at Runcorn, Ian made thirty-three appearances plus three as substitute and scored fourteen goals. He also provided the chances for others, laying on four goals in Runcorn's 9-0 victory over Enfield. Ian held talks with A.F.C. Bournemouth and Leyton Orient, but it was Nottingham Forest who won the race for his signature. The fee of £80,000 was the highest transfer fee that Runcorn had received, and Ian gave up his job as a quantity surveyor to join the ranks of the professional footballer in March 1990.

For the next year, Ian was adjusting to his new surrounding in the reserves. Apart from one game in the Full Members Cup, Ian did not break into the first team until March 2nd 1991 in an away League game at Luton Town. Within a month he was a regular choice and played in the F.A.Cup final against 'Spurs at the end of the season. For the next seven years Ian saw off a number of challengers for his position in the side and twice helped Forest return to the Premiership at the first attempt after relegations. However, by 1998, Ian found himself on the fringes of the team and in the summer of 2000 he was released after more than two hundred appearances.

Ian started the 2000-01 season at Barnsley, but he moved on to Swindon where he helped them avoid the drop into Division Three. At the end of the campaign, Ian signed to play for the Columbus Crew in America.

Caps in the Conference

Many full internationals have spent time playing in the Conference before finally hanging up their boots. Those from the United Kingdom and the Republic of Ireland are listed below:

ENGLAND

Peter Barnes	Northwich Victoria
Kevin Beattie	Barnet
Luther Blissett	Southport
Tony Brown	Stafford Rangers
Steve Bull	Hereford Utd
Martin Chivers	Barnet
Tony Daley	Forest Green Rovers
Peter Davenport	Southport/Macclesfield Town
Gordon Hill	Northwich Vic./Stafford R.
David Johnson	Barrow
Alan Kennedy	Northwich Victoria/ Enfield
Brian Kidd	Barrow
Tony Morley	Bromsgrove Rovers
Stuart Pearson	Northwich Victoria
Mike Pejic	Northwich Victoria
Kevin Reeves	Barrow
Graham Roberts	Yeovil T./ Stevenage B.
Kenny Samsom	Slough Town
Nigel Spink	Forest Green Rovers
Derek Statham	Telford Utd
Alex Stepney	Altrincham
Peter Taylor	Maidstone U./Redbridge For.
Dave Watson	Kettering Town
Steve Whitworth	Barnet
Frank Worthington	Chorley

REPUBLIC OF IRELAND

Gerry Daly	Telford Utd
Tony Grealish	Bromsgrove Rovers
Austin Hayes	Barnet
Jimmy Holmes	Nuneaton Borough
Ray Houghton	Stevenage Borough
Mark Kelly	Farnborough Town
Mark Lawrenson	Barnet
Jim McDonagh	Telford Utd
Jerry Murphy	Fisher Ath
Ray O'Brien	Boston Utd
Kieran O'Regan	Halifax Town
Damien Richardson	Gravesend & Northfleet
Paddy Roche	Northwich Victoria
John Sheridan	Doncaster Rovers

SCOTLAND

Jim Blyth	Nuneaton Borough
Des Bremner	Stafford Rangers
Jim Brown	Kettering Town
Kenny Burns	Stafford R./ Telford Utd
Willie Carr	Worcester City
Andy Gray	Cheltenham Town
Frank Gray	Darlington
Asa Hartford	Boston Utd
Tommy Hutchinson	Merthyr Tydfil
Don Masson	Kettering Town
Steve Nicol	Doncaster Rovers
Derek Parlane	Macclesfield Town
George Wood	Merthyr Tydfil

WALES

George Berry	Stafford Rangers
Clayton Blackmore	Leigh R.M.I
Terry Boyle	Merthyr Tydfil
Les Cartwright	Nuneaton Borough
Gordon Davies	Northwich Victoria
David Felgate	Leigh R.M.I.
David Giles	Newport County
Robbie James	Merthyr Tydfil
Dudley Lewis	Merthyr Tydfil
Chris Marustik	Newport County
Donato Nardiello	Nuneaton B./Stafford R./Telford U.
Peter O'Sullivan	Maidstone Utd
David Phillips	Stevenage Borough
Howard Pritchard	Yeovil Town
Dave Roberts	Bath C./ Trowbridge T./Kettering T.
Tony Roberts	Dagenham & Redbridge
Peter Sayer	Chorley/ Northwich Vic.
Neville Southall	Doncaster Rovers
Nigel Stevenson	Merthyr Tyd./ Yeovil T.

NORTHERN IRELAND

Robbie Dennison	Hednesford Town/ Hereford Utd
Phil Hughes	Telford Utd
John McClelland	Yeovil Town
Sammy McIlroy	Northwich Victoria
Bernard McNally	Hednesford Town
Jimmy Nicholl	Bath City
Jimmy Quinn	Hayes/ Hereford U./Northwich V.
Paul Ramsey	Telford Utd
Ian Stewart	Colchester Utd

Relatively Famous

The following players have come from families where a relative has captured the football limelight:

Player	Club	Relationship	Famous Relative
Craig Allardyce	Welling Utd	son	Sam Allardyce
John Armfield	Runcorn	son	Jimmy Armfield
Steve Book	Cheltenham T/Slough T	nephew	Tony Book
Keith Bowen	Barnet	son	Dave Bowen
Gary Bull	Barnet	cousin	Steve Bull
Tim Clarke	Altrincham	brother	Colin Clarke
Danny Crerand	Altrincham	son	Pat Crerand
David Culverhouse	Dagenham & Redbridge	brother	Ian Culverhouse
Grantley Dicks	Bath City	brother	Julian Dicks
Danny Donachie	Altrincham	son	Willie Donachie
Nko Ekoku	Sutton Utd	brother	Efan Ekoku
Mike Fagan	Altrincham	son	Joe Fagan
Adrian Foley	Maidstone Utd	son	Theo Foley
Paul Foley	Fisher Ath	son	Theo Foley
Danny Greaves	Dagenham/ Weymouth	son	Jimmy Greaves
Paul Harford	Farnborough T/ Sutton Utd/ Welling Utd	son	Ray Harford
Carl Hoddle	Barnet/ Woking	brother	Glenn Hoddle
Gareth Howells	Cheltenham T/ Enfield/ Farnborough T/ Kettering	brother	David Howells
Scott Huckerby	Telford Utd	brother	Darren Huckerby
Wayne Hughes	Bath City	cousin	Emlyn Hughes
Frank Jones	Bangor City	brother	Joey Jones
Mark Jones	Runcorn	brother	David Jones
Mark Jones	Hereford Utd	brother	Paul Jones
Simon Kendall	Altrincham	son	Howard Kendall
Keith Kennedy	Barrow	brother	Alan Kennedy
Gary Kimble	Dagenham & Redbridge/ Welling Utd	twin	Alan Kimble
Ollie Latchford	Kidderminster Harriers	nephew	Bob Latchford
Paul Lazarus	Fisher Ath	nephew	Mark Lazarus
Chris Lewington	Fisher Ath	brother	Ray Lewington
John McMahon	Altrincham	brother	Steve McMahon
Brian Morley	Northwich Victoria	brother	Trevor & Tony Morley
Mark Redknapp	Dagenham & Redbridge	son	Harry Redknapp
		brother	Jamie Redknapp
Dave Regis	Barnet	brother	Cyrille Regis
Bob Ritchie	Northwich Victoria	brother	John Ritchie
Dave Ritchie	Northwich Victoria	son	John Ritchie
Gary Robson	Gateshead	brother	Bryan Robson
Justin Robson	Gateshead	brother	Bryan Robson
Darren Royle	Altrincham	son	Joe Royle
Andy Salako	Sutton Utd/ Welling Utd	brother	John Salako
Dave Sansom	Barnet	brother	Kenny Sansom
Jim Sheringham	Dagenham	brother	Teddy Sheringham
Paul Shirtliff	Boston Utd/Frickley Ath/ Dagenham & Redbridge/ Gateshead	brother	Peter Shirtliff
Edwin Stein	Barnet/ Dagenham	brother	Brian & Mark Stein
Gary Stewart	Altrincham	brother	Paul Stewart
Paul Terry	Dagenham & Redbridge	brother	John Terry
Kevin Thomas	Barnet	brother	Mitchell Thomas
Mark Turner	Telford Utd	son	Graham Turner
Les Whitton	Dagenham	brother	Steve Whitton
Richard Wilson	Lincoln City	nephew	Bob Wilson
Jason Withe	Stafford R/ Telford U	son	Peter Withe

F.A.Cup Giantkillers

Victories: **Conference Victors**
12	Altrincham
11	Telford Utd
7	Yeovil Town
4	Hednesford Town, Hereford Utd, Kettering Town, Macclesfield Utd, Woking
3	Dagenham, Enfield, Maidstone Utd, Northwich Victoria, Stevenage Borough, Sutton Utd
2	Bath City, Chester City, Kidderminster Harriers, Kingstonian, Runcorn, Rushden & Diamonds, Worcester City
1	Barnet, Boston Utd, Bromsgrove Rovers, Colchester Utd, Dagenham & Redbridge, Darlington, Doncaster Rovers, Farnborough Town, Frickley Ath, Halifax Town, Lincoln City, Morecambe, Nuneaton Borough, Southport, Stafford Rangers, Welling Utd, Weymouth, Witton Albion, Wycombe Wanderers

Defeats: **Football League Victims**
5	Cambridge Utd
4	Blackpool, Crewe Alexandra, Lincoln City, Northampton Town
3	Barnet, Chester City, Colchester Utd, Halifax Town, Hartlepool Utd, York City
2	Aldershot Town, Birmingham City, Cardiff City, Exeter City, Gillingham, Hereford Utd, Hull City, Leyton Orient, Peterborough Utd, Preston North End, Rochdale, Rotherham Utd, Scunthorpe Utd, Southend Utd, Stockport County, Stoke City, Swindon Town, Torquay Utd, Wigan Ath, Wrexham
1	Bradford City, Brentford, Brighton & Hove Albion, Bristol Rovers, Burnley, Bury, Carlisle Utd, Chesterfield, Coventry City, Darlington, Fulham, Maidstone Utd, Mansfield Town, Millwall, Oxford Utd, Plymouth Argyle, Reading, Sheffield Utd, Shrewsbury Town, Walsall, West Bromwich Albion, Wimbledon

Season – by Season Giant-Killing

	Clubs per round					
	1st	2nd	3rd	4th	5th	Giantkillings
1979-80	10	4	2			2
1980-1	11	4	2			2
1981-2	10	5	3			3
1982-3	14	7	2			6
1983-4	14	6	2	1		5
1984-5	12	7	2	1	1	9
1985-6	15	8	3	1		6
1986-7	13	6	2			2
1987-8	14	9	4			6
1988-9	14	10	3	2		6
1989-90	13	3	1			2
1990-1	15	5	2			2
1991-2	11	5	2			5
1992-3	14	7	1			6
1993-4	13	8	3	1	1	7
1994-5	9	3	1			2
1995-6	10	2	1			1
1996-7	14	3	3	1		5
1997-8	11	4	3	1		5
1998-9	13	7	3			5
1999-00	12	4	2			3
2000-1	16	9	5	1		11

SOME OF
THE GIANTKILLERS

(Top to bottom, left to right)

1979-80: Altrincham v. Crewe Alexandra (3-0). 1981-82: Enfield v. Wimbledon 4-1. 1984-85: Telford United v. Darlington 3-0.

1988-89: Sutton United v. Coventry City 2-1. 1989-90: Darlington v. Halifax Town 3-0. 1992-93: Stafford Rangers v. Lincoln City 2-1

1994-95: Woking v. Barnet 1-0. 1997-98: Stevenage Borough v. Cambridge United 2-1. 1999-00: Hereford United v. York City 1-0.

Conference Football on the Box

The first arrangement to televise live Conference football came towards the end of the 1990-91 season. British Aerospace Sportscast, which had been launched in August 1990, broadcast to 300 working mens' clubs and social clubs, principally in the North of England. A £50,000 deal to show twelve matches from the championship run-in was agreed with most matches having their kick-off times altered to avoid clashes with other Conference fixtures.

The televised matches were:

30/3	Altrincham v Barnet
5/4	Northwich Victoria v Colchester United
9/4	Kettering Town v Barnet
12/4	Runcorn v Macclesfield Town
17/4	Colchester United v Kettering Town
19/4	Slough Town v Barnet
22/4	Kidderminster Harriers v Colchester United*
26/4	Telford United v Colchester United
28/4	Stafford Rangers v Altrincham
29/4	Wycombe Wanderers v Barnet
1/5	Kettering Town v Sutton United
4/5	Fisher Athletic v Barnet

(* Originally, it was intended that Barrow v Altrincham on 24/4/91 would be shown, but as Manchester United's European Cup Winners Cup semi-final was being televised on terrestrial television, the fixture was switched to this match).

The agreement was to be continued in the 1991-92 season, but the broadcasters ceased trading before its resumption. The baton was taken up by cable station 'Live TV' in the late 1990's, who broadcasted regular programmes showing goal highlights.

In season 2000-01, Sky Television produced a weekly magazine programme to cover the run-in to the Conference title. On March 24th, they broadcast a live match between Yeovil Town and Hayes (3-0). For season 2001-2, an agreement has been reached to televise up to ten live matches at Saturday lunchtimes in addition to the weekly review and preview programmes.

The Conference fixture between Halifax Town and Kidderminster Harriers on 2/5/94 was filmed by Yorkshire Television and some of the action featured in an episode of *"A Touch of Frost"* when a player collapsed in suspicious circumstances after a local derby. The cameras did little to inspire Kidderminster who lost 1-0, five days before securing the Conference title.

The first ever League game, outside The Football League, to be shown live on TV.

Seasons of Conference Football

22	Kettering Town (79-01), Northwich Victoria (79-), Telford United (79-01),
19	Altrincham (79-97, 99-00)
17	Kidderminster Harriers (83-00), Yeovil Town (79-85, 88-95, 97-)
16	Bath City (79-88, 90-97)
15	Boston United (79-93, 00-), Runcorn (81-96)
14	Stafford Rangers (79-83, 85-95), Welling United (86-00)
12	Barnet (79-91)
11	Gateshead (83-85, 86-87, 90-98)
10	Barrow (79-83, 84-86, 89-92, 98-99), Macclesfield Town (87-97), Maidstone United (79-89), Scarborough (79-87, 99-), Weymouth (79-89)
9	Cheltenham Town (85-92, 97-99), Enfield (81-90), Nuneaton Borough (79-81, 82-87, 99-), Woking (92-)
8	Dover Athletic (93-), Farnborough Town (89-90,91-93, 94-99), Southport (93-), Wealdstone (79-81, 82-88)
7	Dagenham (81-88), Frickley Athletic (80-87), Slough Town (90-94, 95-98), Stevenage Borough (94-), Wycombe Wanderers (85-86, 87-93)
6	Hednesford Town (95-01), Methyr Tydfil (89-95), Morecambe (95-), Stalybridge Celtic (92-98), Sutton United (86-91, 99-00), Worcester City (79-85)
5	Bromsgrove Rovers (92-97), Dagenham & Redbridge (92-96, 00-), Halifax Town (93-98), Hayes (96-), Rushden & Diamonds (96-01)
4	Bangor City (79-81, 82-84), Fisher Athletic (87-91), Hereford United (97-)
3	A.P.Leamington (79-82), Dartford (81-82, 84-86), Doncaster Rovers (98-), Forest Green Rovers (98-), Gravesend & Northfleet (79-82), Kingstonian (98-01), Trowbridge Town (81-84), Witton Albion (91-94)
2	Chorley (88-90), Colchester United (90-92), Leek Town (97-99)
1	Aylesbury United (88-89), Chester City (00-), Darlington (89-90), Leigh R.M.I. (00-), Lincoln City (87-88), * Newport County (88-89), Redbridge Forest (91-92), Redditch United (79-80)

* Newport County did not complete fixtures.

Home From Home

On occasions, circumstances have arisen where Conference games have been switched to Football League grounds in order to fulfil the fixtures:

17/1/1982: Barnet v. A.P.Leamington
Due to severe Winter weather, Barnet hired the Q.P.R. artificial pitch a Loftus Road. The match was played on a Sunday lunchtime, and was followed by a F.A.Trophy tie between Hendon and Taunton Town. The Barnet attendance of 1,045 compared favourably with the average home Underhill gate of 760.

17/2/1988: Weymouth v. Wealdstone
Weymouth had their New Year's Day game against Barnet postponed due to heavy rain, and the persistent wet weather caused problems to the pitch at their new stadium. In order to play a match, the home game with Wealdstone was switched to Dean Court, Bournemouth. The crowd of 646 was down on the seasonal average home attendance of 1,491.

3/9/1994: Gateshead v. Yeovil Town
The International Stadium was unavailable for this early season match, so the game was switched to nearby St. James' Park, Newcastle. Gateshead were rewarded with a bumper gate of 2,734, nearly four times the average home crowd figure of 693.

~ Yore Publications ~

Established in 1991 by Dave Twydell, Yore publications have become the leading publishers of Football League club histories. Nearly thirty have been produced, and although many are now out of print, some clubs for which copies are still available include - Scarborough, Wycombe Wanderers and Lincoln City - all with Conference connections; plus the likes of Notts County, Barnsley, Bury and Scunthorpe United. Each history is a large page quality hardback with dustjacket and contains a well illustrated written history, full statistics and line-ups for at least all Football League seasons are included, with many named team groups.

A number of Football League Who's Who books (biography and statistics of every League player) have also been produced, including Chesterfield, Mansfield Town, Portsmouth, Hull City and Reading.

Non-League football is another feature of our publications, especially the 'Gone But Not Forgotten' series (published twice yearly), each of which contains around six (written and illustrated) abbreviated histories of defunct clubs and/or former grounds (also Videos available).

Compilation histories of former Football League and Scottish League clubs (plus a video), and Unusual titles (e.g. 'The Little Red Book of Chinese Football') are also included in our stocks.

Two or three free Newsletters are posted each year. For your first copy, please send a S.A.E. to:
Yore Publications (Ref A/C),
12 The Furrows, Harefield, Middx. UB9 6AT.
Or visit our web sites:
www.yorepublications.sageweb.co.uk... or .....www.yore.demon.co.uk/index.html